Socialism with a Human Face

Socialism with a Human Face

The political economy of Britain in the 1980s

MICHAEL MEACHER

London
GEORGE ALLEN & UNWIN
Boston   Sydney

George Allen & Unwin (Publishers) Ltd,
40 Museum Street, London WC1A 1LU, UK

George Allen & Unwin (Publishers) Ltd,
Park Lane, Hemel Hempstead, Herts HP2 4TE, UK

Allen & Unwin, Inc.,
9 Winchester Terrace, Winchester, Mass. 01890, USA

George Allen & Unwin Australia Pty Ltd,
8 Napier Street, North Sydney, NSW 2060, Australia

First published in 1982

*HC
256.6
M4
1982*

British Library Cataloguing in Publication Data

Meacher, Michael
  Socialism with a human face.
1. Great Britain – Economic conditions –
1945-   2. Great Britain – Politics and
government – 1964-
I. Title
330.9′41′0858   HC256.6
ISBN 0–04–320150–4

Library of Congress Cataloging in Publication Data

Meacher, Michael
  Socialism with a human face.
Includes index.
1. Great Britain – Economic conditions – 1945-
2. Great Britain – Economic policy – 1945-
3. Socialism – Great Britain.   I. Title.
HC256.6.M4   338.941   81–19125
ISBN 0–04–320150–4   AACR2

Set in 11 on 13 point Garamond by Bedford Typesetters Ltd
and printed in Great Britain by
Billing and Sons Ltd, Guildford, London and Worcester

Contents

Contents

Introduction.

Socialism is now back on the agenda for political debate – and for many good reasons.

The compromises of the social-democrat-dominated Labour governments of Wilson and Callaghan have provoked a much stronger revival of socialist ideas within the Labour Party in opposition than ever before. A drive to transform the party under the campaigning leadership of Tony Benn has regenerated debate on the socialist goals of the Labour movement and their practicability. The collapse of consensus politics in 1979 and the rise of the hard-line New Right under Margaret Thatcher have prompted agonised reappraisals of how a strong left response can advance the socialist objectives which were interred by Butskellism and have remained buried for so long. The ascendancy of monetarism as an anti-welfare state, anti-working class economic philosophy, reincarnating old-style capitalism, has forced urgent reassessment of traditional socialist doctrines as a means of grappling with an unprecedented economic breakdown.

It is fashionable on the left, of course, to talk of socialism as the alternative. Yet it is irresponsible to do so without having a clear idea of what it means. Many people regard it as synonymous either with Russian-type bureaucracy and state planning, or with nationalisation, or both. Such views are firmly rejected in this book.

The word 'socialism' is used to describe so many different concepts and policies that it has become virtually meaningless. Yet the fact that it is used to attract support for so many different policies shows that it is a word of power – that socialism is believed to have great appeal for men. In this it resembles 'democracy', so that regimes that are tightly controlled by all-powerful leaders call themselves 'People's Democracies'.

Socialism with a Human Face

What makes socialism a word of such power? At root its appeal is in its repudiation of the value of an exploiting society. On the one hand people are powerfully influenced by habit and custom, by the familiar, so that in countries like Britain large numbers of people accept the necessity for 'incentives' (the justification among workers for wage differentials) and for 'efficiency' in the competitive market struggles in which the strong beat the weak. Yet on the other hand acceptance of these ideas is accompanied by an underlying feeling that somehow they are wrong, that men should work together rather than struggle against each other. Socialism embodies the concept of more just relations among men and women.

How is the concept to be realised? Two basic questions are involved. What are the essential principles of socialism as a different form of society from capitalism, and why and how could such a society serve men's needs better? And what can be done in practice to implement these principles?

Socialism versus capitalism is often discussed as if it were a question of society's choosing at will between two alternative systems. But socialism cannot suddenly spring up fully worked-out and consolidated; it can be achieved only through a historical transition.

The development of capitalism constantly extends and deepens the social relations of production. The competitive struggles among capitalists lead to the victors becoming larger as they swallow up their defeated rivals, so that the general trend is towards larger units of production, leading from competition to monopoly. Today there are whole industries which comprise only one or a few firms, or which are state monopolies.

However, these social relations of production exist in a framework of unsocial control. The giant firms are controlled by a small number of owners and managers. And nationalisation has merely replaced former private owners with an elite of publicly appointed controllers who in practice act as collective owners. Some of the old private owners are, moreover, absorbed into this elite, which continues with the ideas of the capitalist market, organising production to meet the market's tests of profitability and competitive 'efficiency'.

Advocates of nationalisation gloss over these realities and say that it is the way to achieve responsible democratic control of production. But what is 'democratic'? In many industries the technology of production requires workers and productive forces to be concentrated in giant enterprises. If these were controlled simply by the people who worked in them ('workers' control'), on what basis would their mutual relations be regulated? At present these relations are regulated by the capitalist market (which is partly competitive and partly monopolist). But if this were repudiated, how could relationships among the enterprises be regulated other than by the state? Of course, this state regulation might take many different forms. None the less, the idea of 'workers' control' has won adherents because of experiences which have shown that the state can be as oppressive towards workers as the old-style capitalists.

The nature of the state requires it to be a machine for ruling, for making people obey. To this end it relies on both force and persuasion. How far can the state be changed bit by bit from one which is essentially exploitive in character, where one economic class is dominant, into another kind of state which is not exploitive? The answer must be based on experience, and in a number of countries step-by-step reforms have been initiated with the declared intention of changing society fundamentally; but no experiences so far show that this intention can be made a reality.

This is not to say that reforms involving take-over by workers do not have their importance. But it has to be a very different kind of take-over from state take-overs within capitalist society, which are for the purpose of consolidating and protecting the essence of the capitalist mode of production, not of ending it. The state that counts is not Parliament or the complex of activities that are directed to making people feel that the state is under popular control. The state that counts, the apparatus for ruling, comprises the army, police, judges, prisons and similar institutions as well as high-level civil service officials and the controllers of nationalised enterprises. All this machinery is in the hands of people soaked in the ideology of capitalism who are seemingly incapable of working with a different ideology.

For the change from capitalism to socialism to come about there has to be a different kind of state – a state run by people who in their own loyalties and style of living reject the values of capitalism. This kind of state can be achieved only by a decisive break from the old, not by step-by-step transformation. And as a situation that would make decisive change possible could never arise without warning, observable pressures for dramatic change would have to build up over a period during which the state would obviously seek pre-emptive measures.

This book, therefore, is about fundamentals. It is not a programme or a manifesto designed for the next Parliament, but rather an attempt to give people a vision, a sense of longer-term direction, in the light of which they may have a better chance to judge for themselves how to react to events, how to understand the key to what is happening, and how to move forward.

The central problems of today clearly include the economic *impasse,* the unsolved riddle of unemployment and inflation, and the causes of the present drift towards international slump. They also include fundamental questions about peace and war, for most people are very uninformed about the realities of the international situation. It is also timely to take a new look at many old ideas about the nature of government and society in the West – what nationalisation really means, the effects of the growing links between state and business, the results of enmeshing the trade unions at many levels with state machinery, the actual working of the political parties and relationships between rank and file and leaders, and the working of Parliament and its relationship with the Executive.

A further issue concerns finance and money. Workers have experience of industry and know industrialists, but are far less knowledgeable about finance and the City. Yet the City is the dominant section of the British Establishment. The main policies it has wanted have been pursued by governments, both Conservative and Labour, throughout the postwar years. The City upholds two great capitalist freedoms – multilateral free trading, and sterling convertibility and freedom for foreign funds to move in and out of London. This is because the large firms believe that competitive international trading, in which they can use their strength to beat weaker rivals, is in their interest; and because financial freedoms are needed to maintain London as one of the two great centres of international finance, with all the profits resulting from this.

Therefore this book is also about power. More particularly, it is about political and economic power in Britain today. This is a subject of enormous importance for the future of this country, yet one that is greatly misunderstood by the people of Britain. It is not difficult to see why. Not only is the nature of the exercise of power by the country's rulers obfuscated by a stream of propaganda (and Britain is no exception to the general rule here); worse, the political landscape in Britain today is an ideological desert. There is not only a sense of failure, but a lack of clear, detailed, thought-through alternative strategies for charting the future of Britain. Things cannot go on as they are; but what is the alternative, what has to change and how, and who has to do what? These questions are rarely even raised, mainly because the present power structure blocks them. This book seeks to answer these questions systematically and to explore the role of power in creating a movement and leadership capable of bringing about social and political change.

Finally, this book is about ideology. Barrenness of ideas is a major characteristic of present-day Britain. There have been great changes in both British society and the British economy since the mid-1950s, yet very little systematic rethinking has been done since Anthony Crosland's now dated *The Future of Socialism*. The present book, however, does not, and is not intended to, offer a detailed blueprint derived from a general scheme. Rather it seeks to demonstrate, through an analysis of today's problems, that the laws of the system can be mastered (even if they are rather different from what they are often supposed to be); and hence that it would be possible to tackle the successive and changing problems that will need to be faced in the coming years in a new and better way. This is not to suggest that there is any particular 'right' answer. On the other hand, this book aims consciously to avoid either merely offering a forward projection of current events or simply presenting academic political philosophising. Projection is liable to lead into the trap, into which so many contemporary commentators fall, of assuming that improvements in techniques of economic management are all that is necessary to prop up the existing system. Academic philosophising is intellectual escapism.

Between these two poles a way must be found for a new political movement to realise the two pre-conditions for power: a moral philosophy and a capacity to unite for practical action. The idealism of yesterday, which has largely turned to cynicism and apathy today, needs to be rekindled in a manner that is hard-headed, realistic and positive. It is hoped that this book will make a contribution to that end.

Part One
What Has Gone Wrong?

1

Britain's Tailspin of Decline – Economic Failure and the Nature of the State

What has gone wrong? The question is instinctively understood in Britain, where it is almost universally agreed that things have gone very badly wrong, at least over the last two decades. It had become increasingly fashionable to regard these problems as insoluble, indeed to regard Britain as becoming ungovernable – at least until the advent of North Sea oil provided some temporary relief. But even with that benefit it is well recognised that Britain's performance in terms of all the economic indicators – growth, investment, unemployment level, trade shares, inflation – continues to fall increasingly behind that of its main competitors.

Is Britain Then a Special Case?

Certainly the British economy is specially vulnerable to pressure; for example, to imported inflation because of its high trading component of GNP which is around 30% compared with, say, the USA's 9%. Also, the potential disruption of government economic planning by the activities of multinational corporations is likely to be more acute for Britain because, with its history of empire, it forms

3

a centre for such activities second only to the USA. Intra-firm exports as a percentage of total manufactured exports are at an even higher level for Britain than for the USA – 31% in 1979 compared with 21% for the USA in that year – and even more highly concentrated in a few firms than is the case in the USA.

However, the conventional explanation of Britain's decline as a capitalist economy lies rather in the rising demands and increasing militancy of the British working class (though the unprecedented wage cutbacks in the 1975–8 incomes policy and again in that of 1980–1 reversed much of the conventional middle-class wisdom of the early 1970s). For Britain, almost uniquely, possesses the combination of a single united trade union movement and a single main anti-conservative political party. Britain also has one of the highest proportions of trade union membership in the civilian labour force of any major country.

Yet slow growth in Britain cannot be attributed simply to excessive postwar wage pressures. Earnings grew in the UK, according to official Department of Trade and Industry figures, by only 5·7% p.a. compound over the period 1960–70, compared with 7·1% in France, 10·1% in Germany, 10·0% in Italy and 12·6% in Japan. Moreover, Britain's unit labour costs in manufacturing rose more slowly over this same period: according to published Treasury figures they increased 53·2% in West Germany during 1960–71, 54·7% in the Netherlands and 56·7% in France, but only 48·4% in the UK. Yet UK productivity, though equal to that of the USA, was far lower over this period than that of any other main competitor. While output per person employed in all production industries rose only 35% in the UK during 1961–71 (and only 34% in the USA), it rose 53% in West Germany, 57% in Belgium, 64% in Italy, 70% in France, 81% in the Netherlands and no less than 113%, more than three times the UK increase, in Japan.[1] Nor did this pattern change much in the next decade.

4

Over the period 1970–9 the annual compound percentage increase in manufacturing earnings in Britain was high at 15%, certainly higher than in West Germany and the USA (each 8%), but scarcely higher than in France and Japan (each 14%). It is true that the annual compound rise in unit labour costs in manufacturing during this decade were, at 13%, much higher than in Germany, the USA, or Japan (each 5–7%), though slightly below Sweden's (14%).[2] But the key difference remained the widening gap in productivity growth rates. While the annual compound increase in productivity over the period 1970–8 was only 2·2% in the UK (though higher than the 1·2% in the USA), it was 3·4% in West Germany, 3·6% in France and 4·6% in Japan.[3]

Why was British productivity so much lower? Partly this must reflect the cumulative effect of chronically lower investment rates in relation to GDP by UK manufacturers compared with competitors abroad (approximately 15% UK/USA; 20% rest of EEC; 30% Japan). But DTI analysis has found that even when investment in relation to GDP is standardised between countries, the percentage rate of growth of GDP that is generated is lower in the case of Britain: for each unit of growth (1·0) achieved by Britain during 1963–71, Germany secured about 1·3, the USA, France and Italy each about 1·5 and Japan about 2·2. This suggests that not only lower investment overall, but also inefficient allocation and use of resources over a long period of time, lie at the root of Britain's persistent low growth rates. These low growth rates then in turn created further problems which completed the vicious circle by making it progressively harder for Britain to get on to a higher growth rate. Slow growth frustrated workers' expectations of higher living standards and thus fuelled internal inflationary pressures. It can also be seen as damaging industrial relations: far from low productivity resulting from poor labour relations (days lost through industrial disputes are not significantly higher for Britain than the average amongst competitor

5

countries), poor growth, because of its ultimate redundancy consequences, has made workers defensive and worried about job security (justifiably so). And low growth has also tended to be self-perpetuating because of the successively lower yield for reinvestment next time round.

That logically raises the next questions. Why has Britain's (and the USA's) overall level of investment been lower for so long? Why has there been lower efficiency in the long term in the utilisation of this scarce investment capital? How did Britain get into this self-defeating spiral in the first place? The facts suggest that Britain's problem is historical in perspective, and cumulative dating back to its falter in innovative leadership in the industrial world in the period around 1870. From that time up to 1950 Britain's long-run growth of real per capita product, at 1·3% p.a., was higher only than that of countries which were either heavily defeated (Germany 1·2% and Italy 0·7%) or occupied (France 1·1% and the Netherlands 0·7%) in major wars.[4] In comparison, the USA, Canada, Sweden, Norway and Denmark all had rather higher growth rates (1·6–2·0%). But of the countries with low (1·5% or less) long-run growth, Britain showed only a modest improvement in the 1950s (to 2·2%), while all the others increased their rate of growth by between three and seven times (up to 3·5–6·5%).

What caused this watershed for Britain in the last third of the nineteenth century? Certainly 'residual' factors, that is, all those besides labour and capital which affect variations in national output, are relevant here, and have remained so. These include neglect of technical education, the inflexibility of entrepreneurs and dogmatic *laissez-faire* in a class-ridden society. Economic factors which also probably influenced the low level of home investment were the constant supply of cheap labour, which permitted early accumulation of capital but then removed the spur for further technological progress, and the small scale of industrial enterprises.

But a fundamental factor was the massive diversion of investment from home to overseas in the years 1870–1913. For more than half this period foreign investment exceeded domestic, and immediately before the First World War it was more than double, at 9·3% overseas as opposed to 4·1% domestic as a proportion of national income. In fact the total of British overseas investment in 1913, at £3,763 million, stood at a level in relation to domestic GNP which has never been exceeded by any nation before or since, even by the USA today. But the price of this characteristic, reflecting the City's domination of the British economy, was inevitably a major cause of stagnation at home, as well as partly reflecting it. Moreover, this dualism of cause and effect, responding to slow growth at home by investment abroad and thus reinforcing the slow growth at home for the future, has persisted since.

This chronic underinvestment at home has led to profound and accumulating difficulties for the British economy. It has produced structural disequilibrium, creating an economy biased towards the older manufacturing industries, so that the rest of the world has a relatively inelastic demand for British goods. Thus the OECD has estimated that for every unit increase in world income, the world increases its purchase of UK goods by only 0·57. This means that the UK can only grow at around 57% of the world growth rate if equilibrium is to be maintained in its trade balance, though since the British income elasticity of demand for imports is significantly greater than 1 the potential growth rate may rather be only some 35–40% of the world rate.

On top of this basic background, a number of other factors have been layered which have intensified Britain's problems uniquely in its case, mainly as a result of its imperialist past. First, Britain still spends a much higher proportion of GNP on defence than other European NATO countries – nearly 2% more of its GNP than France and West Germany throughout the 1970s (though less in per capita terms because of slower growth and lower GNP). Secondly, it also bears a significantly higher relative level of government expenditure abroad (1½% of GNP, compared with ½–1% of the UK's main competitors). Thirdly, for too long the strenuous British efforts to maintain sterling as a reserve currency exacted their price of holding back domestic investment because of the high interest rates required to keep sterling in London and because financial interests in the City insisted on making the exchange rate of sterling the priority in British economic policy, whatever the costs in domestic deflation and unemployment.

In general, low productivity in British industry has many causes – for example, poor quality of management in organising work, especially in larger factories; proliferation of trade unions at plant level; unpalatable class divisiveness in amenities, status and treatment; and perhaps different attitudes to work throughout the firm compared with abroad. These weaknesses make it less likely that there will be the increase in investment Britain needs or, if there is, that it will be sufficiently productive to encourage yet more investment next time round. Chronic underinvestment, and poor use of what investment there is, interact with each other to their mutual disadvantage. This is Britain's problem from the capitalist point of view.

Why the Present British Industrial Economy Is No Longer Sustainable

This analysis is sufficiently pessimistic to raise the fundamental question of whether the industrial way of life as it is at present organised can continue for much longer. The British are in part suffering from problems which all industrial nations will encounter once they reach the stage that the oldest industrial nation has now reached. In this important sense British shows to other industrialised nations the image of their own future. In its past the oldest industrial nation embraced two kinds of dependence: external dependence on other regions to supply food, energy and raw materials; internal dependence on the institutions and consumption patterns that sustain growth. Both have now turned into weaknesses.

THE THREAT OF EXTERNAL DEPENDENCE[5]

Replacing a world of self-sufficient nations for whom trade was marginal, industrialism has made economic interdependence the basis of the existence of many nations. Since the movement of the terms of trade in favour of manufacturing nations was reversed by the commodity price boom of the 1970s, a series of shortages and escalating prices of commodities such as sugar, oil, coffee and tin, as well as huge payments deficits, have brought home to the British the extent of their external dependence and their powerlessness to control some of the basic supplies on which their security and prosperity rest.

From the repeal of the Corn Laws in 1846 up to the present, the preferred policy of all British governments has been free trade. Free trade has in the past secured for Britain cheap food, cheap energy and cheap raw materials, and so has reaped the greatest possible benefit from the superior productivity of British industry. The crunch came when this lead was overtaken by other nations – Germany, Japan and the United States, and when the empire was finally dismembered in the 1960s. The artificial nature of the British economy was then exposed. Present living standards and the amount of employment in Britain depend upon British industry selling enough exports to pay for the necessary imports. The economy has become highly vulnerable whenever there are sudden changes in the supply or cost of basic raw materials and food, and whenever British industry fails to earn enough in exports or to fend off overseas competition

9

at home. This means that for the industrial way of life to be sustained in Britain, British industry must not fall too far behind world levels of productivity. Otherwise a sudden and cumulative fall in production, employment and living standards could take place.

THE THREAT OF INTERNAL DEPENDENCE

Britain pioneered the first prototype of an industrial society: a free market economy with minimum government intervention; a parliamentary democracy emphasising political compromise, the rule of law and civil liberties; and a cultural system that maintained social cohesion, permitted some mobility and rewarded enterprise highly. Under these conditions industrialism expanded and the institutions adapted to the enormous changes it brought remarkably smoothly for a long time.

Now many of Britain's institutions have lost their former strength and flexibility, and social cohesion has only been maintained at the price of political stalemate. A defensive Labour movement with strong bargaining power was able to commit governments to policies of high welfare spending, full employment and limited nationalisation after 1945, but not to control private investment or City interests. Private industry and finance were able to commit governments to policies of free movement of goods and capital, but not to taxation or industrial relations policies that would have persuaded them to invest more in Britain. The adversary two-party system consolidated this division and hindered consistent and positive policy-making. The outcome has been a relatively unfavourable climate for investment.

By degrees Britain is evolving into a nation of consumers and rentiers. The British place great importance on leisure and quality of life and custom. The competitive instinct is low, there is often hostility or indifference to entrepreneurship and profit-making; management often lacks dynamism.

Many local communities are still strong and there is a dislike of too much mobility and change. Trade unionists fight to defend jobs and restrictive practices, to preserve good working conditions and to delay the introduction of new technology. Local environmental groups oppose new roads, new airports and mining in rural areas. The educational system still tends to celebrate the dilettante rather than the professional or businessman, downgrading subjects like engineering, and often hindering greater social mobility. The British as individuals no longer seem very eager to pay the costs of faster industrial expansion – the necessary mobility and change, the greater pollution and environmental destruction.

Every industrialised nation gradually becomes bound to the treadmill of growth: first because self-sufficiency is given up and competition intensifies; secondly, because new expectations and needs are fostered in the urbanised population, through the institutions which industrialism fashions. The treadmill creates these two kinds of dependence for every industrial nation – external and internal. So long as the economy thrives, the increasing dependence goes unnoticed. Now the British want to leave the treadmill, but find they cannot because they are not yet prepared to abandon many of the benefits the treadmill brings. World shortages may soon compel Britain to reduce its external dependence. Yet the even greater long-term problem remains to find some means of casting off the chains of internal dependence on economic growth. Only that would allow the British to escape fully from the treadmill they have built and establish the first sustainable industrial society.

The Unique Opportunity of North Sea Oil?

But is this analysis not invalidated by the advent of North Sea oil? Certainly oil wealth presents Britain with a very

11

special opportunity. Remaining recoverable reserves on the UK continental shelf at the end of 1979 were officially estimated to be in the range of 2,000–4,200 million tonnes, representing about 1–2% of world reserves, and worth about £350 billion at the current oil price.[6] Output from the fields is expected to rise steadily to over 100 million tonnes a year from 1982 onwards – equal to the annual output of Kuwait or Nigeria. But output might be significantly higher – up to 135 million tonnes. This would make the UK not only self-sufficient but an exporter of oil, since UK domestic consumption in the late 1970s averaged around 95 million tonnes a year, equal in value to almost a fifth of Britain's total import bill. Above all, North Sea oil will make its greatest impact through its effect on the balance of payments and on government revenues. Most economists reckon its direct employment and wealth-creating impact will be slight (about 100,000 jobs). But the other effects will be substantial: the balance-of-payments benefits will add an extra 5% to GNP by 1985, and the government's own estimate of its total revenue from gas and oil (at 1980–1 prices) is £4½–5 million by 1981–2. And current depletion rates suggest the oil will last twenty to forty years.

The oil presents several different policy options. One is to treat it as a bonanza. Certainly the oil could buy for Britain a few more years of high consumption. It puts off the need for hard choices. The present restraints on private consumption, public expenditure and foreign investment would all be temporarily eased. But the folly and irresponsibility of this option are enormous. The international competitiveness of British industry would fall sharply and the country might be back in debt extremely quickly. Far from lasting a generation, the benefits from the oil might only last ten years, and the manufacturing sector would have been further enfeebled as a direct result of the oil wealth.

The second option is the rentier society. Companies would be allowed and encouraged to expand their investment overseas by the amount of surplus on the oil balance of payments once the accumulated debts of the past had been paid off. The oil revenues would be distributed to them in the form of tax cuts to give them extra funds to dispatch abroad greatly increased investments, guaranteeing large flows of profits and dividends to the British Isles in the 1990s when the oil was gone. The oil would have been treated as a capital asset and invested where the highest returns could be expected. This option would not accelerate Britain's industrial decline, but it would not try to reverse it. It would seek a solution to the failing industrial performance by increasing external dependence still further – using overseas assets to claim a living from the rest of the world in perpetuity.

A third option is industrial regeneration. Both the oil revenues and the savings on the balance of payments would be collected in a fund and used to restructure British industry and raise its productivity to European levels (currently they are about 40% below). The chosen instrument of this policy might be either a government agency like the existing National Enterprise Board or direct grants and tax rebates to private companies for approved projects. The aim would be to use the period of oil production to create new industries in Britain that could compete with the rest of the world. A limit would be placed on this rate of depletion of the oil fields in order to spread the benefits over as long a period as possible. During this breathing space great efforts would be made to overcome the internal obstacles to growth. If successful, however, this option would increase the internal dependence on a growth economy.

There is a fourth option – leaving the growth maximisation treadmill by breaking the chains of external and internal dependence. This option, like the third, would place a limit on the rate of depletion and would isolate the oil wealth from the rest of the economy in a special investment fund. The purposes for which this fund would be used, however, would be quite different. The aim would be to invest it in ways that would promote a sustainable industrial society in Britain, so that when the oil fields were exhausted, the external dependence of the British economy on the world economy would have been reduced and a start would have been made on transforming the institutions and culture that sustain growth internally.

But this is not to suggest that the aim should be zero growth, as some environmentalists have suggested. The desire for a modest improvement in living standards over a timespan is a perfectly proper and reasonable desire, and not incompatible with the known availability of resources. What *is* being suggested, however, is that reckless and relentless pressure to maximise economic growth at all costs, over-riding all other factors, is a grossly materialistic distortion of the human personality and in the longer run almost certainly an ecologically unsustainable goal. Rather the aim must be to realise the benefits of economic growth, through the organisation of production as efficiently as possible, but subject to key social and environmental constraints.

No doubt it will be suggested, surveying the bleak UK record of low growth, that what it already has too much of is 'balanced growth': a euphemism for relative economic failure. But this is to misunderstand the concept entirely. There has never yet been a conscious policy in Britain deliberately and thoroughly to instil social and environmental goals as priorities over and above the economic process. Such goals have from time to time been partially and grudgingly conceded, but never positively and comprehensively.

Balanced growth, as the key concept required to escape Britain's increasing vulnerability to both external and internal dependence, will still mean that the UK must be competitive in world trade terms. For there is no other way the country can earn the foreign exchange it will still need to buy the imports that will still be necessary even after a major programme of import substitution, particularly for food, has been put through. What policy is needed to place Britain in the competitive position that has eluded it for so long? The starting point must be that the present Establishment strategy cannot succeed.

The Three Central Economic Policy Alternatives

What, then, are the broad and fundamental economic options now facing Britain? Essentially there are three.

One is to seek to pull Britain back into the capitalist mainstream by jacking up the rate of growth through creating an economic climate which will encourage higher private investment and increased profit-making. This involves stronger investment and tax incentives, especially for high earners, and above all weakening trade union power in order to increase profits. Consonant with this, entry to the EEC was sought as a means to enforce alignment with Britain's more strongly capitalistic competitors on the Continent. But the weakness of this approach is that it ignores how far behind Britain has fallen in the investment race and how difficult (perhaps impossible?) it now is to shift resources from wages to profits on the scale required without a major shift in the pattern of power and rewards in Britain.

A second option would be to make concessions to labour sufficient to get broad consent to switch resources on a major scale from wages to profits and investment. This might involve legislating for an industrial relations climate more favourable to workers (for instance, the Employment Protection Act in 1975) together with some income redistribution towards workers at the expense of wealth-holders and of the highly paid in management and the professions. The trouble with this approach is that it risks getting the worst of both worlds. Any real redistribution in favour of workers contradicts providing incentive for higher private investment, while state intervention to remedy weaknesses

15

left by the private market is resisted by business as unwanted interference – at least, before the stage is reached when business needs state support in rescue operations. Can workers really be expected to accept lower standards voluntarily when the rewards of restraint go disproportionately to the capitalist class? This second option is thus inherently improbable.

The third option is to accept that labour's rejection of anything more than very temporary wage restraint means that workers do not put such a premium on higher growth, from which capital-holders gain most in the short term and for which self-denial by labour is the main pre-condition. Workers give higher priority to improved rights of self-determination at the workplace and to job satisfaction as opposed to output maximisation. In that case, it is the other side of the coin that must be adjusted and some degree of insulation sought against the external pressure of the Western capitalist system as expressed through multilateral free trade and free capital movements.

This would mean imposing industrial (as opposed to purely balance-of-payments) criteria on whether overseas investment was acceptable or not, and would reduce outflows of British capital. It would involve a deliberate policy of increasing British self-sufficiency, in both food and manufacture. It would require backing from workers, which in turn would call for giving them more say in industry. To make use of this, say, there would need to be a massive training programme for shop stewards and other worker representatives. The present negative veto power of workers needs to be transformed into positive influence over decision-making.

The difficulty of this strategy is that by repudiating the capitalist open-market foundations on which the EEC, GATT and the IMF are built it would invite retaliation, even sanctions, from other Western countries. It would meet very strong resistance within Britain itself from the

Establishment (the City, big business and Whitehall top officialdom), who would never willingly agree to real erosion of the power of capitalists.

If these broadly are the options, how have they been used in recent years and what are the practical prospects for the future?

The first option was that adopted by Heath during his 1970–4 government and tried again, in much starker form, by Thatcher after 1979. The Wilson government in its 'social contract' years (1974–5) pursued the second option, and the Labour Party went on after mid-1975, particularly during the Callaghan government, to its own version of option one.

However, there are some major defects in this broad strategy that successive governments have pursued. First, it depended on the long-promised boom in the world economy materialising. But after a faltering and short-lived recovery in 1978, the world was sliding by 1980 into the deepest slump since the 1930s. Alongside this were forecasts of higher rates of international inflation, together with a further sharp rise in European unemployment in the early 1980s. Against this background, when the three most powerful capitalist countries – the USA, West Germany and Japan – refuse to reflate their economies faster, a policy of export-led growth must be doomed to failure. Secondly, the Cambridge Economic Policy Group calculated in 1977 that a growth rate of 5% p.a. until 1985 would be needed to get the level of unemployment below a million. Yet by 1980 Britain was actually experiencing negative growth – 2½% that year, under the whip of monetarist policies. Thirdly, and most important of all, the government's strategy, and indeed the whole future of Western capitalism, depended on solving the inflation/depression riddle. Previously it was believed that Keynesian economic management enabled governments to counter depression and unemployment by public spending and tax cuts to boost their economies. But now, facing the most serious world depression since the

17

1930s, governments were inhibited by fears of unprecedented inflation from having recourse to Keynesian measures at the very time when they seemed most needed. Until, therefore, this strategy – basically a monetarist deflationary policy – is changed, Britain is condemned to be pushed further down the spiral of decline down which it has been steadily slipping for so many years and decades already. Nor is there any limit to how far it can be pushed down. Things will only change if enough people in Britain are prepared to fight hard enough for an alternative strategy that works.

The Power Structure in Britain – Who Controls the State?

All three of the basic policy options outlined above (and no other practicable alternatives seem available) for resolving Britain's economic weakness – which correspond roughly to capitalist, social democratic and socialist approaches – involve sharp conflicts. How these conflicts are settled will depend on the balance of power in Britain at the present time – hence the crucial relevance of the nature of the British state and who controls it. Is power concentrated in too few hands? Is the state a reflection of liberal democracy on behalf of all the people, or an instrument controlled by the dominant class in society? And, above all, is the power structure geared to produce necessary change or an obstacle obstructing it?

BIG BUSINESS – THE STATE

Economic power derives fundamentally from the concentration of production into relatively few enormous corporations. An NIESR study published in the mid-1970s indicated that the market share of the 100 largest UK enterprises rose from 15% in 1909 to 50% by 1970, and since the rate of concentration has accelerated since the last war, it predicted they could become responsible for no less than two-thirds of net output in manufacturing by 1980–5.[7] Certainly their faster rate of development than average national economic growth, plus their global mobility as multinationals and directorate interlock with associated banking institutions, highlight their growing dominance within the power structure of the traditional nation-state.

This acceleration of industrial and financial concentration has brought a convergence of big business and the state towards a new stage, state capitalism, increasingly based on monopoly, whether state-owned or private. This process has ensconced in power a new breed of politico-bureaucrats, in the West as well as the East, who have increasingly displaced both old-style capitalist entrepreneurs and even their big-organisation industrialist successors. The growing importance to national economies of these private or state-sponsored semi-monopolies has forced the state, irrespective of ideology, to intervene to preserve these national giants when they are threatened with elimination – a grudging policy of socialising losses as opposed to appropriating gains.

What is most important of all here is that any intervention by the state to redress defects in the national economy – whether to promote employment, enhance investment, remedy structural distortions, check foreign takeovers, or for any other purpose – naturally redounds to the advantage of business as the major beneficiary because of the bias in the system. For the 'national interest' becomes automatically identified with the health and prosperity of the dominant companies when the nation's success is seen to be so closely tied to their performance. That is inevitably the essence of a capitalist economy. And when export performance, so much the key to modern economic success, is dependent on so few firms – when in Britain in the 1970s some 30 firms controlled 40% of direct trade, 75 firms half and 220 firms two-thirds – it is hardly surprising that any state intervention is bound directly or indirectly, by intention or by result, to assist such firms.

This steady convergence of big business and the state has also strengthened the concentration of power in the hands of the governing class. The democratic governmental forms which exist in many countries disguise this by suggesting that where people have voting and election rights, they can control society through their elected representatives. But the reality is quite different and more complex. Those who have risen in the hierarchy of politics or government administration today achieve positions where the extended role of the state has conferred on them power. This power includes taking detailed decisions affecting the growth and profitability of firms – decisions regarding planning and land development, the award of large contracts, grants and aid, product specifications and safety, financial facilities and interest rates – all of which were previously decided almost wholly within the field of business. This represents a strengthening of the political and bureaucratic elements within the governing sections of society which reflects the consolidation of the old order rather than an escape into new forms of popular democratic control. And this close affinity of interest and similarity of values between business and top civil servants is perhaps nowhere more overtly demonstrated than by the regular interchange of top personnel between Whitehall and the leading boardrooms of industry and finance.[8]

THE POWER OF STATE BUREAUCRACY IN WHITEHALL

Civil service power, and hence utility for business interests, derives basically from the calibre of its administrative class, its sheer organisational weight and control over the Whitehall machine, secrecy, and effective patronage over the vast range of government appointments. Always grounded in its permanence and continuity, it has been growing because of its huge organisational penetration offering unrivalled command over the assembly, use and filtering of information in a more technological age. The slant of this power, while normally not conspiratorial or anti-reformist, is certainly ideologically towards the maintenance, albeit with improved operation, of the existing socioeconomic system.

Tactics used by officials to manipulate ministers take many forms. A chief means is the filtering of information by officials. Papers are progressively screened out as they proceed upwards through the civil service hierarchy, and in contentious issues the 'line' will be decided by the top official, the permanent secretary. Thereafter, in subsequent meetings with the minister other officials will not demur or support the minister against the official 'line', even if they have put strong counter-arguments previously, and the alternatives to the accepted line may not even be put forward because promotion prospects for future postings and future quality of work depend on the support of senior officials.

Alternatively, relevant information may simply be withheld from ministers, partly on the grounds, no doubt, that ministers only have limited time to read papers. Forecasts of economic trends, for example, in the case of unemployment, may be 'doctored', and if forecasts would be 'unacceptable' to a senior minister as being too disturbing, they may not be shown to him, lest he be diverted from policies which might be unpopular with the trade union movement. Again, information may be withheld simply to make life easier for civil servants. Above all, information is decidedly not made available spontaneously to assist a minister's known views where these diverge from officials' preconceptions.

Equally, the timing of the delivery of information to ministers is crucial, and is played to advantage by the civil service. A large Cabinet Office position paper, of perhaps ten to fifty pages, which officials have been mulling over for months, may be put into the minister's night box for his approval for a meeting next morning. The minister may come upon this long, detailed and complicated document for the first time after midnight, and have no time to do more than to glance through it, concentrating on the conclusions. Yet if the document is passed the next day, the whole of it, which most or even all ministers have not properly read and certainly not thought through in depth, becomes 'the agreed policy of the government'.

A second way in which civil service practice undermines the effect of democratic choice is by exploiting ministers' isolation and dependence on the Whitehall machine.[9] As Lord Armstrong, a former head of the civil service, has said: 'The biggest and most pervasive influence is in setting the framework within which questions of policy are raised . . . It would have been enormously difficult for any minister to change the framework, and to that extent we had great power.' Officials retain the 'power of the drafter'. It is not that draft papers cannot always be amended by ministers – of course they can be, provided ministers have time to do so – but rather that much undoubtedly slips through written by officials with particular departmental prejudices, which would never have been *initiated* by ministers in this form. Drafting of papers almost always starts off without prior consultation, oral or otherwise, with ministers, so that by the time that papers reach them they are usually too late and in too final a form for much ministerial input to be introduced.

Any new ministerial inputs into this Whitehall consensus encounter sharp resistance, with every possible objection put forward, many of them fairly trivial or destructive. Usually no attempt is made by officials to be helpful in suggesting how these objections might best be overcome, or how an alternative course of action might lead in the direction desired by the minister. On the contrary, ministers are regarded in Whitehall essentially as spokesmen for their departments – indeed, as one mandarin remarked, 'as our

PR men'. So far from being seen as the political guardians of their party manifesto, they are ranked in Whitehall and the media according to how well they do for their departments. There is a very strong presumption in Whitehall that the role for ministers is to wait for officials to come to decisions on policy issues and then be briefed on what to say in public presentation of the line worked out.

A third way in which Whitehall subverts the democratic process lies in the ruthless use that is made of the inter-departmental network to circumvent an awkward minister. As Richard Crossman noted in his memoirs, 'I have never known a minister prevail against an interdepartmental official paper without the backing of the PM, the First Secretary, or the Chancellor'. One device here is for civil servants who face a minister holding out against them to contact their opposite numbers in other departments and brief them as to how they should brief *their* ministers to oppose their own minister in the interdepartmental ministerial committee discussing the issue. But perhaps the most insidious use of interdepartmental committees, how-ever, is simply to get unwanted ministerial initiatives lost. As an official once said: 'In Whitehall we can co-ordinate anything into the ground.'

A fourth source of civil service power lies in its effective command over the massive range of state appointments. Each department retains huge patronage, the DHSS, for example having within its gift over 3,100 appointments. The actual selection of appointees, though it is nominally in the hands of ministers, is in fact very much a prerogative of the civil servants. For ministerial control is lacking when infor-mation on the full range of personal, ideological and pro-fessional characteristics of suggested appointees is simply not made available. The natural civil service bias is towards self-selection with a 'safe', conservative, centrist slant. This explains why, in terms of social origin, education and class situation, the occupants of the command posts throughout the state sector have been drawn very heavily from business and property backgrounds and from the professional middle class. It explains why the nationalised sector, whatever the ideological facade of public ownership, has since its inception been dominated in practice by private business.[10]

A fifth major Whitehall limitation on parliamentary democracy lies in the enmeshing of the senior echelons of the civil service within the business-finance power structure outside. This occurs at both the administrative and personal levels. Administratively, when ministers ask for a brief on a particular issue, especially in the industrial and economic departments, the source of the information provided by officials is invariably the CBI, top managements of individual companies, the Bank of England, or particular finance houses. Naturally these bodies are a main source of economic data and forecasting, but more significantly it is *their policy slant* rather than that of any other group (since the TUC is not regularly consulted) which permeates the documents put before ministers.

At a more personal level the links between top officialdom and leading industrialists and financiers are very close. They dine together frequently at the Oxford and Cambridge University Club in Pall Mall and at other select clubs around Whitehall. And after their retirement at 60 from the civil service senior officials enjoy in many cases the benefits of lucrative appointments in private industry. Research has shown that no less than twenty-six top civil servants of permanent secretary or equivalent level who retired between 1974 and 1977 were recruited by firms in the private sector.

This close symbiotic relationship with leading representatives of industry and finance must inevitably raise questions about the impartiality of civil service advice. Not that any implication of conspiracy is intended here; it is rather that similarity of class origin and mutuality of interest tends to lead the civil service to a view of what is right in any given situation which closely coincides with the Establishment consensus outside Whitehall.

How far this harmony of interest with industry and finance outside tempts senior civil servants is a matter for conjecture. But there are some pointers. John Pardoe, MP, stated in November 1976 that he had received reliable reports that a number of people from Britain representing both Treasury and City interests had at that time told the US Treasury that it would be better if Britain were to get no more loans from the IMF or the international financial community. On similar lines, Professor Fred Hirsch asserted in 1977 that the IMF was largely the vehicle by which domestic groups, including the City, Bank and Treasury, could get extra power behind their elbows to jog elected ministers, to obtain sacrifices from the people not otherwise obtainable whilst preserving Establishment authority intact. Most striking of all, perhaps, is the story told by Joe Haines of the attempt in June 1975 by the Treasury and the Bank of England, by letting the pound slide down, to 'bounce' the Cabinet into statutory wage controls in defiance of Labour's repeated election pledges. Claiming that the Treasury did nothing to arrest the slump in the pound and used the crisis to force policies on the Labour government which business favoured, though these had already destroyed the Heath government and had been totally repudiated by Labour, Haines describes this action as an attempted 'civilian coup against the government'. Such is the measure of civil service power.

THE POWER OF THE CITY OVER THE BRITISH ECONOMY

The power of the City of London, the third main arm of the troika in the central British power structure, can perhaps best be assessed by examining the key influences on postwar British economic policy. First, in the period of City restriction 1945–51, the central financial feature of the postwar

Attlee government was its 'cheap money' policy which kept down the cost of government borrowing both at home and abroad, and the cost of the great housing drive. It also gave a big boost to investment in basic industries and export industries, not just in those that promised a big return. Despite the postwar difficulties, the recovery of British industry was very rapid under this policy. The trade gap was closed, with exports rising 77% in real terms between 1946 and 1950. It was a policy that favoured industrial capital and so strengthened the national economy.

Criticism of this policy from financial interests and liberal economists was ferocious. Their alternative policy was deflation and high interest rates and high unemployment (*The Economist* called for 5–7% unemployment). This, they argued, would cure inflation and would allow the 'market' to decide how resources should be allocated. The class bias of this approach is evident. But the critics of the Attlee government gained ground because the government found it hard to control inflation. This was partly because of the steep rise in import prices, partly because of the huge re-armament programme (£4,000m.) which the government undertook to satisfy the USA. But it was also because the government took no steps to control the banks. It 'national-ised' the Bank of England in 1946, but the Bank remained the spokesman for the City, and the government lost control of the money market.

In the following period of recovery of the City's dominance, the 'cheap money' policy, which by restricting the freedom of capital gave priority to the government's welfare objectives (like a minimum level of welfare for all and a real commitment to full employment), was replaced by the incoming Tories in 1951 by a regime which might be described as a controlled free market. Lasting from 1951 to 1971, this was a position halfway towards freeing the social power of capital. The Conservatives reactivated monetary policy which had lain dormant since the collapse of the gold standard in 1931, and it soon became their chief weapon of demand management. But recurrent balance-of-payments crises erupted throughout this period because the UK was not earning a large enough surplus on current account to pay for the levels of overseas military spending and foreign investment that were desired by the City, some leading industrial companies and various departments of the government, particularly the military and the Foreign Office. Both policies were related to Britain's traditional role in the world economy. Rather than change these policies, British governments used monetary policy to deflate the home economy whenever balance-of-payments crises erupted. Such deflation hit investment particularly hard and was an important reason for the low investment in British industry during the 1950s and 1960s.

The ascendancy of the City of London was finally restored by the reopening of the commodity markets and the achievement of the full convertibility of sterling in 1958. The reserve currency role of sterling and the position of London as one of the world's two leading financial centres were earned at a heavy price. In every economic crisis in Britain, despite the existence of excess savings, the deflationary policy of dear money was imposed, which only increased the quantity of savings still further. The period saw high and rising long-term interest rates. This suited the financial community, partly because it profited directly from these higher interest rates, and partly because these higher rates protected the sterling exchange rate. But by 1970 the City's interests were no longer indissolubly tied to sterling. It had denationalised itself, and liked to boast of its 'offshore island status' which was recognised and safeguarded by the British authorities.

Finally, the period of the City rampant from 1971 to the 1980s was ushered in by the abolition of the remaining controls that existed over its activities. This new policy of 'competition and credit control' originated as a Bank of

England discussion document in May 1971, and was fully in operation by September 1971. No parliamentary approval was sought or obtained for the scheme, although it had important implications for national economic management. Like so many developments in the City, it was the product of informal discussions. Monetary policy in future would be directed towards regulating broad monetary aggregates, by setting targets like the rate of growth of the money supply. The distribution of the money between different uses was to be left to the market.

The City having secured a degree of free market banking, an orgy of speculation erupted. There was a huge increase in fringe and secondary banking, fuelled by the explosion of the money supply in 1972–3. The market certainly allocated the extra money that the government was pumping in – but not to industrial investment as it wanted. These were the years of the property boom, the share prices boom, the export of capital boom. Indeed it was industrial investment that remained meagre – despite the statutory incomes policy then in force. The monetary authorities entirely lost control of the money supply. Between January 1972 and December 1973 bank lending increased 100%, whilst real economic growth increased 6%. The excesses of the monetary expansion were paid for later in 1975–6: the social contract guidelines on pay cut living standards; the cuts in public spending reduced the PSBR; the exchange rate of sterling fell sharply when hot money flowed out. Stability was restored through the orthodox remedies of deflation and retrenchment. Unemployment stayed high. Apart from the casualties among the fringe banks, the cost of the monetary excesses was not borne by the financial interests. It was shifted to sections of industrial capital and the industrial working class.

What this brief survey of economic and monetary policy over three decades since the war clearly shows is how the financial interests of the City have steadily consolidated their hold on national decision-making, and how at each successive crisis the City's priorities have predominated, gradually at first, but more strongly and overtly later. It is a process taken further still by the massive public expenditure cuts, *laissez-faire* retrenchment and abolition of exchange controls of the Thatcher government, all of them priorities dictated by the City.

Is There a 'Ruling Class' in Britain?

Such are the pivots of the British power structure. But do they collectively really constitute what some have termed a 'ruling class', and if so, is it conducive to the great political, economic and social change that Britain needs to reverse its decline? Answering the first question hinges on four empirical criteria which seem relevant. First, is there a real alliance? Secondly, how comprehensively do they fill the top posts in the command structure of society? Thirdly, does their ownership and control of crucially important areas of the country's economic life also ensure their control of the means of political decision-making in the particular political environment of advanced capitalism? And lastly, what are the key decisions affecting the life of the nation, and how far are they decisively influenced by these dominant groups?

On the first point, not only is there consolidation of the elites horizontally by intensive cross-membership at the top, but they are strengthened vertically by semi-dynastic intra-class recruitment. Guttsman summarised his findings by observing that 'there exists in Britain today a "ruling class" if we mean by it a group which provides the majority of those who occupy positions of power and who in their turn can materially assist their sons to reach similar positions'.[11] Nearly two-thirds of the men in the highest occupational groups, numbering less than 3% of the population, are the sons of men who belonged to the same group. At the institutional level, it is clear that close working relationships exist with the other main elites in society, particularly the armed forces, the judiciary and the press.

On the second point of the extent of occupation of key decision-making posts in society, Miliband has stated that 'what the evidence conclusively suggests is that in terms of social origin, education and class situation the men who have manned *all* command positions in the state system have largely, and in many cases overwhelmingly, been drawn from the world of business and property, or from the professional middle classes'. And Dahrendorf has noted that the 'middle class' which forms the main recruiting ground of the power elite of most European countries today often consists of the top 5% of the occupational hierarchy in terms of prestige, income and influence.[12]

On the third criterion, regarding the effectiveness of economic control in securing leverage over key political decision-making, it is undeniable that the business and propertied interests in the UK, as in other advanced capitalist countries, have generally been able to rely on the positive and active goodwill of their governments; and that even governments who, according to their official party rhetoric, cannot thus be relied upon turn out in practice to have an approach to affairs which either greatly reduces or even virtually eliminates any dangers which these interests are supposed to face. This is not, of course, to suggest that governments always or necessarily act in perfect congruity with these dominant economic interests. Governments may sometimes wish to pursue policies which they themselves believe desirable for capitalist enterprise but which powerful economic interests find objectionable; or governments may be subject to pressures from other classes or interests which they cannot altogether ignore. But the 'bias in the system' does operate strongly – strengthening 'the economy' means in practice consolidating a capitalist economy and the particular social order built upon it, both internally and via the international economic pressures of the IMF, GATT and the EEC.

The fourth criterion focused on how decisively the dominant interests identified – business, City finance and the state apparatus – could be said to influence the key decisions of the nation. Control over the main investment decisions in the economy lies squarely in the boardrooms of leading companies in the private sector. The distribution of income reflects a mixture of market forces and traditional differentials, so that employers can use competitive pressures as a means of holding down wages or, where that fails, call on government incomes policies in aid; equally the distribution of wealth is heavily monopolised by business interests. The allocation of tax revenues in public expenditure has traditionally provided the main funding for the so-called welfare state, but only so far as key business goals (in terms of economic growth, investment levels, anti-inflation measures) have not been threatened. The regulation of the overall level of economic activity, and the key issues deriving from it such as the level of employment and the movement of living standards, reflect the market cycles of capitalism, with business only investing if it sees prospects of future demand and profitability, and government seeking to stimulate or damp down the economy in order to meet business requirements. Similarly, government's regulation of the money supply and fixing of the exchange rate normally reflect Bank of England advice and hence the interests of big-scale finance in the City. Control over the instruments of coercion, notably the army and the police, is used explicitly in ways that serve business interests – to protect property, to quell social unrest or disturbance, to keep essential services going if blocked by strikes, to spy on 'subversives', and so on. On the handling of fundamental conflicts which in capitalist society involve labour–capital struggles, governments have consistently acted to abate or routinise conflict in the interests of business. Incomes policies, deflationary economic management and industrial relations legislation, though regularly defended as essential to the national interest, the health of the economy, the defence of the currency, or the good of workers, do in practice put organised labour in a weaker position relative to employers. And the making of top appointments to key posts in the command structure of society lies directly in the hands of the owners or managers of capital as regards their own companies, and indirectly, through the support of leading officials in the Whitehall departments of state, as regards most key positions in the public sector.

What all this evidence suggests is that, despite a century or more of the political franchise, private economic power continues to exist in ever more concentrated form, and those who wield it, in close alliance with the controllers of the state machine, exercise massive power in society and in the determination of the state's policies and actions. Yet this symbiosis is concealed by the prevailing ideology. For the prevalent view is that the state, in advanced capitalist societies like Britain, is the agent of a 'democratic' social order, with no inherent bias towards any class or group, and that any occasional lapse from impartiality must be ascribed to an accidental deviation external to its 'real' nature. But this is a fundamental misconception. The state is primarily and inevitably the guardian and protector of the economic interests that predominate in it. Its real function is to ensure their continued dominance, not to over-ride them. For these reasons, given the fulfilment of the four criteria specified to a high degree in each case, it can be properly and objectively asserted that there does exist in Britain today a close-meshed set of dominant interests, located primarily in the top industrial boardrooms, the City of London and the top ranks of the state bureaucracy, which collectively fulfils the role of a 'ruling class'.

Values and Ideology: How Does the Power Elite Maintain its Hold on Society?

How is this power *used*? Does it act as a catalyst for needed change, or as a brake on it? How compatible is this power of the governing class with policies required to reverse long-term economic decline?

Whilst the securing of willing compliance is always the most effective means of legitimating rule, it is not the only means available to the dominant class, nor the only one actually employed. The legal authority of the state, for example, can be brought into operation against political or social opposition through the application of an ideology of the state which is propounded as impartial, but which is in fact highly conducive to the interests of the ruling elite. This liberal-democratic theory of the state, which asserts that the state acts as neutral arbiter, has an important legitimising function because of the implication that the state acts for the benefit of society as a whole. This is highly convenient to the ruling Establishment because it places working-class political action firmly in the context, not of the confrontation between capital and labour which it is, but of action against the interests of all.

This has repeatedly enabled the Establishment to claim 'national interest' cover for its own self-interested policies. Many recent instances can be quoted. One was the uniting of the ranks of the Establishment in advocating British entry into the EEC on the grounds that it would boost employment and incomes – the contrary to what actually happened – though its real motive was to restore declining capitalist power against an increasingly strong trade union challenge. Similarly the move in 1978–9 towards currency stabilisation and a European Monetary System was publicly welcomed by the British Establishment because it would sharpen market pressures on the UK economy and thus further curb trade union restraints on capital. For these reasons the

Establishment continued to urge this course even though it would sell out Britain's interests by consolidating a Deutschmark zone and German economic power in Western Europe.

A second example concerns the absolute priority which the Establishment consistently attributes to 'the commercial judgement of companies' in national economic decision-making. It is the British version of 'what is good for General Motors is good for America'. It explains the rationalisation consistently put forward by official spokesmen, both in industry and finance and in government, in favour of maximally unregulated freedom for overseas direct investment, even though the long-term growth and employment potential of the UK economy continues to be undermined by the substantial chronic excess of outward over inward direct investment in manufacturing. It explains why inflation is regularly pronounced to be public enemy number one, rather than unemployment, even when (as in 1978 and 1981) inflation has been reduced to a tolerable level and unemployment has increased to a wholly intolerable level. It explains the rhetorical facade of Labour's so-called 'industrial strategy' in the late 1970s (a medley of work creation, job saving and sectoral planning schemes) which in practice means a rejection of interventionism in favour of private enterprise profit priorities, with the state confined to an adjustment role at the margin. It explains the pretence of the so-called 'social contract' which in reality has meant wage restraint without the corresponding pressure to require increased investment on the managerial side.

A third dimension of this ideological cleavage between the interests of the ruling Establishment and those of the mass of the people lies in the repeated implicit preference of the former for accommodating foreign international pressures rather than asserting the primacy of what is nationally advantageous to the British people. It is symptomatic of the deference of the British authorities in favour of the main

Western capitalist powers that they sided with the USA,
Germany and Japan in vigorously opposing the slide into
world trade protectionism in the late 1970s, though it is the
strong economies that chiefly gain from free trade, and
weaker economies like Britain whose domestic industries
would benefit most from trade regulation.

A fourth way in which the British Establishment (like
those in other countries, only more so) exercises power in its
own interests, not those of the people, is in its manipulation
of the laws against emerging movements of political opposition and in favour of the status quo of the British state. The
Official Secrets Acts guard state secrets, leaving the mass of
the people in almost total ignorance of the state's actions.
Incitement laws have been developed in such a way as to
ensure the loyalty of the armed forces at the disposal of the
controllers of the state. Attempts to introduce democratic or
syndicalist ideas among the police or the military have
historically been viewed as directly subversive to the interests of the state and punishable as sedition. In addition,
the conspiracy laws have been used to ensnare political
militants opposing the state. Since proof of incitement and
conspiracy does not require proof of any actual crime having
been committed, it can be, and particularly since the 1960s
has been, used to catch persons where the evidence to con-
vict under the laws relating to public order, public morals
and political conflict may not be available. Thus the 1875
Conspiracy and Protection of Property Act was used, as a
far-reaching precedent, against the building workers' pickets
in the Shrewsbury trial in 1972 on the grounds that they
'wrongfully and without legal authority intimidated divers
people with a view to compelling these people to abstain
from their lawful work'. Political or trade union dissent thus
becomes indictable, given a determined judiciary, as conspiracy. Furthermore, the Emergency Powers Acts, whilst
ostensibly being directed at preventing civil disorder and
revolution, have all been used to pre-empt what most would

regard as legitimate political opposition. What is most significant here is that the wording and construction of each of these Acts 'offend widely accepted democratic rights under the normal rule of law',[13] and are overtly political in their implications and use, backed up by the partiality of the judiciary in giving interpretive judgements that favour the Establishment.

A fifth illustration – and clearly many other examples could be quoted – of the elitist and self-interested ideology of the controllers of the British state lies in their instinctive anti-trade unionism. This obsessiveness is revealed in their constant railing at trade union power as being overmighty and excessive (though in fact the City, industrial management and Whitehall monopolise all the key instruments of political and economic control like money supply, investment and exchange rate policy, in their united hostility to industrial democracy (demonstrated by their successful emasculation of the Bullock proposals in 1977–8), in their interminable harping on the need for wage restraint without any accompanying *quid pro quo* on which to base a genuine 'social contract', and in their sedulous fostering of the image of the trade unions as responsible for all Britain's ills. The root of this class hatred of the trade unions is the recognition that the latter constitute the single focus of power in Britain which is not part of an otherwise homogeneous class Establishment, even though efforts are constantly made to incorporate it.

It is this regular use of power by the dominant established class in Britain, in favour of its own class interest even where this clearly diverges from the national interest, that constitutes the central impediment that has brought about, and prevents escape from, Britain's persisting economic decline. How to overcome this critical obstacle to change, which would open the way politically and socially to reversing the country's long-standing economic decline, is tackled in Part Four.

NOTES: CHAPTER 1

1 These Treasury figures, from *Hansard*, 22 October to 8 November 1973, are compiled respectively from the ILO *Yearbook of Labour Statistics*, 1971, and from the UN *Economic Survey of Europe in 1969*, pt II, 1971.

2 Treasury, *Hansard*, 7 November 1980, compiled from OECD *Main Economic Indicators*.

3 Treasury, *Hansard*, 13 November 1980, from OECD sources.

4 M. Fores, 'Britain's economic growth and the 1870 watershed', *Lloyds Bank Review*, January 1971, p. 28.

5 I am indebted for the substance of this section to A. M. Gamble and D. E. Gamble, whose essay *Towards a Sustainable-State Economy in the United Kingdom* won the 1977 Mitchell prize, and to the publishers, Woodlands Conference, Inc.

6 All the figures in this paragraph come from the Department of Energy (*Hansard*, 8 December 1980).

7 S. J. Prais, *A New Look at Industrial Concentration*, Oxford Economic Papers, vol. 26, no. 2 (July 1974).

8 Better-known recent examples include the transfer of Sir William Armstrong, former head of the civil service, to chairmanship of the Midland Bank; of Richard Marsh, former Labour Cabinet minister, to head British Rail; of Anthony Barber, as Tory Chancellor the greatest postwar money supply inflator, to chairmanship of Standard and Chartered Bank; of Sir Don Ryder, chairman of the huge Reed International corporation, to head Labour's National Enterprise Board. Most revealing of all is the number of Treasury or inland revenue mandarins who over the last two decades have been translated to chairmanships or managing directorship of some of Britain's foremost companies – Sir Henry Wilson Smith to GKN, Paul Chambers to ICI, Sir Maurice Bridgman to BP, Lord Plowden to Tube Investment, Sir Leslie Rowan to Vickers, Sir Edward Playfair to ICI and Glaxo, Francis Cockfield to Boots, and others.

9 See further details in M. Meacher, 'Whitehall's short way with democracy', in K. Coates (ed.), *What Went Wrong?* (Nottingham: Spokesman Books, 1979).

10 It explains, for example, how Mr Nigel Vinson was appointed in November 1973 to the British Airports Authority Board when a council member of the virulently anti-nationalisation Aims of Industry, how Mr Peter Matthews was appointed in 1973 as deputy chairman of the nationalised BSC when managing director of Vickers and leading the anti-nationalisation campaign of the SRNA, and how Mr Ralph Bateman was a non-executive board member of BSC when, as the newly elected president of the CBI, early in 1974, he led private industry's attacks on Labour's nationalisation plans. It also explains how the RR(71) board as at 1974, almost totally lacked members with industrial management experience and was top-heavy with former civil servants and service officers (e.g. the deputy chairman was a retired civil servant with a £25,000 salary, the vice-chairman was a retired service officer also on a £25,000 salary and the project director was another retired civil servant drawing a salary, in addition to other directorships, of £20,000 a year).

11 W. L. Guttsman, *The British Political Elite* (London: MacGibbon & Kee, 1965), p. 356. He has documented the extensive cross-membership of elite groups, and illustrated it by the careers of such 'pluralists of power' as Willink, Pilkington, Stedeford and Sir Philip Morris. Such cross-hierarchical

careers frequently embrace multiple membership of a major company board, board of the Bank of England, Royal Commission, advisory committee, board of governors of the BBC, CBI, vice-chancellor of a university, and so on. Another recent striking confirmation of this trend is the later career of Sir Denis Greenhill. After retiring as permanent under-secretary at the Foreign Office in 1973, he was appointed a director of the merchant bank S. G. Warburg, a government director of BP, a governor of the BBC and also a director of British Leyland.

12 R. Miliband, *The State in Capitalist Society* (London: Quartet Books, 1973), p. 61, and R. Dahrendorf, 'Recent changes in the class structure of European societies', *Daedalus*, vol. 93, no. 1 (Winter 1964), p. 238.
13 T. Bunyan, *The Political Police in Britain* (London: Julian Friedmann, 1976), p. 56.

Part Two
Why Things Cannot Go On As They Are

2

Slump

Britain's predicament needs to be seen in two contexts. One – what has gone wrong internally in economic, power, ideological and social terms – was the subject of Part One. The other is the international economic situation within which Britain is located, and this, the current state of Western capitalism, is the subject of Part Two. In this wider context at least three main factors can be identified which, singly or collectively, clearly pose profound challenges to the maintenance of an international capitalist system, and *a fortiori* therefore to Britain. These factors are examined in the next three chapters. The first, and potentially most serious, is deepening slump.

What Has Caused the International Slump?

On the fundamental question of the causes of the slump, and therefore on prescriptions for its reversal, there is considerable controversy. For the world capitalist economy one of the severest problems has always lain in ensuring sufficient consistent growth in demand. Violent oscillations in the trade cycle between boom and slump were the common experience in the nineteenth century until the First World War, followed by deep and persistent depression in the interwar years. However, the long boom in the West from the Second World War until the early 1970s seemed to prove that the instability inherent in capitalism could be cured by Keynesian demand management techniques. Only stagflation – the simultaneous existence of high unemployment and high inflation – and the renewed world slump of the mid-1970s have now suggested otherwise. But if the capitalist cycle has returned with a vengeance, why was it kept relatively under control for the quarter-century 1945–70? There are two questions, therefore, which any satisfactory explanation of the slump must answer: it must explain why the Western economies flourished for two and a half decades after the Second World War and why they gradually succumbed to a deepening slump in the 1970s and 1980s (as well as of course during the 1920s and 1930s).

A Kondratieff-type explanation, postulating long-wave movements involving several normal cycles, is inadequate here. This has been used to explain the quarter-century stagnation 1913–39 followed by the quarter-century boom 1945–70, the implication being that capitalism has now entered a further quarter-century depression 1970–95.[1] However, whether causation is quite so mechanistic seems rather doubtful. There can at least be no doubt that the avalanche of innovation and the shrinking interval between invention and manufacture were main causal factors associated with the long postwar boom. There are perhaps two main types of view about the cause or causes of the gradually unfolding post-1973 depression. One holds that it results from a combination of technical factors which, if correctly identified, can be reversed by a new mix of technical instruments. The other believes that deepening stagflation derives from structural factors inherent in the nature of capitalism itself which is seen as prone not only to recurring violent fluctuations but above all to a fundamental tendency to stagnation.

Explanations Based on Technical Factors

THE ESTABLISHMENT VIEW

Perhaps the most eminent recent expression of the former view, representing the conventional wisdom of the Western capitalist Establishment, is the McCracken Report[2] commissioned by the OECD and published in June 1977. The authors, eight economists led by a former chairman of the US Council of Economic Advisers, attribute the post-1945 decades of steady expansion to postwar reconstruction, a remarkable increase in technological change, an expansion of international trade and relatively cheap raw materials and energy. They trace the origin of the present crisis, which they see as beginning in the USA in the mid-1960s, to Washington's financing of the Vietnam War largely by the creation of surplus dollars unsupported by increased real wealth. This began to disrupt monetary stability in the USA and, via the US balance-of-payments deficit, in the rest of the Western world. The economists did not, however, consider aggressive wage claims by trade unions a primary cause of international inflation; but they believed that the remarkable growth in the power of organised labour, matched by the growing international concentration of business, provided an obstacle to the ready correction of inflation once it had got a grip.

Such a relatively superficial listing of the main economic difficulties of the last decade offers little or no *explanatory* power as a guide to policies for the future. The McCracken Report simply recommends direct measures to create jobs at a time of serious unemployment, particularly among school-leavers, together with some broad kind of prices and incomes policy, a redress of imbalances of which inflation is one of the main symptoms, better functioning of private markets and a system of constant review of the claims of public expenditure on economic resources. This is, of course, very much the existing pot-pourri of policies of the conventional wisdom. It does not, however, explain why economic recovery has been so uncertain and hesitant during the second half of the 1970s, nor why Keynesian demand management techniques now seem inappropriate for use at a time of the deepest and longest post-Second World War recession.

THE COMMODITIES PRICE EXPLOSION AS A CAUSE OF DEPRESSION

A similar type of explanation is propounded by Professor N. Kaldor.[3] He selects several specific factors – trade union militancy, the abandonment of fixed exchange rates, the failure of US grain stocks to play their former role, OPEC, Western fiscal and monetary policies – due to their fortuitous coincidence in the early 1970s, as the factors which collectively produced the fundamental discrepancy between the output of the primary (commodity-producing) and secondary (manufacturing) sectors of the world economy from which it had previously been shielded for half a century. Kaldor suggests that any large change in commodity prices, whether in favour of or against primary producers, tends to dampen industrial activity. On the one hand an oversupply of primary products causes a fall in their price, which is determined by the level of effective demand, and therefore a fall in primary sector incomes and hence their capacity to buy manufactured products. On the other hand, undersupply of primary products, while causing a rise in their price, also causes a disproportionate rise in the price of manufactured goods since the latter prices are cost-determined; and raw materials (including food for industrial workers) are an industrial input to which customary fixed profit margins are automatically added. So, either way, primary producers' real incomes are cut, thus depressing demand for manufactured goods. The Kaldor solution is therefore to stabilise commodity prices through the creation by leading governments of international buffer stocks for all the main commodities, and to link the finance of these stocks directly to the issue of international currency such as Special Drawing Rights (SDR) which could thus be backed by, and directly convertible into, major commodities comprising foodstuffs, fibres and metals.

Such a one-way ratchet hypothesis does usefully explain why less developed countries' (LDCs') incomes are consistently depressed relative to those of industrialised countries, and hence suggests one important reason why there is a persisting tendency to stagnation in the Western world. But this theory cannot by itself explain why deepening recession is simultaneously accompanied by unprecedentedly high inflation. Nor can it be regarded on its own account alone as a sufficient explanation of the depth and prolongation of the recession in the developed world in the middle and late 1970s. The balance in total output between the developed world (including here the Soviet bloc) and the under-developed world is approximately 80:20. Given an imbalance of this magnitude, it is implausible to assume that growth could not be adequately stimulated within the industrialised countries themselves, and deficiency of LDC demand could not in global terms be more than a further aggravating factor (though very serious, of course, in its own right on political grounds). Nor does a commodity prices destabiliser theory explain why in the second half of the 1970s, when commodity prices had largely steadied, the recovery from deep recession faltered and stagnated throughout the capitalist world in 1976–8 in the midst of still-rapid inflation.

Explanations Based on Structural Factors

For these reasons, whilst the McCracken and Kaldor theories certainly draw attention to events and processes which have aggravated economic instabilities, identification of 'technical' factors of this kind clearly cannot explain adequately both why the history of the capitalist economies for the quarter-century after 1945 was one of relative stability and why the succeeding decade of the 1970s has shown such marked signs of chronic instability. A more 'structuralist' explanation seems to be called for. Of these, there are perhaps two main types. One assumes a basic underlying stability in the framework of capitalism and seeks to explain how this has been undermined. The other assumes a fundamental tendency to instability in the capitalist system and thus seeks to indicate why this phenomenon was suppressed for almost three decades after the Second World War before its 'natural' propensity manifested itself. A major advantage of the latter type of explanation, however, is that it can much more easily accommodate within its theory the Great Depression and the prolonged instability of the interwar years.

THEORIES OF STRUCTURAL ADJUSTMENT ASSUMING A
BASIC STABILITY OF CAPITALISM

On the former view, there have been two main theses advanced by those who accept the stability model of capitalism and offer a rationale for structural adjustment to remedy current instabilities. One stresses internal institutional maladjustment, and the other emphasises distortions in external trade, as the basic cause of breakdown.

Excessive power of unions and corporations
The first of these two views, most notably advanced by Professor Galbraith, is that the decisive weapon of economic policy is the national budget, and this, interacting with the power of large corporations and labour unions to set more or less any prices they like irrespective of market conditions, produces the inflation-recession combination.[4] Since

monetary policy cannot then be effective, Galbraith asserts, except at a price in unemployment which is beyond the political tolerance of democracy, a permanent incomes policy is necessary to combat the permanent market power of corporations and unions, plus a government capacity to raise taxes or cut expenditure as quickly as the reverse. Galbraith also asserts that 'a more consciously egalitarian income distribution will become an indispensable aspect of successful economic management'. At the same time the physical supply of strategic products and services will have to be planned nationally and supranationally. International currency arrangements cannot be stabilised until national economies have been stabilised.

However, while excessive institutional power may well constitute one of the prime aggravations of inflation, it is not clear why on this view these long-term phenomena should have produced such a serious slide into depression specifically in the 1970s, nor why these factors, operative throughout the two previous decades, were not more destructive of growth then. Secondly, this theory propounds a theoretical solution – permanent control over the distribution of incomes by state authorities – for which there is no historical precedent and which there is every reason to believe is in practice unattainable. Market pressures, or the need to make in some cases quite large-scale adjustments according to market requirements, would seem on the basis of experience to be irresistible beyond at maximum a three- to five-year period. Thirdly, permanent wage controls would ossify an income distribution which can only be validated by historical tradition, not by equity or social principles, and it must be highly doubtful if the authorities would sensitively reflect changing popular ideas about differential occupational values. Fourthly, the sheer rigidities of a permanent price-fixing bureaucracy cause the imagination to boggle.

Another variant on this general theme, which seeks a

compromise between the 'free market' solution involving intolerable unemployment and the permanent planning solution involving unmaintainable rigidities, has been advocated by Peter Jay.[5] This suggests that our existing political economy is inherently unstable because it insists on a level of employment which is unattainable without accelerating inflation under present labour market arrangements. Therefore those arrangements must change so as to remove the general influence of collective bargaining and to enhance the general efficiency of the labour market. The only potentially acceptable alternative is a change in company law which gives ownership and ultimate control of enterprises to the people employed by them. They would then have to sink or swim in a market environment. Inflation, it is claimed, would subside, employment would be high and the sovereignty of the consumer would be assured. Adam Smith's 'hidden hand' would continue its benign dispositions, and the corporate state and its handmaiden, the national trade union, together with the bureaucracy of the mixed economy, would wither away. The democracy of the ballot-box, of the market-place and of the workplace would prevail over the otherwise oppressive power of giant organisations, especially of government itself.

Jay's vision is an appealing one and the advocacy of industrial democracy is attractive, but as a proposal for resolving the fundamental recession-inflation conundrum it is based on a false analysis. Like the Galbraithian approach, it concentrates on explaining accelerating inflation rather than deepening recession and this cannot by itself explain why the West fell into the grip of a profound depression in the 1930s and then again in the 1970s to 1980s. Even on the inflation side it is limiting because it implicitly assumes that the sole or at least main cause of inflation lies in the monopoly power of the trade unions. This is clearly contradicted by historical experience. Relevant factors, varying in importance from time to time, have included devaluation leverage on import prices, increases in indirect taxation, monetary policy upward push on interest rates and extensive below-capacity operation in many industrial sectors which sharply raises unit costs. In many recent years wage rises have in fact accounted for less than half of increased prices.

Severe trade imbalances inhibiting growth
Another view of the need for fundamental adjustment, whilst implicitly accepting the inherent stability of the system, is that the GATT rules, which fuelled the world boom for a quarter-century after 1945, no longer engender a system of world trade which induces adequate growth. This conclusion was reached by the Cambridge Economic Policy Group in 1979 on the basis of a market-by-market examination of trade in manufactures and on separate consideration of volumes and prices for trade in fuels and for food and other raw materials, so as to take account of the particular pattern of interdependence between every pair of blocs in manufactured trade and of the sensitivity of each bloc's trade balance to world prices of oil and of other primary commodities. This showed that low growth in the world economy was not primarily due to high oil prices, but rather to a persistent and growing surplus on the part of Japan and a few European countries, notably West Germany.

What is therefore most needed to restore rapid growth in world trade and GNP is, firstly, a sharp reduction in the growth of Japanese exports, secondly, reductions in the import propensities of the USA and certain other countries such as the UK, and thirdly discrimination in favour of exports of manufactures from developing countries on the part of importing countries which have strong trade balances or themselves control imports.[6] Contrary to much received wisdom, the Cambridge study showed that two widely denounced contingencies – higher oil prices and retaliation against US or UK import controls – would not be particularly harmful to world trade. It also reached several other important conclusions. One was that the required changes in structural trends in the 1980s were larger than could be achieved by exchange rate adjustments. Another was that whether or not the growth of world trade accelerated, the USA would need to restrict growth of imports in order to achieve internal growth and full employment, and provided such restrictions were used to maintain internal growth rather than to cut the US trade deficit, they would not reduce the trade of other countries.

However, whilst it cannot be doubted that excessive trade imbalances do undermine overall levels of international growth, it is not clear why on this theory such profound dislocations of the previous growth pattern should have occurred in the 1970s when substantial chronic surpluses and chronic deficits were already being registered in the boom years. And the enormous reduction in the Japanese trade surplus after 1979–80 did not seem to have any appreciable impact on world growth.

THEORIES OF STRUCTURAL ADJUSTMENT ASSUMING A
BASIC INSTABILITY IN CAPITALISM

The alternative view of recurring slump is that the system itself is fundamentally unstable, and its viability is preserved from slowdown and collapse only by major structural interventions. There are two main theories of this kind that have been put forward.

Arms expenditure as the engine of demand
Arms expenditure has undoubtedly been one of the main engines of growth of Western capitalism in the postwar period. In 1978 world military expenditure reached a staggering £212,000 million, having already nearly doubled over the decade to 1973, whilst over the same period the world arms trade almost tripled in current money terms to US $8·7 billion (or doubled, after adjustment for inflation).[7]

Kidron has seen in this permanent arms economy the major factor offsettting the long-run tendency of the rate of profit to decline.[8] Certainly the significance of arms expenditure has been massive. It corresponds to about a half of gross capital formation throughout the world.[9] Even before the Vietnam War boosted US military outlays, arms expenditure was equivalent to some 8–9% of world output of all goods and services at that time, and approximated to almost the entire national income of all backward countries. It was also, to use yet another illustration, very nearly equal to the value of the world's exports of all commodities. It has been estimated that the US military-industrial complex creates one in nine jobs in the USA, generates one-tenth of GNP, involves 100,000 companies and provides huge profits without clear reference to performance.[10]

Overall figures conceal the full significance of defence expenditure specifically for manufacturing industry, for both investment and markets. As a proportion of gross domestic fixed capital formation it constituted nearly 60% for the USA, and even 42% for the UK.[11] OECD figures for the 1960s also indicate the paramount importance of the military budget for particular industries. In the USA more than 90% of final demand for aircraft and parts was on government, almost exclusively military, account, as was nearly 60% of the demand for non-ferrous metals, over 50% of the demand for chemical and electronic goods and 35% of the demand for communication equipment and scientific instruments.

The significance of arms expenditure in Western capitalism is not only that it is claimed to be a massive source of demand in a system otherwise prone to stagnation because of need saturation (even given the Galbraithian artificial stimulation of needs by commercial advertising); it also has three other special characteristics as a stabiliser. One is that demand for new defence equipment and new weapons systems is open-ended: there is potentially no end to improvements that can be sought in military security networks. Secondly, arms production has a 'domino' effect: initiatives by one side have to be countered by equal or preferably superior responses by the other, and all the major economies are thus drawn inexorably into a competitive arms race which in demand terms within each economy is self-perpetuating. Thirdly, arms expenditure has produced considerable civilian 'spin-off', and thus has made an important contribution to stimulating the general rate of technological advance.

The strength of the argument for the arms economy as the main engine of capitalist growth can be further strengthened by considering the alternatives. It could, of course, be argued that there is nothing unique about arms expenditure, and it could be replaced by other forms of government spending – on houses, schools, hospitals, roads, or power stations – which could serve the same demand-expanding purposes. The difficulty with such proposals is essentially a question of size and impact: as a US government report noted at the end of the 1960s: 'Our objections to [welfare expenditure are that] . . . As an economic substitute for war it is inadequate because it would be far too cheap.'[12] The report maintained that war was a stabilising force for which it would be very difficult to find a satisfactory substitute in US society. Significantly, the New Deal in the 1930s, despite unprecedented state expenditure of the 'social service' and 'hole-filling' kind, did not prevent the US economy from relapsing into a second slump, on top of an already high level of unemployment, in 1938–9.

How far, then, can armaments expenditures be expected to provide the needed growth stimulus in Western capitalism? The possibilities of a limited international war cannot be excluded as an economic booster – there is none better – but, without being too dangerous (as in the Middle East), such a war is unlikely to last long enough for this purpose. No doubt the most favourable prospect of all would be served by a Sino-Russian war, with both sides preferably, or at least one, being furnished by the West with arms, the classic form of waste expenditure that needs constant and urgent replenishing. This may seem a somewhat far-fetched prospect, but perhaps no more so than the efforts of the Western powers in the 1930s to manoeuvre fascist Germany and bolshevik Russia into war (hence appeasement in the 1930s and the 'phoney war' on the western front till after Stalingrad, 1943), with Western-supplied armaments to lead recovery from the depression.

However, there are clear limitations to the arms economy argument as an explanation of growth and slump. It is true that on the arms front Western military expenditure is gradually but steadily losing its proportionate share in each national GNP. Even the Vietnam War did not reverse the declining share of armaments in government spending in the West from 25% in 1955 to 17% in 1965.[13] But such a decline can hardly by itself explain the slide into depression in the 1970s, given that military expenditures still remained at extremely high levels. Moreover, it has been argued that a permanent war economy, as in the USA, is actually inimical to productive growth: the USA, with the highest proportionate military spending at 9·2% of GNP in the 1960s compared with Japan's mere 0·8%, attained an annual growth rate of only 2·6% per employee during this period, compared with Japan's very rapid 9·5%.[14] Japanese concentration on medium-level technologies, with low-cost overheads, spread over huge export runs, proved a much more effective and enduring postwar growth formula, at least until 1971.

Major new technologies generating massive investment cascades

Whilst arms expenditure has undoubtedly played a major role in sustaining growth in the Western economies, it is better understood as one – a large one, but not the only one –

53

amongst a *set* of massive investment generators. Whatever limited influence government measures to stimulate growth may have had on the cyclical fluctuations, the basic underlying trend of growth has been due to the emergence, stage by stage, of *real* sustaining factors.

Historically, the accumulation process within capitalism has been buoyed up by successive fundamental innovations involving far-reaching changes in economic activity and employment patterns. These centred on the steam engine in the late eighteenth and early nineteenth centuries, the railways in the second half of the nineteenth century and the automobile in the early and middle twentieth century. From the 1850s onward until the depression of 1907 the railways in the USA directly absorbed about as much capital as all manufacturing and extractive industries combined, and provided employment for a large part of the great waves of immigrant workers entering the country in that period. During the 1920s reasonably full employment in the USA (unemployment averaged 4·5% during 1916–29) was attained on the back of the first great wave of automobilisation, a major sweep of new technologies which included not only the development of car manufacture itself, but also many related industries such as oil, glass, steel, rubber, highway construction and suburban growth.

Then after 1945 there was, first, pent-up consumer demand and investment in reconstruction, financed heavily by Marshall Aid in 1947. Then came the Korean War and the accompanying commodities boom. The Cold War of the late 1940s and 1950s also ushered in a period of huge arms expenditures. Furthermore, technological innovations in the 1950s elicited massive investments in new fields such as synthetic fibres, computers and petrochemicals. Another major factor was the spread of ownership of motor cars to the working class in the main industrial countries, leading not only to important social changes, but also to large-scale investment in building and communications. The changing patterns of international trade – notably the decline of the British Empire and of Commonwealth connections, the huge expansion of US overseas penetration and the establishment of the EEC – similarly encouraged investment to take advantage of new opportunities chiefly centred on the advanced technological markets of the West.[15]

At the end of the 1950s the Russian launching of Sputnik precipitated a huge US missile build-up, particularly in the early 1960s under Kennedy and with a major boost of demand for several sectors of the domestic economy. Similarly, the American NASA moon programme provided substantial civilian spin-off from space projects throughout the 1960s. Most of all, the Vietnam War, especially in the 1965–70 period when the cost to the USA soared to some $80 billion a year, provided an enormous boost to demand (though the 1973 Middle East War was too short-lived to replicate these beneficial effects to the US economy).

Historically, therefore, the postwar period was characterised by a succession of *real* investment factors which strongly underpinned growth. But is such a bunching of technological innovation – what some have identified as a third industrial revolution – likely to recur regularly? The emergence of new technologies with massive applications and thus feeder effects throughout the entire system can never be discounted – for example, possibly new petroleum marine extraction technologies with reverberations throughout the huge worldwide offshore supplies market, or new pervasive anti-pollution techniques or materials conservation systems. Such developments are indeed possible, but at the start of the 1980s there was still no sign of them on anything remotely like the scale required.

What is more directly relevant is that the USA has never previously experienced unemployment at the 1970s rate except in 1915 (9·7%) and in the 1930s up to 1941 (9·9%). On both these occasions periods of deepening stagnation were only ended by war – after the depression of 1908–15 and the revival of deep depression in 1938–9. In the latter case it is highly relevant that after the normal business upswing of 1933–7 which, aided though not caused by the New Deal, brought unemployment down during this period from 24·9 to 14·3%, unemployment shot up again to 19% in the sharp recession of 1938. War, not the New Deal, removed unemployment from the face of America in the 1930s. What, then, will perform the same function in the 1980s, when first a repeat New Deal may be no more efficacious than the earlier version, and secondly, and more important, the credit-boosting mechanisms must operate by accelerating inflationary pressures already unprecedentedly and dangerously high?

NOTES: CHAPTER 2

1 After N. D. Kondratieff, the Russian economist, whose theory was developed further by Josef Schumpeter.
2 P. McCracken (ed.), *Towards Full Employment and Price Stability* (Paris: OECD, June 1977).
3 N. Kaldor, 'Inflation and recession in the world economy', *Economic Journal*, vol. 86 (December 1976), pp. 703–14.
4 J. K. Galbraith, *Money – Whence It Came, Where It Went* (London: Deutsch, 1975).
5 P. Jay, *Employment, Inflation and Politics* (London: Institute of Economic Affairs, 1976).
6 *Cambridge Economic Policy Review*, no. 5 (1979), p. 1.
7 'US Arms Control and Disarmament Agency', *World Military Expenditures and Arms Trade, 1963–1973* (Washington, DC: US Arms Control and Disarmament Agency, January 1975).
8 M. Kidron, 'An Arms Economy'; *Western Capitalism Since the War* (Harmondsworth: Penguin, 1970), ch. 3.
9 UN, *Economic and Social Consequences of Disarmament* (New York: UN, 1962), p. 3.
10 ibid., pp. 55–7.
11 A. Yarmolinsky, 'The problem of momentum', in A. Chayes and J. B. Wiesner (eds), *ABM: an Evaluation of the Decision to Deploy an Anti-ballistic Missile System* (London: Harper & Row, 1969), pp. 144–9.
12 *Report from the Iron Mountain, on the Possibility and Desirability of Peace*, ed. L. C. Lewin (London: MacDonald, 1968), p. 92.
13 M. Kidron, *Western Capitalism Since the War* (Harmondsworth: Penguin, 1970), p. 62.
14 S. Melman, *The Permanent War Economy: American Capitalism in Decline* (New York: Simon & Schuster, 1975).
15 A. N. Silver, *Politics and Money*, vol. 6, no. 4 (August–October 1975), p. 8.

3

The End of Full Employment – the Counter-Attack of Monetarism

Not only have the events of the 1970s presented the capitalist authorities with an extremely dangerous combination of deepening inflation-slump for which they have no remedy, but they have also given grounds for reconsidering one of the main premises for predicting, from Marx onwards, the eventual demise of capitalism. This has been the assumption that the increasing productivity of capital would so shrink the employment base as to bring the class relations on which the system depended to an explosive end. The road to socialism is paved with bad predictions, and the evolution of employment opportunities within Western capitalism has, in fact, proved far more complex than Marx expected. Nevertheless, the inflation-slump combination poses a dilemma for policy-makers, both right and left, which shows every sign, whatever the policy option adopted, of abandoning full employment as a practical target and leading strongly towards 1930s-type levels of unemployment throughout the Western world.

The Steady Contraction of Manufacturing Jobs

In the decade and a half from 1960 employment in manufacturing decreased in Britain by 12·1% (i.e. by nearly 1·25

57

million), while jobs in central government over the same period rose 6·7% (up by 0·1 million) and in local authorities by no less than 62·6% (up by nearly 1·25 million). It may be argued therefore that even if labour is increasingly made redundant by automative technology in manufacturing, it may be absorbed elsewhere in the economy, particularly in the services and government sectors. However, there is a limit to the extent that such a large movement of labour can take place with impunity when it represents for the economy both the contraction of the market base, shrinking in Britain's case from 56% of output in 1961 to 39% by 1974, as well as a marked shift into a sector where marginal productivity is tiny or nil.

There is also another caveat which is sometimes entered against the end-to-full-employment thesis. This is that workers are anyway beginning to show preference for a shorter working week, so that as long as the reduced total quantum of work is shared out fairly the net result is not increased unemployment but increased leisure. But apart from the technical difficulty of sharing out many types of work and the economic disincentive in many cases (in higher labour costs to employers through increased national insurance contributions, and so on), this preference is of course predicated *also* on a demand for adequate, not to say annually improving, real living standards. This can hardly be guaranteed by large-scale and growing *structural* unemployment. Thus, though the increase in *frictional* unemployment arising from the liability of the increasing scale of industrial enterprise to mass redundancies can be resolved, albeit by slower redeployment, there seems very little prospect on present trends of such extensive job restructuring that the full employment economy of the 1950s can be regained in the West.

The Impact of Microelectronics on Employment

On top of these pre-existing trends, the West is now under-going a quantum leap in technology. But the silicon chip is not the only example. Nuclear energy, molecular biology, genetic engineering and charge-coupled devices are all starting to bear the fruits of their development, and these too will have impacts on work and society. But the chip remains the main problem, because of the enormous range of its potential applications. There are not many industrial processes, either batch or continuous track, commercial processes or clerical and administrative processes, that will not be affected. All jobs with repetitive elements, or which are totally repetitive and where individual discretion is at a minimum, risk either massive job changes or job losses. Industries particularly affected by the new technology have been identified by the Advisory Council on Applied Research and Development (ACARD) as energy, agri-culture, fisheries and food processing, transport, tele-communications, manufacturing plant and machinery, cars, security equipment, domestic equipment and the service industries. Thus the facets of the new technology – cheap-ness, reliability, flexibility, application to all stages of production (since the actual production process is automated as well as the components) – will not only affect, as in past automation, the manufacturing sector, but will have a huge impact on the service sector as well; for example, word processors replacing typists and visual display transmission eliminating the need for postal communication.

Very different projections have been made as to impact of the microelectronics revolution on employment. On the one side, a study by US consultants published in 1979 con-cludes that 1 million net extra jobs are likely to be created in Western Europe and the USA during the next decade.[1] On the basis of a study of four industries – consumer home appliances, business communications, industrial test

59

equipment and cars – they calculate that extra wealth created in these industries by 1987 will be £15–17 billion (at 1977 prices). Whilst some industries will decline, the fast growth of newer sectors will provide a *net* increase of at least 1 million extra jobs overall. About 60% of the extra jobs can be expected to be in the USA and the rest of Europe, though application as between different European countries may vary considerably.

On the other side there have been many pessimistic forecasts about the employment impact. APEX research, for example, has estimated that electronic equipment could put an end to a quarter of a million office jobs by 1983.[2] In Japan the top seven TV manufacturers cut their labour force by almost 100% between 1972–6, whilst increasing the output of sets by 25% and improving their reliability and quality and reducing the need for servicing and running costs. Siemens, the giant German firm, predicted in an internal report in 1978 that in West Germany 40% of clerical jobs (i.e. 2 million) would disappear within ten years (1980–90).[3] In the UK the unpublished report of the Department of Industry's Computers, Systems and Electronics Requirements Board forecasts job losses in the information sector as 'in the 10–20% region'.

However, accurate forecasts of the net effect are uncertain because of the imponderables involved. On the one hand, the extent of job creation will depend partly on factors like the overall level of demand in the economy, the speed at which the new technology is introduced and the actions of our competitors. On the other hand, the destruction of jobs can occur in a more sudden, concentrated and substantial manner than the longer-term creation of new jobs through the development of new products.[4] What cannot be assumed, despite the complacent optimism of the CPRS (government's Think Tank) report on the employment implications of the micro-processor, is that the service sector will continue to absorb the labour displaced from manufacturing. For it is precisely in the former area that jobs will disappear. Thus a CES study has concluded that unless public expenditure on health and education is increased, productivity improvements in the service sector mean that 'the service industries can no longer be relied upon to soak up jobs lost from other sectors'.[5]

Significantly, though paradoxically, one major study has pointed out forcefully that the greatest danger to jobs comes, not from the direct effects of the new technology, but from its probably slow diffusion in the UK, given our poor innovation record.[6] In other words, Britain stands to lose more jobs by *not* introducing microelectronics into British industry than by adopting the new technology, because its international competitiveness will decline further. The sharp fall in UK manufacturing employment (de-industrialisation) has resulted much more from low productivity and changes of demand than from an over-vigorous introduction of labour-saving machinery.

There are really three main options for the UK response to the new technology. The first is to opt out and say it cannot afford the introduction of microelectronics because of the massive job losses involved. Yet this is actually no choice at all because if no other action were taken, we would lose these jobs *anyway* through reduced competitiveness at home and abroad. Thus if job preservation were the aim, then abandoning microelectronics must mean a total siege economy geared to the maximum resource self-sufficiency. It also means giving up the potential benefits of automation such as higher material living standards, less arduous work and more leisure.

A second alternative is to pursue the route being followed at present by Japan and Korea, and to a lesser extent by the USA and Germany, and go all out to reap the material benefits of the new technology, whatever the consequences, including the probable net job loss. In the absence of countervailing state action, this option is likely to involve a major polarisation of society between the employed elite and the unemployed, between rich and poor, and so on. Social conflict would be maximised.

A third and more positive option would aim at maximising the benefits of microelectronics while minimising the adverse costs resulting from their use. Provided the UK does strongly develop the productivity of micro-processor technology, this could, and should, be seen rather as an opportunity to reduce the burden of work and enhance the quality of life. An essential part of this, however, would be government action to ensure that the logic of micro-electronic production does not lead to unacceptable concentrations of wealth and power.

A determined policy for maximising the benefits of micro-processors would go much further than the Government's £70 million scheme to encourage the production of microelectronic components (which compares with £500 million which Japan has poured into micro-processor development during the 1970s). A more effective policy would be active use of planning agreements, backed with statutory powers over financial assistance and prices, to ensure that all the top companies did raise productivity by introducing the new technology. This would be reinforced by a concerted programme to expand the supply of technicians trained in microelectronics technology.

In practice, however, given Britain's private enterprise economy and traditional power structure, it is much more likely that the potential of microelectronics will be grasped half-heartedly because of fears about immediate jobs displaced, while on the other hand the siege economy strategy will be rejected on political grounds. Compensatory manpower measures will be all the more difficult as the total number of jobs available falls. This prediction of market drift is supported by the poor showing of British industry so far in failing to invest in the new technology. Until the late

1970s there were no plans for domestic production of standard chips, the building blocks for microelectronic automation, and even the NEB-backed INMOS and joint GEC-Fairchild project scarcely fill this gap.

However, even if labour-intensive public spending were expanded and industrial planning instruments used to harness locationally mobile manufacturing and services to help provide alternative employment wherever possible, it is still likely that, other things remaining equal, unemployment would rise quite substantially; in other words, the inevitability of the microelectronics revolution simply emphasises further the need for an alternative industrial strategy.

The Response to the Inflation-Slump Dilemma: Unemployment through Monetarism

By far the greatest threat to full employment, or the prospect of any return to it, arises from the authorities' reaction throughout the Western world to the inflation-slump syndrome.

The fundamental Keynesian problem, it is alleged, is that demand management can hold unemployment below the level to which it would tend under balanced fiscal and neutral monetary policies only by adding more to the flow of monetary demand than the underlying growth of productivity in the economy warrants. In the short term this stimulates output and employment, but as the extra demand interacts with the slower growth of output capacity, it begins to force up prices and employment starts to fall back to its long-run equilibrium level. To prevent this, government then has to inject further inflationary demand sufficient not only to outweigh the effects of rising prices on real effective demand, but also to bring about the additional real stimulus needed. Thus any given employment target above the long-run equilibrium level requires progressively more and more stimulus, always running ahead of the expected and discounted rates of inflation. In the long run the target is unattainable because ultimately along this process a threshold of hyper-inflation must be reached (indeed quite quickly as the process gathers momentum) at which money breaks down and violent economic contraction sets in. Monetarists would add to this scenario that this process is all the sharper where collective bargaining is prominent; for by raising labour costs above their 'free market' level, labour monopolies reduce employment and thus add to the pressure on governments to 'reflate' and thereby accelerate further the inflation rates. Political imperatives, it will be said, are likely for a time to over-ride economic imperatives, but in the longer run the latter must prevail.

When they do, the more fundamental policy options of left and right present themselves. But either way, it is argued,[7] the result is the destruction of the postwar balance of price and employment levels, which for three decades underwrote the broad political consensus in the West. Whether draconian pay controls, with the abolition of collective bargaining, lead to the 'planned society', or whether the restoration of the 'free' economy (or fear of adequate reflation on grounds that it will lead to excessive inflation) ushers in mass unemployment or underemployment, the full employment regime in a mixed economy with free collective bargaining is likely to be extinguished.

The attractions of monetarism as the political economy of the ruling groups in society are considerable. It reduces the ability of governments (especially left-wing governments) to intervene decisively in the management of the economy, by limiting the government's role purely to the management of the money supply. Secondly, monetarism puts the City and the money markets in an extremely powerful position. For it will be they who are daily passing judgement on the government's economic policies (as was shown in April 1978 for a few weeks, which produced a sudden increase in the M3 figure and thus forced a major change in the announced budget strategy). Thirdly, monetarism does, of course, operate very much in the interest of bankers and money-dealers. By manipulating the money supply and the sale of government securities, they can force up interest rates, as they did in February 1979. Monetarism is simply the device to ensure that the government puts the City's interests ahead of those of manufacturing industry. Above all, monetarism is seen not merely as a way of controlling prices, but as the spearhead of an intellectual counter-revolution aimed at wresting the state from the neo-Keynesians and restoring it to the traditional propertied classes dependent on more *laissez-faire* market forces. After the failure of successive incomes policies and industrial relations legislation, it offers the authorities a new and more potent means to suppress working-class demands and to preserve their own control, albeit at the price of severely exacerbating the depression already gripping the economy from other causes. Indeed, the imposition of arbitrary but low fixed and monetary ceilings, ostensibly in response to inflationary wage demands, has had the merit – from the point of view of this philosophy – of forcing up unemployment levels 'to teach workers a lesson for their wage militancy'.

Whatever its ideological attractiveness to the powerful forces of reaction, monetarism as a theory to explain the real world is riddled with flaws.[8] First, there is the obvious difficulty of deciding what should fall within the definition of money itself, since there is nothing sacrosanct about the M3 concept used by the British government and different definitions would produce very different results for the theory's underlying relevance. Secondly, even if a definition were generally agreed, the application of monetary targets in terms of the simple measure of quantity ignores the fundamental point that the demand for money is not merely a function of the change in its supply, since traders

65

accommodate to this via the velocity of its circulation. Thirdly, there is the difficulty that the connection monetarists postulate between money supply and inflation rates is subject to time-lags which are unpredictable. Also the transmission mechanisms put forward for converting increases in the money supply into increases in the rate of inflation are far from plausible – mechanisms such as the exchange rate favoured by the international monetarist school, where research has failed to establish an automatic connection between export and domestic prices.

Fourthly, there is a great deal of evidence to suggest that the long-run inflation of the postwar period has come from sources other than increased demand which would have been prompted by excessive money supply. Thus the very high inflation rates of 1973–5 were not only due to the substantial Barber expansion of the money supply, but to other factors such as the explosion of world commodity prices (especially oil) in 1973, a low real level of the exchange rate which increased demand for goods and services and a wage indexation scheme which transmitted those externally produced cost increases directly through into domestic prices. Fifthly, international comparisons do not bear out the monetarist case. The case of West Germany, for example, certainly shows that a rapidly increasing money supply does not necessarily lead to more inflation.

Sixthly, the monetarist theory of inflation is built on the Phillips curve, in either its original or its modified form, yet the Phillips curve hypothesis is false because it assumes that market forces play the dominant role in wage determination, ignoring the fact that the reality lies rather in workers attempting to compensate for reductions or for inadequate increases in real net earnings. Empirical evidence[9] supports the view that money wages are determined, not by market forces, but by institutionalised bargains where both employers as well as employees seek to maintain and improve real net earnings. Indeed the 'cure' of monetary or fiscal deflation advocated by monetarists and other supporters of the Phillips curve may even perpetuate high unemployment and worsen inflation, not abate it. In the Western industrialised economies heavy social overheads and maintenance of the unemployed are largely financed by taxation of those who remain at work. Thus, as the level of unemployment rises, so does the squeeze on living standards of wage-earners and hence the pressure for larger compensatory pay increases.[10]

If, then, it is true in a modern industrial economy that wage-price inflation arises acutely when socially determined real wage norms cannot be fulfilled, the solution must rather be sought either in improved economic performance which will more closely equate real wages with norms or in institutional agreements to modify wage targets. Both are more likely to be achieved in conditions of full employment than in times of low output and high unemployment; hence the limited durability of income restraint policies, illustrated most recently in Britain in 1969, 1974 and 1978. If this analysis of inflation is correct, and if Friedmanite measures continue to be applied, then renewed monetary restriction will undoubtedly produce a very high persisting level of unemployment.

There is a further paradox of restrictive monetary policy designed to keep price rises in check, namely, that when applied to an economy already very understretched it cannot restrain a rise in inflation without destroying the possibility of economic growth. It is a necessary pre-condition for the success of deflationary policy – which is what monetarism is at root – that a certain proportion of resources should be kept out of use. But in these circumstances growth can never be achieved because as soon as the under-utilised resources are drawn into use the necessary pre-condition for success has been removed. Moreover, even on the anti-inflation side of the equation, monetarism contains within itself the seeds of its own destruction. It is precisely in the conditions of nil or slow growth produced by deflationary policies that a pay policy is most difficult to sustain. Since there is no room for a real increase in wages, the pressure for a money increase is so much greater. Also, when output is static or falling, unit costs are unlikely to be reduced and every small increase in costs becomes inflationary. For, as international comparisons of the annual average increase in output per worker strongly suggest, productivity is a function of growth, and not the other way round.

For these reasons the monetarist future in the 1980s can only be one of deepening slump and much higher unemployment, with unpredictable consequences for the political and social stability of the West.

The Response to the Inflation-Slump Dilemma: Unemployment through Fear of Reflation

The alternative to the monetarist scenario is a return to some variant of neo-Keynesian principles, for stimulating demand and reducing unemployment. But this option too for averting hyper-unemployment now seems increasingly blocked by the dangers of excessive inflation and credit overhang.

Until the 1930s it had always been the case that during the prosperity phase of the business cycle debts grew faster than real production and income, partly because prices rose and debts were based on monetary values, but mainly because it paid to proliferate debts when the profit rate was rising faster than the inflation rate. Once the squeeze on profits from both slowed demand and rapidly rising costs (the combined under-consumption and over-investment aspects of the same situation) brought about the downturn, prices began to fall, the debt superstructure was squeezed by bankruptcies and unemployment, and real and paper values were once again restored to a viable relationship.

In the postwar world, however, it was believed that the damaging extremes of boom and depression had been greatly mitigated by Keynesian demand management techniques. These required substantial amounts of government spending, suitably provided by the huge and rising postwar military budgets, plus a flexible money and credit system involving both deficit government spending and increases in the money supply, with the penalty initially of a creeping inflation confined to 2–3% per annum. Amid the triumph through the 1950s and 1960s of 'the new economics', whether Keynesian or monetarist, which with certain theological differences agreed on the controllability of economic fluctuations, it was only fiscal conservatives on the right and Marxists on the left who recognised that this convenient strategy necessarily involved a vast secular increase in the debt structure within the economy, with a parallel decline in corporate and individual liquidity. The danger that arose from these consequences was that the economy became more vulnerable again to the kind of shocks that previously set off panics.

At the same time, the rapidly increasing concentration in industrial assets since the last war – the largest 100 manufacturing enterprises produced 21% of net manufacturing output in 1949, but no less than 46% by 1970[11] – together with the increasingly close interconnections both within and between industrial sectors meant that a single major bankruptcy could precipitate shock reverberations throughout the entire system, with unpredictable consequences as to how many other firms might be dragged down at the same time. Hence the role of the state became ever more urgent in extending massive government credits to guard against this recurring threat, but only at the expense of greater inflation in the short term and of deferring a still bigger explosion in the longer run.

The problem for capitalist institutions is that the solutions adopted paradoxically serve only to intensify the problem for the longer term. The economic boosters have been applied more and more strenuously, but with less and less impact on underlying inflation. As the magazine *Business Week* put it in 1974:

> the US economy stands atop a mountain of debt $2·5 trillion high . . . $1 trillion in corporate debt, $600 billion in mortgage debt, $500 billion in US government debt, $200 billion in state and local government debt, $200 billion in consumer debt. To fuel nearly three decades of postwar economic boom at home and export it abroad, this nation has borrowed an average of $200 million a day, each and every day, since the close of World War II.[12]

Yet, as the article goes on, 'there are signs of tension everywhere: corporate debt ratios way out of line, consumer installment debt repayment taking a record share of disposable income, the huge real estate market in desperate trouble despite all the federal government has done to save it'.

This bloated credit/debit structure and long-run decline in liquidity formed the background to the near-panic triggered by the Penn Central Railroad bankruptcy in 1970. Similarly, there can only be conjecture as to how far or fast the chain reaction resulting from the actual as opposed to merely threatened failure of Chrysler in 1970 would have gone. But a leading US Senator declared at the time: 'My recent conversations with financial leaders have convinced me that the economy has just skirted the edges of economic disaster, and that for some days it was a matter of touch and go.'[13]

For these reasons therefore – the very real risk of a massive credit collapse bringing down major companies and financial institutions in its train, plus deep fear of the destabilising effects of hyper-inflation if any counter-recession stimulus of demand were pressed too far – it is very likely that

Keynesian techniques of demand management, at the very time of worsening slump when they are most needed, will continue to be left in abeyance by Western governments in the 1980s. What will give instead will be the target of full employment as a serious goal of economic policy. But once abandoned, as it has been, there is no natural ceiling within which it is bound to be contained – other than that imposed by political resistance.

Thus the combination of reducing growth and deepening recession with rising inflation (aggravated by steeper real OPEC oil price increases designed to recoup losses from the weakening dollar) is likely to worsen through the early 1980s. This itself will then increasingly call in question the foundations of the postwar Western political concordat between capital and labour. For this depended on the achievement of steady economic growth on a sufficient scale to generate enough extra resources to sustain near-full employment as a means to soften or postpone class conflict.

This is a second reason why things cannot go on as they are, and why there must be a change.

NOTES: CHAPTER 3

1   *The Strategic Impact of Intelligent Electronics in the US and Western Europe, 1977–87*, ed. Arthur D. Little, US consultants, March 1979.
2   *Financial Times*, 20 March 1979.
3   T. Forester, 'Society with chips and without jobs', *New Society*, 16 November 1978, p. 388.
4   TUC interim report, *Employment and Technology* (London: TUC, 1979), p. 28.
5   D. Harris and J. Taylor, *The Service Sector: Its Changing Role as a Source of Employment* (London: Centre for Environmental Studies, 1978).
6   J. M. McLean and H. J. Rush, *The Impact of Micro-Electronics on the UK: A Suggested Classification and Illustrated Case Studies* (Brighton: University of Sussex Science Policy Research Unit, June 1978).
7   For example, P. Jay, 'Ending the age of full employment', *The Times*, 8 April 1975, p. 21.
8   B. Gould, J. Mills and S. Stewart, *The Politics of Monetarism* (London: Fabian Society, May 1979), p. 6.
9   S. G. B. Henry, M. C. Sawyer and P. Smith, 'Models of inflation in the United Kingdom', *National Institute Economic Review*, August 1976; W. W.

Daniel, *Wage Determination in Industry* (London: PEP, 1976); K. Coutts, R. Tarling and F. Wilkinson, 'Wage bargaining and the inflation process', *Economic Policy Review* (Cambridge), no. 2 (1976); D. A. S. Jackson, H. A. Turner and F. Wilkinson, *Do Trade Unions Cause Inflation?* (Cambridge: Cambridge University Press, 1975).

10   F. Cripps, 'The money supply, wages and inflation', *Cambridge Journal of Economics*, no. 1 (1977), p. 111.
11   S. J. Prais, *A New Look at the Growth of Industrial Concentration*, Oxford Economic Papers, vol. 26, no. 2 (July 1974).
12   Editorial, 'The debt economy', *Business Week*, 12 October 1974.
13   Senator Jacob Javits, *New York Times*, 28 July 1970.

4

An Ecological Crisis?

Another, very different, threat to the survival of capitalism, or indeed of any industrialised system inherently dependent on endless growth, has been posited by ecological analysis. It became a credo of the political economy of certain social and physical scientists in the 1970s that it would take only another short finite period (perhaps fifty years?) of population growth and economic expansion at present rates to cause a collapse of the ecosystem sustaining life on this planet, bringing mass famine in some areas, industrial breakdown in others, and a drastic shortening of lifespans almost everywhere. How serious is this threat?

Are There Natural Limits to Growth? – Raw Material Shortages

In the early 1970s the 3½ billion people of the world produced a gross world product of around US $3½ trillion a year, or US $1,000 per head. Americans at that time earned on average US $5,000 a head, and world population is now doubling about every thirty-four years. So to achieve an average world income per head increased to the then US level, and to achieve this within forty years from then (i.e. by about 2012) it would require a 6% growth in real GNP per year (very rapid, but theoretically possible), and this implies an increase in annual world production of slightly over tenfold.[1] Even if this were achievable, would it not generate shortages of materials in short- or long-term inelasticity of supply?

Food is unlikely to become subject to any sudden overall world shortage (however much the present ill-distribution persists) when some 60% of the world's population still works on farms, and the application of modern techniques would render most countries self-sufficient in agriculture with only about 5% of their workforce in farming. On the other hand, within a half-century absolute shortages of certain minerals, petroleum, timber and some other raw materials are predictable – have been predicted – and such predictions do carry some plausibility.

The most pessimistic scenario stems primarily from the work of Jay Forrester and fellow scientists at MIT who projected through computerised models the complex inter-actions of human activity and the environment. These projections, which formed the basis for both 'A blueprint for survival'[2] and the Club of Rome's *The Limits to Growth*,[3] show that even if population growth halts within two generations, even if 'unlimited' new resources are discovered, and even if three-quarters of the pollution generated is removed, continued industrial growth *per se* will still bring about a condition of self-destruction within the lifetimes of our grandchildren. But more compelling still, these studies argued that even those premisses on which such doomsday prophecies were built were grossly optimistic. The *Limits to Growth* study argued (1972) that of the nineteen mineral and energy resources vitally important to any industrialised society, ten had such low known reserves that they would run out within forty years at current consumption rates, including nine within twenty-two years. Moreover, even if new reserves were found so that total reserves were increased fivefold, they would still only last thirty to seventy years.

However, against this projection of imminent doom,

requiring major and early adjustments in industrial patterns, several counter-arguments have been advanced. First, the amount of proved reserves relative to trend rates of consumption has varied little over the last forty years. Secondly, potential reserves in the first mile of the earth's crust, as determined by geological sampling techniques, are many thousand times proved reserves. In this layer aluminium, for example, is estimated to be present to the extent of 10 million times proved reserves, tin 1 million times, and copper and zinc over 100,000 times.[4] The resource depletion argument is really therefore a claim that it will become increasingly, perhaps prohibitively, costly to discover new deposits and to exploit them.

Thirdly, breakthroughs in technology have offset, at least partially, cost increases due to falling grades. Taking the three most important metals in terms of the value of world metal consumption, the real price of iron has remained fairly constant over the last forty years, that of aluminium has actually fallen, while in the case of copper average ore grades being mined today are almost half those mined forty years ago, yet the real price of copper has risen only some 40% during this time. Totally new techniques of exploration (geophysical techniques, use of satellites) and exploitation (nuclear blasting, deep-sea mining, hydro-metallurgical processing) promise vast savings in production costs.

Certainly it is quite likely that the world will soon run out of known and easily tappable sources of such materials as mercury and tungsten. But with the exception of those necessary for the production of extreme heat-resistant alloys, synthetic substitutes have either been invented or in most other cases can be reasonably conceived as likely to be invented within a given future time-period. Coupled with this is the fact that a much larger part of the world will be opened to mining both because of the use of new observation platforms, such as space satellites and deep-sea equipment, and because of the magnified power of new electronic

75

sensors linked to computer processing of the results. More futuristically, man's capacity to assemble matter by its molecule components is growing, though nobody can yet predict how far this could resolve problems of world shortages of materials within, say, the next half-century. On the key question of the exhaustion of fossil fuels, it might be expected that nuclear fission would become a substitute source for many forms of energy, given advances in magneto-hydrodynamics which will make electricity transmission much more efficient. Further into the future, the fusion process, using the oceans as a virtually endless source of fuel, should provide man with almost limitless industrial power.

It is very difficult to weigh the balance of these arguments with complete confidence, but there seem to be strong grounds for doubting the reliability of arguments based on lengthy previous experience. One point is that the enormous and indeed exponential growth of consumption today is without precedent. Only in the last two decades or so have all countries simultaneously concentrated to the present degree on maximising economic growth. A second issue is that the exponential growth in the world's population, shown by the accelerated shortening of intervals within which the world's population has doubled, suggests that the earth's population, now 3¾ billion, is unlikely to stabilise on the most optimistic control assumptions at less than three times today's total, that is, 11–12 billion. It has been calculated that to raise such numbers even to present British or US living standards would require respectively twelve to thirty times the present level of industrial production. It must be extremely doubtful whether the ecosystem could sustain such vastly increased demands, especially in view of the enormous rise in energy consumption required and in pollution emission per unit of production.

A third query is that the price mechanism of the private enterprise system is particularly ill-suited to the need to reduce the rate of resource depletion as scarcity grows. Such a situation provides competitive enterprises bound by a short-term profit horizon with an incentive to pre-empt remaining supplies, which could well result in accelerated depletion. A fourth question is that though economists have traditionally regarded substitution as the panacea for scarcity of a particular resource, in today's world the opportunities for substitution often ensure only that scarcity is contagious. There is a long list of extended networks of resource interdependence.

The argument about the finitude of the world's resources remains therefore controversial, though with the combination of an accelerating rate of resource depletion, geometric increase in energy consumption and pollution emission, and an exponential increase in population (so far), it is difficult to believe that the world's industrial system can cope indefinitely. Once that is agreed, the issue then becomes what politico-economic adjustments are required, minimally and optimally, and how quickly they can be set in hand.

Are There Artificial Limits to Growth? – Suppliers' Cartels

As the global economy has become more integrated, as a result of growing monetary interdependence and rapidly expanding international trade, it has become extremely difficult for individual countries to isolate themselves from scarcities elsewhere. The USA, for example, which previously benefited by relative self-sufficiency of resources, is now not only dependent on imports for 45% of its oil requirements, but is also experiencing growing dependence on imported minerals. Thus, of the thirteen basic raw materials required by a modern economy – copper, tin, lead, iron ore, cobalt, nickel, potassium, sulphur, phosphorus, aluminium (bauxite), chromium, manganese and zinc – the

USA was already by 1970 dependent on imports for more than half of its supplies of six. By 1985 it is projected to be primarily dependent on imports for supplies of nine of these thirteen basic raw materials, including three major ones – aluminium (bauxite), iron ore and tin – and by the year 2000 for more than half its imports of no less than twelve out of the thirteen.[5] This means that the USA, importers of US $5 billion of metals in 1970, would have to import US $18 billion by 1985 and no less than US $44 billion by the year 2000. Could an economy, even the USA's, withstand such pressure on its balance of payments, even if the supplies were obtainable?

How far are countries likely to go in denying others access to an indigenous raw material of which they are the principal global suppliers? Several motives lie behind this increasing tendency to limit exports of raw materials. It may be to cope better with internal inflationary pressures, to extend the foreign-exchange-earning lifetime of a non-renewable resource, to increase the share of indigenous processing, to improve export terms, or to take advantage of anticipated future price rises. Above all, the developing countries (LDCs) are likely to use scarcity of raw material supplies as weapons in the sharpening international economic competition between the poor South and the rich North of the world. Increasingly in the 1970s the LDCs have shown determination to face up to the multinationals and to seek means to control their own destiny.

Whilst international negotiations in the so-called North–South dialogue have largely proved desultory, the developing world has become more conscious of its potential bargaining power and more deliberate about its actual use. Thus Western Europe, according to Claude Cheysson, EEC commissioner in charge of relations with developing countries, relies on external imports for 95% of its energy needs, 75% of its raw materials for steel-making, 65% of its copper, 57% of its bauxite, 99% of its phosphates, virtually all of its cobalt, 86% of its tin ore, 100% of its manganese, 95% of its tungsten, 92% of its coffee, 100% of its cocoa and 100% of its oil seeds.[6] Along similar lines, a report by a group of Europe's major mining companies to the EEC Commission in 1976 estimated that Europe would have to invest a minimum of US $58,000 million over the next twenty years simply to maintain its supply of essential non-ferrous metals.[7] The problem for the LDCs remains one of translating this formidable armoury of potential negotiating weapons into real levers of political and economic influence.

There are several conditions that have to be fulfilled before circumstances favour a producers' alliance. First, there must be a limited number of countries involved, and perferably a near-monopoly. Secondly, there must be no real competition from substitutes or alternatives to the raw material. Thirdly, none of the countries should be of 'banana republic' status, or wholly dependent on that single product. Fourthly, in the case of agricultural goods, it must be possible to store them. Among the products that would lend themselves to this type of alliance are rubber, pepper, jute, sisal, copper, tin and phosphates. Some alliances have already been formed, such as the Asian Rubber Producers, the Asian Pepper Community and CIPAC (the copper producers' alliance), but most are not yet geared to a tough and concerted campaign. Also, powerful constraints on such LDC action lie in the fact that some primary producers are themselves large importers of other essentials that could be cut off in retaliation, and that excessive restriction of supply strongly stimulates the search for a substitute or a techno-logical way of bypassing the need.

Nevertheless some of these conditions for cartelisation exist and tempt LDCs to exploit them. One of the necessary, though far from sufficient, conditions for effective collective bargaining – that a small number of countries control most of the exportable supplies – is met in the case of several raw materials other than oil. Four poor countries – Chile, Peru,

Zambia and Zaire – supply most of the world's exportable surplus of copper. Three others – Malaysia, Bolivia and Thailand – account for 70% of all tin entering international trade channels. Australia, Mexico and Peru provide 60% of the exportable supply of lead. Cuba and New Caledonia have well over half the world's known reserves of nickel. Known reserves of cobalt are concentrated in Zaire, Cuba, New Caledonia and parts of Asia. Exportable protein food-stuffs are concentrated in even fewer countries. Thus Peru, for example, alone supplies most of the fish meal entering the world market. By contrast, however, in the balance between poor and rich countries in command over raw material sources, North America dominates cereal exports, both foodgrains and feedgrains, to an even greater degree than the Middle East dominates in energy. The world is more dependent on North American food supplies than ever, and indeed the USA is not only the leading supplier of wheat, but the leading exporter of rice as well.

It is difficult to believe, therefore, that artificial raw material scarcities induced by political restrictions on supply are likely to be on a scale to choke off world economic growth altogether, though they may well produce deepening and ever more serious dislocations. It is doubtful if the full requisites for OPEC-type price-boosting or supply restric-tions exist in the case of any other raw material besides oil, even where this seems most likely. The copper producers' organisation, CIPEC, is too sharply divided between political ideologies, and though nearly half the non-communist world production of bauxite (the source of aluminium) is provided by four underdeveloped countries (Jamaica, Surinam, Guyana and Guinea), Australia has now pushed Jamaica into second place in the world's bauxite production league, thus effectively denying the others the chance to dominate world markets and prices.

USA-EEC-Japanese hegemony remains, however, potentially vulnerable to Third World leverage over their increasing reliance on foreign metals. Given that all the Western countries are affected, though to a varying extent, by the same trends, the balance of power in the world must shift in favour of developing countries rich in raw materials, provided they can be politically mobilised.

The Western Political Response to Resource Scarcity

There would seem to be three main alternative directions in which the resources control question may develop over the next few decades and these may be set out in order of probability.[8] The most likely perspective is that economic growth mania (subject to the inflation constraint) will continue unabated in the industrialised countries, though because the latter will become increasingly dependent on the Third World for their resources input, bargaining by the Third World to secure a fairer *quid pro quo* in the gains of industrialisation can be expected to become much tougher. Stronger efforts to improve recycling performance will be made and energy conservation measures, based on both fiscal and physical constraints, will be multiplied, with the ultimate aim of preserving growth patterns as closely as possible.

The Fourth World, lacking large-scale resource availability, will be excluded from the fruits of the bargaining stakes, and may only be saved from negligible or even negative growth by the need to maintain and improve its real income as a growing market for processed goods and manufactured exports. Otherwise global inequalities may even be increased, and redistribution will be limited to the extent that developing or semi-developed countries that are richer in raw materials may be able to use their period of indispensability from their resource endowments to shift the geographical focus of industrialisation more rapidly and decisively to their own area.

A second possibility, however, is that if over the next decades sudden shortages or unpredictable breakdowns, localised at first, do indicate that the ecosystem cannot in fact cope with the accelerating strains of industrialisation, the growth maximisation target of the richer countries may have to be cut back. There were already some signs of the beginnings of this in the USA following the Iranian crisis in 1979. Immediately, much tougher and more radical conservation and recycling techniques would be compulsorily imposed.

No doubt it would be premature to represent these developments as the first serious moves towards a 'steady-state economy', that is, one in which the total population and total stock of physical wealth are maintained roughly constant at some desired levels by a minimal or low rate of maintenance throughput (by physical production and consumption rates that are equal at about the lowest feasible level). But this stage would certainly mark the beginning of the end of the so-called affluent society, characterised by Galbraith in its 1950–70 heyday as dependent on artificial demand creation.

It is here too that ecological and socialist perspectives begin to dovetail. Industrial production would have to be systematised for prior social uses, and employment and investment would need to be channelled towards the nation's most essential requirements. International planning, both of the distribution of limited resource inputs and of pollution control, energy use and marketing of finished products, would become essential, at least to a moderate degree. Some redistribution to poorer countries might become implicit, though it might well be made conditional on much tougher standards of population control. Even at this stage, however, it is unlikely that national rivalries would be absorbed into any executive international agency, and no doubt pooling arrangements would be confined only to those countries directly or imminently affected.

A third and more distant perspective is that a world in which the finite limit of particular resources or the finite capacity to extend industrialised processes has become demonstrably and painfully apparent – a vision of perhaps fifty to a hundred years on – must react by empowering intergovernmental agencies with executive control. But in practice it will only be taken when catastrophe really looms and confronts the richer industrialised countries so that the latter will finally submerge their rivalries (or else, of course, fight them out) in a UN-type environmental agency equipped with full powers. Such a body would oversee the totality of remaining supplies of particular raw materials and would be responsible for worldwide planning of resource use. No doubt in previous situations where failure to co-operate would have left all nations worse off, institutional frameworks would already have been created for specific goals scarcely impinging on national sovereignties, for example, in managing oceanic fisheries to avoid depleted stocks, declining catch and soaring sea food prices, through some agency like the UN-sponsored Law of the Sea Conference.

The difference at this new stage would now be generalised planning powers uniquely vested in one central world supervisory agency designed to regulate in outline the exploitation of known limited world resources through industrial conversion into finished products. In the face of over-riding resource or energy shortages or pollution over-flow, markets would need to be fully stabilised, and com-prehensive worldwide control over scarce resource depletion would have to be balanced by countering demand fluctua-tions through stockpiling (for instance, world food reserves). Balanced world development might then become possible through planned international trade exchanges linking with the industrialised economies not only the resource-rich primary producers, but also the less-endowed developing countries, since ecological restrictions would necessitate universal co-operation in a single broad-based development plan.

But Is a 'Steady-State' Growthless Economy a Serious Possibility, and What Would It Mean?

The first requirement in obtaining a proper assessment of growth is that account should fully be taken of externalities. If man achieves apparently healthy economic growth, but impoverishes the land and forests, exhausts the mines and quarries and strata of oil or natural gas, lowering the water-table, killing the fish in the rivers and coastal waters, and desecrating such wilderness as remains, the diseconomies may well in the longer term outweigh the gains.[9] Even in the shorter term, are living standards really rising with GNP if the air is more foul, the quality of the water declines, social violence increases, diseases like emphysema, bronchitis and cancer multiply, or if there is a need to travel farther for solitude on more crowded roads, more shoddy trains, or more delay-prone airlines?

Because they believed that the modern industrial way of life with its ethos of expansion was not sustainable, the authors of 'A blueprint for survival' and *The Limits to Growth* believed that zero population and zero industrial growth were imperatives. To this end they advocated every technological means to reduce waste, expand resource availability through recycling and lower pollution. But for them the only real solution for ecological equilibrium was a stationary, growthless state.

This was an odd conclusion when a 'stationary' state, where industrial growth had ceased, would not necessarily be in ecological balance and could anyway still be polluting the environment. Also, more important, a stationary state would impose an enormous and unfair penalty on the great mass of the poor world who would remain shackled in their poverty, while also imposing severe institutional strains in the industrialised world. The target for elimination should not therefore be growth *per se*, but pollution-generating growth. The aim must surely be technological change which increases output without further damaging the air or water or soil, or increases output by shifting from a less to a more abundant resource, again without increasing pollution.[10] This is politically and socially practicable in a way that compulsory birth control in the underdeveloped world, halting the green revolution with its huge agricultural increases, or stopping new capital formation in the West, surely are not.

Yet having said that, however alarmist the data on which the 'blueprint' and MIT models are based, however ingenuous their call for social change on a scale that is not realistic, it must eventually become true that the exponential curves of human and industrial growth will one day overtake the finite capabilities of the biosphere, with semi-catastrophic effects on the population and quality of life. At that point, whenever that is, the extension of public control required will be to an intense degree which has scarcely yet been envisaged. Environmental stability will require governmental control not only over the volume and composition of industrial and agricultural output, but over family size and consumption habits as well. Whilst therefore it is possible to be sanguine about the technological possibilities of continuing industrial growth for a considerable period, the vast increase that will afterwards be required in the scope and penetration of regulatory authority is much more difficult to foresee. The social transition needed is quite breathtaking, not only marking the end of the routinised self-aggrandisement of the industrial corporation, but fundamentally altering the social values at the micro level of individual behaviour.

While it is necessary to prepare for these changes now, in the shorter term it is possible for socially necessary production to be better weighed against environmental impact. Thus Commoner has recommended an 'ecological impact inventory' for each productive activity, in order to put a pollution price-tag on each product. Such an inventory would more clearly reveal the true relative social value of different products. Commoner concluded that the technological factor, that is, the increased output of pollutants per unit of production resulting from the introduction of new technologies since the 1940s, accounted for no less than 95% of the massive rise in pollution in the USA since the last war.[11]

While this certainly underestimates the contributions of popular growth and increased affluence to environmental deterioration, and conveniently avoids the now desperate need to face the harsh problems of population control and redistribution of wealth, it rightly draws attention to the fact that after the Second World War huge sections of the technological-industrial machine shifted to much more environmentally destructive patterns of production, primarily because they saw new markets, new openings for growth and new profits. By emphasising the whole resources–production–consumption–waste chain, Commoner has shown how ecologically vital are solutions which may nevertheless be inconvenient, bristling with technical problems, expensive and low on profits. Otherwise, Western technological progress seems destined steadily to diminish the probability of small inconveniences at the cost of increasing the eventual probability of very large disasters. Economically, we have so far been too ready to discount the future.

The concept of Spaceship Earth calls for profound political rethinking. At present nearly all politicians are entirely committed to quantitative growth, rather than the socialist idea of the redistribution of wealth, as the cure for poverty, unemployment and other social evils. But before long the rich nations will have to start reducing many of their energy-hungry and resource-draining technologies and stop selling them or their products to poor countries, which cannot usually pay for them and anyway have more urgent needs. Besides, industrialising the world along present lines simply is not possible; the resources are not available and the pollution would be appalling. Also, developing countries need industries which produce jobs but do not demand vast capital investment. But Third World efforts at such simple, labour-intensive 'intermediate technology' cannot proceed very far while the West plays super-factory to the globe, buying cheap raw materials and selling them back as expensive finished goods. In the spaceship economy trade will be more rationally ordered, with India, for example, supplying not cheap raw cotton but finished fabrics and clothes, West Africa supplying not palm oil but soap and Malaysia supplying not natural rubber but tyres.

To provide for these rational long-term solutions, huge counter-pressures will be needed to curb present underlying forces – population increase, rising expectations, the drive for 'growth', the profit motive, the runaway linkage joining extra industrial growth to extra capital which then produces more industrial growth. There are several possible scenarios. One is that the affluent nations press on with growth, and the world's North–South, rich–poor gap widens. The world becomes more sharply split into two groups, one living in bursting shanty cities and enduring mass unemployment and recurring famines, the smaller group very wealthy, but highly armed and increasingly dependent on the other group for its supplies; tensions will be enormous and war inevitable.

A variation on this scenario is that the industrial world fights to cut pollution and to conserve resources, but in a framework that is still founded strongly on material growth. The cost of such efforts rises inexorably, with diminishing returns. Either environmental deterioration or resource depletion overtakes the industrial world within a few generations. From a 'golden age' now when living standards have never been higher and from which they can only decline, the West and North of the world adapt, but to ever-worsening conditions. Or, thirdly, the rich world develops a quite new set of social goals, clamping down hard on resource use, consumption and waste, and helping the Third World to avoid its own mistakes.

Central to the last scenario and to reversing the trends now driving the world towards the environment crisis is abandonment of the idea that what matters most is consumption, or the flow of goods and services – the commodities that now swell the GNP. Much more important is maintaining our capital stock of 'satisfactions' that derive from what we do and what we have, and slowing the rate at which these satisfactions fade. There are, of course, deep social and political implications in all this. It hits at advertising, which exists partly by creating dissatisfactions. It hits at planned obsolescence, the new-model-every-year syndrome and the electric tin-opener brand of gimmickry. It undercuts private ownership in favour of communal services. Most of all, it hits at consumer one-upmanship, keeping up with the Joneses.

For the solution of the spaceship economy is not so much recycling (except for perhaps paper and packaging) as designing and making longer-lasting goods which are also easier and cheaper to repair, and much easier to discard to other users. Indeed, the energy crisis implies a need to create a production system which is consciously intended to serve social needs and which judges the value of its products by their use – in a word, socialism. Such an environmentalist regime will require meticulous planning, firm controls and probably a reduction in all the traditional ways of accumulating capital, making profits and spending wealth. Not, however, that the dominant classes of Western society will agree so readily to their political euthanasia.

What prospect, therefore, for socialism? This is the central question to which Parts Three and Four of this book seek to provide practicable answers.

NOTES: CHAPTER 4

1 N. Macrae, 'The future of multinational business', *The Economist*, 22 January 1972, p. xiv.
2 'A blueprint for survial', signed by thirty eminent British scientists, *The Ecologist*, January 1972.
3 D. H. Meadows, D. L. Meadows, J. Randers and W. W. Behrens III, *The Limits to Growth* (New York: Universe Books, 1972).
4 R. Perlman, 'Is the world running out of raw materials?', *International Affairs*, July 1974.
5 C. F. Bergsten, US Interior Department, *Guardian*, 29 December 1973, p. 14.
6 *Observer*, 29 December 1974.
7 *Guardian*, 5 August 1976.
8 M. H. Meacher, 'Global resources, growth and the political agency in the next decades', paper delivered to the Institute of Workers' Control Conference, January 1975.
9 H. V. Hodson, *The Diseconomies of Growth* (London: Pan/Ballantine and Earth Island, 1972).
10 R. L. Heilbroner, 'Growth and survival', *Insight*, May 1973, pp. 31–2.
11 B. Commoner, *The Closing Circle* (London: Cape, 1972).

Part Three
Does Socialism Offer an Answer?

5

Is There a Socialist Alternative? – What Do We Mean by Socialism?

Most people, one suspects, when asked what they understand by 'socialism', immediately think of nationalisation or of East European-type bureaucratic centralisation. It is an identification sedulously fostered by the enemies of socialism, not only in politics, but far more damagingly in industry, finance and the media. Although such lurid image-mongering reflects the ideological dominance in capitalist society of the controlling interests outlined in Chapter 1, it is also true that the advocates of socialism do have themselves also largely to blame because of the great uncertainty and haziness so often attaching to their own descriptions of the kind of society they plead for.

The Definition of the Socialist Alternative

The alternatives that are traditionally posited to the capitalist concept are normally described as social democracy, socialism and communism. None of these descriptions, however, is precisely analytical in any universally agreed sense, and indeed all of them have acquired, or had ascribed to them, emotional prejudices strongly favourable or pejorative depending on the viewpoint of the speaker or writer. To that extent it is impossible to formulate definitive specifications of these systems except in terms of the basic aspirations and underlying moral values which broadly reflect the consensus of proponents of each of these political philosophies.

SOCIAL DEMOCRACY

Social democracy has perhaps best been described in recent times by Anthony Crosland in his revisionist thesis *The Future of Socialism* published in 1956. There he identified five key motifs – though without making a distinction between social democracy and socialism, he ascribes them to the latter concept.

> First, a protest against the material poverty and physical squalor which capitalism produced. Secondly, a wider concern for 'social welfare' – for the interests of those in need, or oppressed, or unfortunate, from whatever cause. Thirdly, a belief in equality and the 'classless society', and especially a desire to give the worker his 'just' rights and a responsible status at work. Fourthly, a rejection of competitive antagonism, and an ideal of fraternity and co-operation. Fifthly, a protest against the inefficiencies of capitalism as an economic system, and notably its tendency to mass unemployment.[1]

With the possible exception of the fourth goal, which portends a different non-capitalist type of society (though Crosland discusses it in the much more limited application to personal motives and workplace relations rather than in terms of the central dynamics of the system), this list might be said to portray well the essential concerns of social democracy. What is significant is that none of them is inherently incompatible with a capitalist framework, albeit one that has been severely modified by government intervention or trade union collective bargaining. The type of society posited is still moulded by an economy governed by market exchange for profit which determines the production and distribution of goods and services and the movement of capital. It is the consequences of such a system which it is sought to mitigate and rectify, not the system itself. The aim is a more humane, more just modification of capitalism, not socialism as such.

SOCIALISM

The essence of socialism (Latin *socius*, meaning friend or ally) lies rather in the ideal of sharing, co-operation, altruism. Its values are characterised by much more equal sharing of the material benefits of society, greater sharing in the making of key social decisions rather than subjection to artificial hierarchies of command, and greater sharing of opportunities to develop one's full potential. It abhors class domination and individualist self-aggrandisement at the expense of others. Because production for profit maximisation is replaced by production to satisfy people's needs, work ceases to be simply a means of 'making one's living' and is no longer alienated in that it becomes rather a part of one's living. Arbitrary distinctions by race and sex (or language or eye colour) cease to be criteria for particular forms of oppression or for tracking people into limited opportunities. Ultimately imperialism, the unequal relations of national dominance and subordination, would be replaced by the co-operative ethic involving a much more balanced and fairer world division of labour, thus promoting a more uniform spread of industrialisation and its required technologies.

However, while it is one thing to list the objectives of a socialist society, it is quite another to harness the political and economic power and popular consent to realise these aims. But socialism is anyway more than a set of humane values – it is a process. Socialism means democratic, decentralised and participatory control for the individual. Such a

participatory form of socialism certainly requires a much
more equal access for all to material, educational and cultural
resources, and this in turn requires the redistribution of
wealth and the ending of the use of the private ownership of
capital as an instrument of personal economic power. But
above all it calls for men and women with a socialist consciousness to transform productive, consumer, educational
and social relations which alienate them and others around
them from their full creative potential.

Moreover, socialist values and process will not develop in
accordance with any predetermined theoretical blueprint,
but only out of specific struggles against elements of the
prevailing capitalist order that alienate and oppress. Nor is
the development of a new non-alienating productive framework to be expected somehow automatically from the so-
called 'contradictions' of the existing order, but only on the
basis of a self-conscious and self-educated political movement. That is why the conditions necessary for the mass
development of a new political consciousness are emphasised
later at such length and so strongly. Ethically, this importance of consciously organising to overcome alienation has
well been caught in Paul Tillich's memorable phrase defining
socialism as 'a resistance movement against the destruction
of love in social reality'.[2]

To the philosophical rationale of socialism as a system
creating the conditions for a truly free, rational, active and
independent man, the riposte will no doubt be made that
this is exactly what modern capitalism does. It will be said
that the big corporation seeks to serve the needs of man,
hence the market surveys and motivational analysis as a
pre-condition of advertising. But such a response is precisely
to underline the lopsided approach of capitalism (quite apart
from the very relevant question of motives) in treating man
unidimensionally. It fails to perceive the distinction between
the true needs of man and the synthetic, artificially elicited
needs of man. Of course, to assert that man's true needs are

those whose fulfilment is necessary for the realisation of his essence as a human being is akin to an existential proposition: it does not permit the concept of 'true needs' to be verified empirically. Moreover, purely subjectively, false needs are experienced as being as urgent and real as true needs, and from a purely subjective viewpoint there could not be a criterion for the distinction.[3] While, therefore, it is the role of socialists (as of others convinced of the spiritual and philosophical potential of man) precisely to awaken man so that he can become aware of illusory false needs and of the reality of his true needs, for those who doubt such aspirations there can in the last resort be no compulsion but to think and judge for themselves the conditions necessary for man to realise his full and real potential. Socialism is not a provable thesis. Ultimately it must remain the prerogative of each person to decide for himself whether capitalism does, or ever can, recognise and satisfy the fullness of man's true nature, or whether that is only possible where production serves exclusively the interests of the community, not the profits of a few, and where capital ceases to enhance and exploit one dimension of man's needs at the expense of others.

COMMUNISM

It must be added here that the other central alternative to the capitalist system is, of course, communism. However, perhaps even more than the concept of socialism, this is a term that has been massively abused by its users on innumerable occasions to suit their loaded propaganda. On the one side, it has been crudely identified in the West with totalitarianism, regimentation and bureaucratic excess; on the other, with the Eastern bloc it is extolled as a system uniquely offering freedom for the masses against the exploitation of capital. Either description may serve partisan cold war interests but neither, of course, suggests any objective definition. In so far as it is not purely a term of convenience, it is certainly a heuristic concept, that is, knowledge of it proceeds by discovery and experimentation rather than its being susceptible to precise blueprinting in advance. For in its pure sense it has never existed anywhere, though certain societies have perhaps manifested some characteristics that might be regarded as precursors of communism. Pure communism may be defined as 'a society in which people do not work for wages, but for the social good, and there are no prices, but people take according to need'.[4] This roughly corresponds with the famous slogan 'from each according to his ability, to each according to his need'. But it has always been held by Marxist ideologues that such a system could only evolve out of socialism, and not directly from capitalism itself. Certainly a communist society (in the pure unrealised form described here, and not the bowdlerised pretences sometimes claimed to exist now), involving free sharing and a very high level of social commitment as opposed to socialist payment according to labour done, does seem logically to presuppose a level of political consciousness, social psychology and type of political economy which require gradual, stepped evolution rather than immediate transition from capitalism, whether by revolution or otherwise. To this extent discussions of communism are theoretical at this stage, and in terms of realistic prospects of direct alternatives to capitalism discussion is therefore confined here to the issue of socialism.

How Is Socialism To Be Realised in Practice?

Whatever precise nuances are attributed to the socialist goal, it is notoriously more difficult to establish practical procedures for operationalising such ideas. But if the fundamental premiss is accepted that the key essential of a socialist economy is the principle of sharing and co-operation, seven forms in which this principle might be realised and consolidated present themselves.

(1) PRODUCTION FOR SOCIAL USE

Under capitalism it is pressure for profits as the central dynamic of the system which determines the basic character of the society created, evaluating relationships by the criteria of the market. The economic system dominates the rest of society rather than being submerged in it. Other institutions – the state, the family, schools, the media – are subordinate to, and hence developed in accordance with, the primacy of the economic sphere. It is the market that determines social classes in accordance with their economic relationship to it, and by fixing their income it also determines their rank and position in society. The work process, rather than being established by collective decision, is settled according to market criteria of profitability, even though this produces its own internal contradiction, when under conditions of advanced capitalism the growing social character and consequences of production increasingly conflict with the existing private control and ownership of production, now more concentrated than ever before.

Secondly, the exaggerated role which commodities (goods produced for exchange on a market) and commodity relations assume within capitalist society transform even workers into commodities in a market. Thus all production relationships are reduced to the character of exchange relationships. For example, the relationship between the capitalist owner/manager and the worker is not the human relationship based on a co-operative work activity, but an exchange relationship in which the worker seeks to maximise wages from the owner and the capitalist owner/manager to maximise profits from hiring or firing the worker. On the consumption side, the status of commodities is likewise inflated. Instead of commodities serving as instruments for worthwhile human activities, commodities themselves become ends. The accumulation of commodities and the exaggerated consumption of commodities replace rational use.

Under socialism, on the other hand, production is determined by the social needs of the community, not by what happens to offer prospects of profitability at any given point of time. This is not, of course, to suggest that the product of a socialist economy will not overlap quite closely in many respects with that of a capitalist economy, but only that the balance of emphases will be different (for instance, on improved housing rather than office property, on domestic manufacture rather than imports, or on better health and educational facilities rather than Concorde). Nor is it to suggest that socialist production will not normally be profitable, but only that this is not the single, exclusive, or main determinant. Nor, less still, does it mean that the expression of 'the social needs of the community' requires a weighty central bureaucratic apparatus: to the degree that the spread of individual incomes is made more equal rather than highly skewed in distribution, market exchange will require less supervision by over-riding bureaucratic controls. Nor is this a utopian and unrealisable ideal. In some of the planning techniques used by large distributive chains in their relations with manufacturers, and in, for example, China's development of flexibility (under Mao) between producing and consuming organisations using market relationships of a different kind from those of capitalism, there does exist relevant experience of planning production to maximise use of available resources while at the same time working for sensitivity to consumer needs and preferences.[5]

(2) POLITICAL DEMOCRACY AND INDIVIDUAL FREEDOM

Quite apart from the implicit false premiss that the private ownership of property is a *sine qua non* of individual freedom, socialism is by no means synonymous with the bureaucratic state framework currently espoused in the USSR and many Eastern European countries. Political democracy – indeed with more direct, regular and effective accountability of political leaders than exists, for example, in contemporary Britain with its quinquennial all-embracing single ballot – is an essential attribute of socialist society. The existence of central planning for particular specified functions is no more an eliminator of individual freedoms within a socialist state than within present-day Western capitalist states: it is in either case a matter of balance of power in decision-making between the centre and the various peripheries, and the form of market socialism posited in this book is decisively biased towards the decentralisation of power.

For similar reasons the traditional *canard* against the socialist state of lack-lustre greyness and loss of variety and choice is equally inappropriate. Nor can even the spectre of wholesale nationalisation and alleged consequential subjugation to the state be levelled against the system proposed here. These proposals exclude both the private ownership of industrial capital and the bureaucratic national ownership of capital as the predominant form of control of industrial enterprises (though both would still survive significantly), and instead they favour an intermediate form of social ownership. It would be pitched locally, would be more amenable to control by those affected by its operations, and would be subject to a wider range of direct influence (because of part-ownership by the local community) than the present structure of capital ownership permits in Western capitalism today.

(3) INDUSTRIAL DEMOCRACY

Economic decision-making is decentralised to the extent that makes a reality of worker democratic demands at plant level. There is no categoric blueprint for workers' control, but rather a need for workers collectively in each plant, salaried and technical as well as manual, to devise their own framework for involvement in the corporate strategy of their enterprise. There are already a number of models that have been developed along these lines, including the Yugoslav self-management system, the Israeli kibbutzim and the Chinese communes, and there is the precedent of the Lucas Aerospace shop stewards who in 1976 challenged the strategy of their company with an alternative, detailed, full-length corporate plan involving new products and techniques.[6] But preparation of their own corporate strategies by workers in individual enterprises would still require close co-ordination with a central planning agency to ensure gaps are covered, to avoid overlaps and to seek optimum allocation of resources.

However, this certainly does *not* imply authoritarian directives from the centre of the 'command economy' type. Power would still be chiefly vested on the periphery, and only minimum essential controls (monetary, fiscal, planning) would lie at the centre. The problem of this reconciliation has been identified as the key issue of a positive alternative system:

> how to define *community* economic institutions which are egalitarian and equitable in the traditional socialist sense of owning and controlling productive resources for the benefit of all, but which can prevent centralization of power, *and* finally which over time can develop new social relations capable of sustaining an ethic of responsibility and co-operation which a larger vision must ultimately involve.[7]

This raises crucial questions about the nature of the state: how to prevent those who should serve society from acting as its masters. This issue is explored in the specific British context in Chapter 9.

(4) REAL FULL EMPLOYMENT

Full employment is provided, that is, the state guarantees either a job or retraining to *every* adult who requires employment. This contrasts with the goal under Keynesian capitalism of seeking to maximise employment compatibly with the controlling interest of capital in determining the level of economic activity. Making real full employment a primary objective rather than a subordinate desideratum (leading to the 95±% pseudo-'full employment' of the postwar Western democracies) has several important implications:

(*a*) Since *ipso facto* unemployment cannot be used as a regulator of the level of demand, alternative means must be found to damp down inflationary pressures. This probably implies acceptance of some degree of regular price and income restraint, though this presents a different prospect in an economy built on a redistributive framework and one which has consciously forsaken devil-take-the-hindmost competitive greed.

(*b*) If jobs (or training) are state-guaranteed, new means must be found, other than merely closures or redundancies, for securing flexibility in the deployment of resources and personnel to match technological improvements and changes in the pattern of demand. This implies a much more massive system of retraining and voluntary mobility than the UK Manpower Services Commission has yet committed itself to, indeed on a scale at least akin to the performance of the Swedish Labour Market Board which retrains some 3% of its workforce each year (compared with Britain's less than 0.5%).

(*c*) A state guarantee of a job would require a wide-ranging government-controlled capacity for job creation, in far greater depth and scope than that suggested by current direct (National Enterprise Board) or indirect (sectoral

103

planning) instruments. Nor is it sufficient, as in Sweden, to require firms to provide breakdowns of their labour force by age, sex and skills, in order to ensure that the balance of employment responsibilities is fully met by all main companies. If fiscal pressures and monetary incentives proved insufficient, it might be necessary for the state to have some limited reserve powers of job placement in respect of both public and private enterprises. Conversely, closures or redundancies over a certain minimum level could not take place without the approval of the state employment agency.

(*d*) If real full employment is to be achieved (that is, structural unemployment is to be eliminated), it must require a steadying of the market environment of demand and some insulation from violent fluctuations in international trade pressures. For the purposes of a more self-contained economy (not in any sense a 'siege economy'), one main objective here must be much fuller utilisation of Britain's own resources. In the case of food, for example, only slightly over half of UK requirements is produced domestically. Of the imported balance, nearly half is composed of food not suitable for domestic production, but the rest (nearly a quarter of the total) is made up of indigenous-type foods. If this were produced in the UK rather than imported, some £1,500 million in imports would have been saved annually, for example, in the mid-1970s. In general, since much of world trade consists of industrialised countries exchanging almost identical products, it would be much more rational for Britain to plan for actual volume targets for specific products, with a division between domestic production and imports that suited its particular national capabilities, resources and employment requirements rather than the unplanned, disaggregated profit interests of private firms operating independently.

(*e*) This explicit placing of people's jobs and the nation's resources before private profits would still involve a high degree of market flexibility (though not of the capitalist type) and in no sense implies a 'siege economy' (except in the sense that capitalism = struggle = economic war). The requirement that would still remain to sell output in the market would impose standards of competitive efficiency that are not over-ridden by the jobs guarantee. Rather, worker control of enterprises implies either remedial productivity measures being taken at a much earlier stage (perhaps through regular efficiency audits) – anyway, well before collapse; or else where technology or market demand has irreversibly shifted, it implies deliberate phased dissolution and redeployment of assets and of personnel through retraining.

(5) LIMITATIONS ON INEQUALITY

A further essential requirement if the sharing and co-operative ideal is to be realised is very much greater equality in the distribution of income and wealth. The mainspring of this demand is both ethical and economic. It is ethical in seeking to secure social justice between individuals, to minimise social resentment, to equalise opportunities and to erode deep-seated class stratification and the feelings thus generated of envy and inferiority. But it is also an economic appeal in as much as a more equal spread of income and wealth produces a spread of output much more closely aligned to the real needs of the great mass of the people, without the intervention of distorting physical controls.

The question as to how far the process of egalitarianism should go to satisfy these purposes cannot, of course, be answered in any objective sense. The issue can, however, perhaps best be posed as: do the institutions of society so operate as to give some people in it more than they either need or deserve and other people less?[8] This is very different from asking for all differentials to be abolished, all labour to be directed, all savings to be taxed away, all gifts or bequests to be prohibited, or whatever else might be implied by a quest for literally total equality. What it implies is not that all inequalities are unjustified, but that until *none* is unjustifiable the institutions of society ought to work towards reducing them, provided that the basic liberties of each individual are not improperly infringed.

The desirable span of differentials must ultimately reflect a consensus on the relative value of different occupations, and this is a developing, never a static, process. One crude indicator of the extent of movement on this question in Britain has been constructed by comparing the range of pre-tax salaries in the public sector in terms of the ratio of highest to lowest over the period 1939–74.[9] This shows that in England just before the Second World War the income of a judge of the Supreme Court or a member of the Cabinet was thirty-five times that of a municipal street cleaner. Less than four decades later the ratio had shrunk to only nine or ten to one. In the Scandinavian countries and Switzerland, however, the ratio, which had been only six or seven to one in 1939,[10] remained remarkably constant over the next thirty-six years. This is not to suggest, however, that there is anything politically sacrosanct or sociologically stabilising about such a ratio. In China, for example, the ratio is rather between three and five to one. All that can be said with assurance is that a socialist economy would exhibit a distribution of income, and even more so of wealth, substantially more equal than that currently prevailing in Western societies.

(6) WORKER WELFARE AND JOB SATISFACTION

A corollary of the socialist emphasis on the worker's welfare rather than on the maximisation of his output *per se* requires new patterns in job structuring. Capitalism involves a constant relentless pressure for maximising profit, with severe penalties for less profitable enterprises, irrespective of their merits in other aspects of organisation or in personnel welfare. While profitability (the capitalist criterion of efficiency, but not the only possible criterion) no doubt always remains a desirable characteristic, its unqualified and automatic pre-eminence over all other considerations cannot be justified. Now that Western societies have achieved their present levels of wealth and technological mastery over their environments, it is neither self-evidently requisite nor rational to continue to place such total stress purely on increasing output at the maximum rate rather than on more satisfying aspects of the productive process. At a certain level of affluence a guarantee of security of income from employment, a sense of purpose in one's occupation, shared control over decision-making in the immediate job locality and satisfaction from the intrinsic interest of work become more important than raising output for its own sake. Socialism thus redresses in favour of the former the obsessive drive towards the latter which has always been a hallmark of capitalism.

Of course, it has often been argued that these two opposed alternatives – job satisfaction versus efficiency – are by no means necessarily contradictory, in that workers who are motivated by securing greater control in organising their own job environment also normally respond by significantly increasing productivity. Thus the Volvo experiment at Kalmar in replacing the assembly line altogether by 'island assembly', whereby teams of workers are responsible for a large chunk of the production of each car, also achieved high productivity and substantial profits. Similarly, the switch from a conventional line by Saab at its engine plant at Södertälje to autonomous group construction of a unit reduced personnel turnover by 20% and cut assembly costs to 5% below budget.[11] But this will not, of course, always necessarily be the case. The distinctive feature of a socialist economy is that, even if it did not improve productivity or profits, the human factors of satisfaction and self-determination would be over-riding in the organisation of work.

A fortiori, workers' health would be accorded an automatic priority which it does not receive when it has to compete with profit pressures. Under the existing capitalist system safety legislation is pitted with compromises. Thus harmful emissions and pollutants are to be prevented by the manufacturer by the 'best practicable means',[12] which implies that environmental health is interpreted in the light of costs and competitive pressures rather than as an absolute, and industrial safety is still limited by the standard of what is 'reasonably practicable',[13] which is a great deal weaker than the standard of what is 'physically possible'. Industrial processes known statistically to yield a quantifiable sequel of debilitation and death via the forty or so 'prescribed diseases' (pneumoconiosis, byssinosis, asbestosis, and so on) and others as yet unacknowledged are still permitted to continue, with greater or lesser safety precautions, as the price for maintaining industrial output at competitive costs.

An economic system that put a premium instead on workers' safety, health and satisfaction would not pay this blood price in ill-health, disability and death. Although risks can never be totally eliminated from all industrial operations, nevertheless there can be no doubt that where profits form the mainspring of economic activity the risks are substantially increased, both of individual injury (e.g. the continued production of thalidomide by Distillers despite medical evidence in Germany and elsewhere of its deforming effect) and of environmental pollution (e.g. the Seveso poison cloud, July 1976, and the Avonmouth smelter at Swansea, 1972–3).

A further aspect of job restructuring within a socialist system concerns the redressing of overspecialisation in the interests of fostering a stronger sense of wider community commitment. At present capitalism entails an early choice of occupation within one of a range of finely scaled hierarchies, and initial choices, often taken on irrational or contingent grounds, tend to limit later opportunities within a narrow employment sphere. Above all, this process of excessive specialisation tends to rigidify status stratifications, particularly between the manual and non-manual sectors. A socialist economy that emphasised instead individual sharing and community co-operation would seek to minimise status discrepancies and to widen work experiences for each person.

One means of producing this result might be to require a period of, say, two years of community service at the start of working life. This might involve helping with municipal services, factory work, participation on building or maintenance projects, or whatever boards appointed to supervise such activities might assign young persons to. The weakness of such an approach is that it might simply be regarded as a kind of initiation ritual into adult life, a token preliminary to be gone through before the real business of getting a foot on one of the main career ladders. To prevent its purpose being thus neutralised, it might be necessary to consider repeating the exercise at least once during each person's later career. It would then be far more likely to achieve its real purpose of deepening appreciation of other people's working lot, of scaling down the excessive status pyramid that enormously divides people and classes at present, and of inducing a more equal sharing both of income and of occupational facilities. However, there can be no pretence that such an arrangement would commend itself to a society where there was not already strong opinion in support of socialist values such as sharing, community co-operation and altruism. Hence the mobilisation of such values remains an integral part of a socialist system and of the transition to such an economy.

(7) PROMOTION OF A CO-OPERATIVE ETHIC

To entrench co-operative economic values it is clearly necessary to foster social institutions that will develop such an
ethos. This means countering the mechanisms in capitalist
society which propagate a selfish individualism and generate
a drive for egoistic advancement. It means emphasising the
egalitarian rather than the meritocratic option in comprehensive secondary schools and beyond; expanding adult
education as a continuing process available throughout life
to increase social, psychological and spiritual awareness;
cutting back the crass materialism and unbridled appeal to
personal snobbery flaunted by contemporary advertising,
and replacing it by a much stronger emphasis on contribution to society and on the primacy of relationships over
commodities; and ensuring that the broadcasting media –
press, radio and television – should be free to explore and
project these values, which would require determined resistance to conditioning by profit pressures from advertisers
and by direct personal influence from the established authorities. Of course, these goals imply to some extent an
already advanced stage of struggle in support of a new
ideology but their attainment cannot be considered logically
prior to the struggle for economic change towards socialism.
In practice they interact and are mutually reinforcing.

To paraphrase Illich, capitalist institutions tend to be
highly complex and costly production processes in which
much of the elaboration and expense is devoted to convinc-
ing consumers that they cannot live without the product or
treatment offered by the institution. Socialist institutions on
the other hand tend to be networks which facilitate client-
initiated communication and co-operation.[14] But neither set
of biases can proceed far without being profoundly influenced by the pull of the other, and to that extent the
development of socialist values – whether through the
radicalisation of political or social consciousness, the

struggle for new mores (for example, the democratisation of marriage), the forging of new rights for the traditional underprivileged such as blacks, the poor, women, and so on – must at each stage prove compatible with the evolution of the economic base of society. Of the course of this process of transition there can be no advance blueprint, only the assurance that the creation of new economic foundations must go hand in hand with the widespread stimulation of a new co-operative political consciousness. Chapter 7 therefore returns to this critical problem of transition.

NOTES: CHAPTER 5

1 C. A. R. Crosland, *The Future of Socialism* (London: Cape, 1956), p. 103.
2 P. Tillich, *Protestantische Vision* (Stuttgart: Ring Verlag, 1952), p. 6.
3 E. Fromm, *Marx's Concept of Man* (New York: Frederick Ungar, 1961), ch. 6.
4 H. Sherman, *Radical Political Economy* (New York: Basic Books, 1972), p. 334.
5 A. N. Silver, *Politics and Money*, vol. 6, no. 4 (August–October 1975), p. 15.
6 These products, already prototyped in the health, safety and transport sectors, included kidney machines, sight-substituting aids for the blind, body monitoring devices, automatic braking devices for heavy road vehicles, telechiric or remote control devices for mining, deep-sea diving and fire-fighting, a new roadrail freight vehicle, etc.
7 G. Alperovitz, 'A long revolution', unpublished manuscript.
8 W. G. Runciman, 'Equality', *Observer*, 29 August 1976.
9 Lord Taylor, *The Times*, 14 April 1975, p. 12. This technique has obvious and major limitations in that it leaves out the self-employed and the private sector, it omits the equalising effects of taxation and it disregards the increasing use in the 1960s and 1970s of surrogate methods of payment, especially sizeable fringe benefits. But the broad conclusions it yields are unmistakable.
10 E. Simon, *The Smaller Democracies* (London: Gollancz, 1939).
11 'Sweden outdates modern times', *The Economist*, 9 November 1974, p. 78.
12 Alkali Act 1906, s. 7.
13 Health and Safety at Work Act 1974, ss 2–5.
14 I. D. Illich, *De-schooling Society* (London: Calder & Boyars, 1971).

6

Does a Socialist Society Already Exist Abroad as a Model for Britain?

Chapter 5 outlined a model of socialism for an advanced industrialised state at a stage of development like that of Britain. Has such an economy been created anywhere in the world from which lessons of practical guidance might be derived?

Broad Types of Socialist Society

Within the varying degrees of incomplete socialist order that exist it is perhaps possible to identify three main distinct types, according to level of economic development and the pattern of power in society. One of these is typified by the industrial socialism of the USSR and much of Eastern Europe today. Here the industrial apparatus closely resembles that of capitalism, both in structure and outlook (though the techniques of control differ), and it is accompanied by a highly centralised, bureaucratic, and repressive social and political 'superstructure'.[1] A second type is represented by the underdeveloped societies which lay claim to a socialist approach, where political centralisation and social repression exist (strongly in South-East Asian

112

countries like Vietnam or Cambodia, least in some African countries like Tanzania and Algeria), but where the framework of industrialism is absent. This reflects, of course, the simple fact of underdevelopment itself, though it is by no means yet certain that these nations will develop along industrial lines characteristic of the first socialist type.

A third type of socialism may be identified as that which seeks to combine a high degree of industrialisation with a substantial amount of political freedom and decentralisation of control. This model was perhaps most closely realised in the Czech reforms of 1968 seeking explicitly to create 'socialism with a human face', and also with fluctuating success in the Yugoslavia of the 1950s and 1960s. It is also envisaged by many as the direction in which Western socialism may be expected to move in the future, so that, though unrealised in practice, it does exert influence as a historical force.

For the purposes of offering a possible model for Britain, clearly the second category can be discounted. This leaves, for the purposes of illustrative comparison, five main countries: the USSR, China, Czechoslovakia (during the 1968 reforms), Yugoslavia and Cuba. How far does each of these exhibit the seven key principles of socialism identified in the last chapter?

Is the USSR Socialist?

In conventional terms the Kosygin reforms of 1965 have sometimes been claimed to be a reversion to capitalism. But this seems a curious description when the means of production are owned by the state, when there is no rentier class receiving income from property and when the basic direction of the economy is controlled by the state.

(1) Production for social need exists in the USSR only in the formal sense that both production aggregates and

divisions are determined by central plans collectively agreed. It is, of course, a very different system from the market mechanism which allows producers guided by profit to determine their own output and consumers constrained by their income to determine their own consumption, while prices act as signals guiding the allocation of resources. But production for social need in a socialist sense implies a high level of political and social accountability over basic investment and production decisions. By this key criterion the Soviet economy is not socialist, not because profits have increasingly been substituted for gross value of output as the central index for incentives, but because there is an absence of any real degree of accountability to the workforce at large. A socialist description cannot be applied to the Soviet economic framework, not because the 1965 reforms introduced a Soviet analogue to the Western managerial bonus schemes (without, of course, any analogue to the functionless rentier shareholder), but because Soviet national economic plans are drawn up without regard to the wishes of the broad mass of consumers and Soviet enterprise plans are drawn up independently of the wishes of the producers.

(2) The USSR is a society lacking in intellectual and political freedom where political power concentrated in the hands of a small self-perpetuating oligarchy makes a nonsense of pretensions to individual equality and self-determination. Class divisions still exist in the USSR, based less on relations to production than on membership of the Communist Party hierarchy and access to bureaucratic privilege. Nor are conditions of political democracy present in the USSR. Rather it is a country dominated by a new kind of governing class, but one as determined as its rather different counterparts in the West to use state power to serve its own interests.

(3) Though the 1965 reforms were intended to strengthen the authority and independence of local management against the central planners, there were no proposals to extend

decision-making rights further down the hierarchy to shop-floor level. The Soviet worker is still confronted by an employer and must still accept a subordinate role in the productive process. He is in the same position as a worker employed by the National Coal Board (which also has no shareholders) or GEC, but with the important difference that unlike the British worker he has no effective trade union rights. Certainly there is no decentralised decision-making over investment, monetary and production matters for the Soviet worker to participate in, or even systematically over working conditions.

(4) Providing jobs for all who want them is, however, a major task of Soviet economic planning. Whilst the overall employment level is not the dependent variable of economic decision-making that it is in the West, so that in the USSR there are no permanent pools of jobless adults, there is still nevertheless extensive disguised unemployment. This occurs not only in Soviet agriculture, but also in industry. There is further a lack of jobs in small and medium towns, and a lack of female employment in some centres of heavy industry, like the Kuzbass. To put this in perspective, however, it should be added that by Soviet standards Britain, for example, has a substantial pool of disguised unemployment (quite apart from high visible unemployment) in the form of women who do not go out to work and those made redundant who fail to register for benefit, in addition to its statistically recorded unemployment. With these provisos (though there must be some doubts about the truthfulness of Soviet statistics and the true position in the countryside), it is true to say that the Soviet system does largely secure full employment in the absolute sense.

(5) Income can be said, on the best available evidence (sketchy though it is), to be distributed more equally in the Eastern bloc countries than in Western market economies. It is true, however, that published data omit collective farm families, who represent about 18% of the Soviet labour force

115

and are the lowest-paid workers in the USSR. This omission overstates the degree of equality implied by the statistics, but with this caveat it has been estimated that the share of per capita income received by the top 10% of spending units was in 1966 about four and a half times the share of the lowest 10%.[2] This needs to be compared with the 1940 Soviet ratio of fourteen times. It is also to be compared with the 1967 differential for the whole US economy of twenty-eight times.[3] The main reason for this latter dramatic discrepancy is that there is no property income in the USSR, where all income-earning property, with some minor exceptions, is owned by the state (though of course it is a small governing group which controls the state and benefits from that control). There are also, it should be noted, some other factors which tend to complicate evaluation of Soviet income distribution. On the one hand there is the widespread use of official cars, dachas (official residences), foreign vacations, special shops with special goods and other fringe benefits by upper-income groups that does not enter Soviet estimates (as also, of course, in the West). On the other side, many medical, educational and social services are provided free of charge to low-income groups which equally are omitted from the overall distributional data (as also, again, in some Western countries).

Overall, therefore, income is distributed more equally in the USSR than in, say, the USA, largely owing to the absence of property income in the former. But the differentials are still substantially greater than might be defensible in a socialist society, and moreover inequality is strongly defended in the USSR and there is every emphasis on perpetuating it.

(6) As regards job welfare and work satisfaction, certain factors unique to the Soviet industrial system of production provide the Soviet worker with special opportunities for control of the work situation. These include the numerous workers' commissions and the participation of workers in

rationalisation and invention. Moreover, the more paternalistic attitude of the state to the worker, the absence of structural unemployment and the unions' legal right to veto sackings (though it is doubtful what practical effect this has) all tend to underpin the Soviet worker's sense of greater job security.

Nevertheless, feelings of powerlessness and of the meaninglessness of labour still seem to persist in the USSR. Empirical Soviet research appears to show work attitudes not significantly different from those under capitalism.[4] There is the joke: 'they pretend to pay us, so we pretend to work'. Bettelheim, indeed, has described the alienation and resistance of Soviet workers as amounting to a gigantic go-slow movement.

Also the role of the unions in the USSR in protecting workers' rights is rather different from that in the West. Unions in the USSR are organised on the basis that society is politically homogeneous and that a union member as such can have no individual interest apart from that of society as a whole as represented by the government. Rather than articulating the workers' interests as in the West, Soviet trade unions seek to resolve disputes and to see that the law is enforced in favour of the worker. Certainly the union newspaper *Trud* has often complained that unions do not protect workers' rights, and one study has shown that of requests for dismissal of workers, about half were agreed to by the unions.[5] However, research also shows that of industrial disputes referred to labour disputes boards (though these referrals were no doubt suitably sieved), regarding holidays, wages, dismissals, subtraction from pay, bonus, transfer to other work and disciplinary procedures, nearly twice as many decisions went in favour of the worker as against him. But the fact remains that the unions accepted the required terms of work (over pay, and so on) and in so doing they were controlled by the party, not the workers (in a manner not wholly unlike the Nazi Labour Front).

117

(7) It is true that 'socialist emulation' or comradely co-operation and mutual assistance in the labour process is officially encouraged in Soviet industry, partly to improve output, but also to develop a co-operative spirit towards work. But the emphasis of the ideological programme of the Communist Party remains less on radical change than on traditional capitalist growth competition, on catching up with the West. The 'official goals' are not to abolish money or the state, but to increase the GNP within the framework of a publicly owned, but more decentralised, industry. Even in the 'coming of communism' as envisaged by 'The Programme of the Communist Party' (adopted at the Twenty-Second Congress in 1961), money as a means of exchange was to continue; income differentials would persist, but decline; some services and commodities (especially transport and public catering) were to be taken out of the price system; and one-man management was to be modified by various advisory committees within the factory; but no far-reaching proposals for workers' control were put. The ideas of inter-personal sharing and community co-operation were not keenly pursued.

In summary, therefore, the USSR cannot properly be described as a socialist society. Only one of the seven principles enunciated in the last chapter is effectively implemented, that being the condition of real full employment. Even production for social need cannot really be said to be achieved when the basic production choices reflect the personal judgements and prejudices of the politico-bureaucratic elite unencumbered by democratic constraint and unresponsive to popular demand.

Was Maoist China Socialist?

China, at least till the death of Mao in 1976, pursued a very different path from that of the USSR. The Cultural

Revolution in the late 1960s aimed to cut back the privileges of government and party hierarchies, and also attacked accepted views on political and social stratification. No doubt it is true that the means chosen to achieve the total politicisation of the masses – 700 million of them – were crude and elementary, but the sheer ambition of the social objective remains without precedent in history. Above all the purpose of the Cultural Revolution was to prevent the emergence of a new elite appropriating state power to its own advantage, separated from and standing over the people in the manner of past rulers. How far, then, can the results be described as socialist?

(1) The essence of Chinese planning is the central programming of production combined with a framework of direct consultation and bargaining between enterprises, especially at the provincial level. All profits are transferred to the state, since there is no self-financing of enterprises from ploughed-back profits and depreciation reserves. Prices are uniform and administered; with profits transfer to the state, there is less need for fluctuating prices and taxes.

In the Chinese view the aim of socialism is not the maximisation of economic growth. Having achieved a level of adequate food, clothing and shelter, the Chinese have preferred to try to decide what is the 'good society' and then to plan the basis of its social organisation and needs. Here the substitution of moral and ideological incentives for financial ones – the new motivation engineered by the Cultural Revolution – is crucial. Not only has the profit motive been rejected, but even profit as a criterion of efficiency has been rejected. In terms, therefore, of both economic objective and social-psychological incentives, it can be properly said that China's economy is geared to production for social use.

(2) China has a great deal of popular participation, but not democracy, at least in the Western sense. The National People's Congress, China's parliament, is not elected; its

delegates are nominated by the local party organisations. It might be said that there is democracy inside the Communist Party. But the Party Congress rarely meets – only in 1958, 1969 and 1973. Even when these bodies meet, their deliberations are not publicised, so it is impossible for the people to know what is being decided in their names.

Nor do personal freedoms such as the freedom to travel and the freedom to seek alternative employment exist in China as in the West. But the Chinese leaders would insist that freedom has been transmuted into a self-sacrificing commitment to community goals. If political democracy and personal freedom are the corollary of individualism, 'serving the people' is the equivalent predicate of Chinese communism.

(3) Following the Cultural Revolution, China's political philosophy has been geared to the replacement of material by moral incentives. The immense educative effort required to fulfil this goal has required the mobilisation of social-political consciousness and participation on a scale unprecedented in any comparable society. Moral incentives have been used as an essentially practical way of getting people to take a more active part in deciding how their material production is to be used and how to arrange their social lives without subordinating the mass to the elite. Nevertheless, evidence is scant as to what degree of participation is actually exercised in decision-making by industrial and agricultural workers through the so-called 'revolutionary committee' which replaced appointed managers.

In the case of communes, while the state sets prices and receives 6–7% of total revenue from crop sales, decisions about how to run commune activities and about income distributions are made either by the commune itself or by the brigades which are the main internal unit.[6] Wages, previously allocated by the brigade on a works-point system, are now settled by discussion. In the case of factories, output plans are decided by consultation with the next highest authority, whether other enterprises, central ministries, or state trading corporations.

(4) Chinese policy has consistently been to keep wages relatively low and to provide employment for all who can work.

Nevertheless, despite extensive state planning, unemployment in China, as in other poor countries, remains a key index of underdevelopment. It has been estimated that the population is growing by around 1·5% a year, which has added some 20–25 million people to the labour force every year since 1968. Thus, taking into account the number that go into higher education, the armed forces, and so on, the system needs to find 10–15 million jobs a year to keep up the level of employment of 1968. One observer has guessed that there are only about half a million new jobs created in the cities each year,[7] and few on the land except briefly at harvest-time (though many big projects located in the countryside, like irrigation and drainage works, are labour-intensive). In the cities there is a higher chance of getting a job, but for this reason the cities are tightly controlled against illegal entry and against the spontaneous movement of people by means of the pass system and elaborate regulations. But though stringent efforts are thus made to reduce actual or potential urban unemployment, and though unemployment is concealed by extensive work-sharing and over-manning, it is also true that maximisation of output growth through pressure to mechanise has been deliberately subordinated to a certain preference for labour-intensive processes to mop up the huge and swelling reserves of labour. To that extent there is approximation to the real full employment goal.

(5) Despite the emphasis on moral rather than material incentives, considerable differentials have continued to exist in China (though much less than in Kuomintang China). One analyst has collected data on differentials within factories in different provinces which show an overall ratio

121

(highest to lowest) of 5:1 in 1948, 5:1 in 1956, 7:1 in 1957 and 7:1 in 1972.[8] The same evidence suggests that wages and salaries in the government service were cut from a ratio of 31:1 in 1955 and 20:1 in 1958. In the cities, Karol reckoned in 1967 that there were eight wage-grades among workers, ranging from 40 to 120 yuan per month, with factory directors getting 150–90 and one chief engineer of a chemical plant receiving 250.[9] On top of these basic rates, an incentive premium was paid of 6–10% of salary. Also these figures are internal to the factory and exclude the higher pay of higher management staff outside the factory, banking and merchanting, and party, city and government officials. Nevertheless, though basic inequality in China remains not insubstantial, considerable and at least partly successful efforts were made to reduce it during the Cultural Revolution period so that the broad mass of the working population was paid within a 3:1 band.

(6) A main aim of the regime has always been the philosophical, but almost immensely practical, one of making the demands of industrial work compatible with human dignity. One facet of this has been the requirement that intellectuals and administrators should not segregate themselves into an elite out of contact with the masses – that they undertake regular work at the bench or on the farm. Since the Cultural Revolution students must have had two years' practical experience in industry or on the land before they can be enrolled. The object of the exercise is 'to improve feeling for labouring people by manual labour'. In other words, if the agrarian economy is overwhelmingly dependent on human labour and therefore the opportunities for job satisfaction are very limited, at least the burdens of the multitude are regularly shared.

The quality of workplace facilities is little known. Big character posters in 1974 complained, amongst other things, of inadequate health and safety conditions and poor compensation for accidents.[10] Others have reported, for example, that each commune has at least one clinic, reasonably well equipped with simple medical equipment, and capable of performing relatively simple operations like appendicectomies.[11] A proper assessment would seem to be that the Chinese have been at pains to make the benefits of worker amenities, limited and even primitive though they may be, as widely and fairly diffused as possible.

(7) An essential aspect of 'politics in command' under the Cultural Revolution was the gigantic experiment in human motivation, to make the planning system work not by appeals to self-interest or material incentives, but by moral incentives. Partly it was inspired as a bulwark against what the Chinese regard as a Soviet counter-revolution in economic administration, leading to the restoration of a bureaucratic manipulation of the economy through selfishness campaigns. The Maoist principle of 'fight self, fight self-interest' provided the counter-strategy against a similar development in China. The Chinese noted that in the first stages of Soviet industrial development centralised planning seemed to provide the most efficient form of utilising scarce trained personnel but it also perpetuated and intensified inegalitarian tendencies: power, authority and privilege flowed from the top down. Also, the Soviet model of rationality of production re-created the conditions of alienation from work so characteristic of bourgeois society.

It is necessary to add, however, that the means of internalising moral incentives – education, debate and criticism – need to be understood in terms of the actual social context in which they occur. Critics have interpreted the verbal pressures of education and debate as forms of social, psychological and even physical coercion. But whilst those elements of Chinese moral incentives which impinge on the individual's freedom to think and act, especially the cult of Mao and the intensity of group pressures, can be properly criticised, so (the Chinese would argue) can excessive emphasis on individual values which in market economies can be used by a minority class to dominate the majority. In practice, the Chinese through moral incentives have stressed the priority of 'serving the people' as a means of serving oneself, whilst Western societies through material incentives characteristically reverse the priorities.

In summary, on this analysis China, within its own parameters (which it is not to say that it is directly reproducible in different socioeconomic conditions elsewhere), displays many of the characteristics of socialist society as defined in Chapter 5: production for social use, industrial democracy, real full employment, considerable limitation on inequality, attention to worker welfare, and above all a massive drive to recast political consciousness through instilling moral incentives and combating class elitism. Only political democracy and personal freedom in the Western sense are lacking, and the latter correlates of Western individualism have been replaced by a concept of social commitment which is the necessary analogue to the supersession of materialism by moral motivations.

Was Czechoslovakia at its 1968 Reforms Socialist?

The Czech Communist Party proposals of April 1968 were aimed at creating a society which would be both socialist and profoundly democratic, devoted to humanist ideals in revulsion against a Soviet-dominated dictatorship which exploited them. A commentator said at the time that 'Dubcek seeks to marry Communist rule with political democracy, a Socialist economy with economic efficiency'.[12] It was thus proposed that the Communist Party should give up its legal monopoly of power, and aim only at broad direction, not direct intervention in local economic or cultural issues. Other existing political parties were to be allowed to function effectively and to promote different programmes, provided only that they remained socialist. Criticism of the leadership and real elections were to be permitted within the Communist Party. Moreover, new organisations – new political groupings and new trade unions – were able to be promulgated, and the old trade unions were given a new lease of real life. In all organisations nomination from above was ended. Political prisoners were rehabilitated and economically compensated, and the requirement of party membership as a condition of eligibility for certain jobs was abolished. The special list of 'good' people within the party, who had automatically been given first choice of all the best jobs, and who were in effect self-chosen and self-perpetuating, was ended. The real salaries of top leaders, which were previously of unknown size, were lowered and fixed. How socialist, then, was the Prague Spring?

(1) The goal of market socialism, which the reforms avowed, necessarily involves something of a self-contradiction, the market being the central institution of capitalist society and socialism being a society which substitutes conscious control for blind automatism. But the term may not be inappropriate when the phenomenon it designated in Czechoslovakia was also inherently self-contradictory. Ota Sik, its main proponent, envisaged many features characteristic of Western market economies, including the extensive use of material incentives, the relatively free formation of wholesale as well as retail prices, the application of anti-monopoly measures wherever possible, the use of imports to exert competitive pressure on prices and quality of home products, the relating of incomes to individual as well as their firm's economic performance, and so on. In summary he stressed that 'the need to subordinate production to society's priorities . . . is justified only under special conditions, when the economic standpoint must be explicitly and temporarily subordinated to serious political purposes'.

Nevertheless, in this formulation the market was restricted almost entirely to microeconomic decisions. The relative proportions of consumer and capital goods in overall production and the share of total investment to be allocated respectively to agriculture, industry, transport and other sectors were still to be decided by the central planners. This model of a 'regulated market' thus went some way towards reconciling the socialist requirements of flexibility in economic activity with central controls over macroeconomic allocations. The remaining question is whether these central budgetary and planning controls were democratically accountable, and here there was not sufficient time before the Soviet invasion in August 1968 for the political evolution, rapid though it was in 1967–8, to secure the relevant mechanisms.

(2) The elements of democracy introduced into political life after January 1968 ran deep. Inner party democratisation involved real debate at all levels of the party, with pressure from below playing a considerable role in influencing higher party appointments. Censorship virtually withered away, and whilst editors were still appointed by the top party leadership, the latter no longer determined the contents of the papers. The press, radio and television, offering a virtual explosion of information, stimulated a new level of political awareness, while political scientists as well as journalists used weeklies to publish pungent and perceptive political critiques. The decision to federalise meant a greater measure of autonomy for the regions. New organisations were permitted to develop completely free from Communist Party tutelage, including KAN (the Club of Committed Non-Party Members) and Club 231 (of former political prisoners), and a genuine religious freedom was re-established.[13] The role of public opinion was recognised in ways such as the publication by the mass media of opinion poll results on some of the most sensitive political issues. Also the secret police powers of the Ministry of the Interior were curbed by efforts to begin its conversion into a more limited protector of national security, such as exists in any state.

Furthermore, the old fixed election system was terminated, and new election laws were to be written. Effective freedom to strike was granted to the trade unions. Workers' councils were proposed to institute participatory democracy in the factories – though the Russian invaders gradually reduced their powers or dismantled them. Restrictions on individual freedoms were lifted. Thus any checks on travelling abroad were removed. Again, censorship was ended. The media, including films and publishing, were made independent agencies, with government subsidies granted without strings. Whilst one publishing house was to be run by the Communist Party, others were to function as non-profit co-operatives to serve the interests of other parties, groups, or private persons. Such groups, and particularly students, could start new journals and newspapers as non-profit co-operatives.

(3) In the summer of 1968 the proposal was accepted for enterprise councils to be set up and for over 50% of their members to be elected from among the employees of the enterprise in secret elections organised by the trade unions, plus 10–30% drawn from outside organisations such as the bank providing credits, or scientific institutions. The manager was also to sit on the council, though having been nominated by it, he was also subject to recall by it, subordinate to it for all major decisions (including his own salary and investment plans) and accountable to it for annual assessment. In 'important enterprises' the state would also be represented, though by no more than 20% of the members.

In addition, following the announcement of enterprise councils, workers began defending their rights and wishes by strikes or threats to strike. A new labour code introduced ideas, highly innovatory in a communist state, of mobility of labour, elimination of the cadre system, access for a worker to his personal files, protection by contracts, rights to take grievances to court, and other practices which increased worker freedom, protection and rights.[14] Trade unions

127

themselves were to be reformed to make them genuinely representative of workers' interests in factories rather than agencies of the state.

(4) Since it was a principle of the market-oriented 'improved system of planned management' that unsuccessful enterprises were to close, the corollary would be the emergence of unemployment, at least in the short term. Its length would depend on the central handling of demand management and the extent of job creation by the state and of direction of labour. How far the continuing state responsibility for long-term planning designed to predict trends in supply, demand, costs and resources might in practice have prevented any significant emergence of structural unemployment can only be conjectured, since the invasion of August 1968 meant that the reforms were never put to the test in this respect.

(5) Similarly, the espousal of the market system would presumably have generated greater income inequalities over time. The former scheme of wage equalisation was replaced by a system whereby wages were to be differentiated according to the workers' tasks and merit (a market rather than a social test). The level of wages was to depend on the success or failure of the plant, though the state would establish minimum wages along with price categories, levies and certain key investments, so that it would retain some influence on overall wage developments. The thrust of the 1968 reforms cannot therefore be said to have been towards equality, but to a moderate degree in the opposite direction.

(6) Nor in the impact of the reforms on the trade unions, where their main role was towards liberating them as organs of state power, were the 1968 upheavals directed specially at securing advances in workers' health and safety conditions or welfare or job satisfaction. It may be that the new enterprise councils would have developed along this route, but they were disbanded too soon to tell.

(7) The central cultural motif of the reforms lay in

establishing freedom of expression for all the main interest groups. Again, therefore, the values of sharing and co-operation were not a primary objective, and the shift from command-economy controls to much greater enterprise autonomy was bound in the first instance to emphasise rather the separation and individuality of pluralist interests.

In summary, therefore, the Czech 1968 Action Programme can be seen to have broadly incorporated the first three of the socialist principles enunciated in the last chapter – overall social planning of production, democratic freedoms for political, cultural and religious organisations, and worker democracy and managerial accountability in the factories. On the other hand, the market orientation of the reforms might have meant, if allowed to mature, the emergence of at least some structural unemployment, a certain growth of income inequalities, and even a possible weakening of a co-operativist value system, though all these conclusions must be tentative in view of the enforced briefness of the experiment.

Was Yugoslavia in the 1950s and 1960s Socialist?

Claiming that the USSR had deviated from socialist democracy towards bureaucratic overcentralisation, the Yugoslavs began in 1950 to decentralise their economy, and focus on workers' councils in each factory. Farming reverted to private ownership, and private enterprise began to play an increasing role in the catering and service sector, though only a very small role still in industry. Apart from this latter small enclave, factories are run as producer co-operatives, each under the control of its own workers' councils directly elected by all the workers of the enterprise. Managers are appointed by the local government, though the workers' council has veto power over this and can also fire the manager. Furthermore it sets wages and prices within limits laid down by central agencies, establishes production targets, determines technology and can dispose of its profits after taxes through wage increases, collective welfare projects or reinvestment. Having constructed this edifice, the official Yugoslav view has been that its self-management system, by giving balanced emphasis to the citizen's rights as producer, consumer and politically involved member of society, offers the nearest approach to direct democracy yet achieved anywhere in the world. But how socialist is it really?

(1) Initially, prior to the 1960s reforms, it was believed that a socialist government should prescribe the basic trajectory of a socialist society, requiring centralisation of investment decisions, while short-run allocation decisions were too numerous and too unimportant to be made effectively at the centre. However, after a decade of experience with this dichotomy, the Yugoslav authorities became convinced that much the same arguments could be made against centralised investment decisions as against short-run allocation decisions because in practice a great many 'political' factories continued to require substantial operating subsidies to survive at all.

This does not mean, however, that the state has abdicated all control over economic planning. It retains powers to intervene to control prices and to influence investment policy. But the norm is now the market, and state intervention is seen as an exceptional and declining factor. To that extent the first criterion of socialism in the last chapter is not met.

(2) The political system based on self-management clearly has significant democratic potential since the elected delegates to the local assemblies are directly accountable by mandate to their voters and can be recalled at any time. But there are limiting factors. At the level above the local councils, delegates to the republican and federal assemblies are chosen by the local-level delegates, so that democracy is indirect. On another dimension, inside the enterprises the

'informal groups' may not willingly cede their power. Secondly, party control has been strengthened and recentralised throughout the country, in contrast to the decentralisation of industrial and local power. Nevertheless, it must be accepted that sufficient democratic choice exists for the ordinary citizen so that the second criterion is met.

(3) Constitutionally, the workers' self-management system developed from the basic law on enterprises passed in April 1965 whereby an enterprise with thirty or more workers is obliged to set up a workers' council in each branch of the production process. Elections of council members, averaging some twelve per council, are held by secret ballot every two years, when a proportion of council members are obliged to retire. The powers of the unit council include dividing the income of the unit between investment funds and personal incomes and setting differentials and rates of pay. Central workers' councils for the whole enterprise fix prices for internal products and services, establish the overall production plan and adopt the programme for technological development. A board of management is elected by the workers' council with a minimum of five members, including *ex officio* the manager. The main function of the board is to implement the council's decisions and to supervise all technical services, but it can also initiate policy. The members are obliged to change every two years. The manager is appointed by the workers' council in conjunction with the local government body for a four-year term, which is renewable only once.

Despite the sometimes vaunted claims made for self-management, is the worker really in charge in Yugoslavia? Whether workers actually take over and run enterprises depends on such factors as the level of education, the political climate, the quality of management and the level of economic development. Predictably, workers in more developed areas put more emphasis on consultation and other forms of participation, while those in poorer regions still feel most strongly about pay and conditions. But even in developed regions an independent sociologist in Zagreb (Shutt) concluded in 1970 that only 2–3% of all decisions in the enterprise represented genuine acts of self-management adopted after a proper process of consultation.[15]

Undoubtedly the self-management system offers many advantages when compared with either corporate capitalism or bureaucratic socialism. Work rules have been adapted to the needs and wishes of the workforce in an atmosphere that is not rigidified by the bureaucratised bargaining of management–union relations. The system of technical commissions appointed by worker councils has proved a substantial counterweight to technocratic information hoarding. Above all, the workforce is genuinely able to offer serious and effective challenge against unwanted decisions being made, not only through the right to strike, but through the right to dismiss management. There can be little doubt that these rights, slowly but steadily expanded, have provided a more effective check on the technocratic-bureaucratic coalition than has yet been achieved under alternative economic systems.

(4) An important feature of the 1960s reforms was the closure of a number of uneconomic factories built in the period of 'administrative socialism' in the late 1940s and early 1950s. This in turn created heavy unemployment, despite extensive waves of emigration. Though it was estimated that about 1 million Yugoslavs were working in the West, there were still in the summer of 1974 some 400,000 unemployed in Yugoslavia itself. In order to prevent unemployment growing as marginal firms go out of existence, it would be necessary to maintain the rate of investment at an arbitrary level, especially since a centrally determined price-cut to dispose of goods is not open to a market socialist system. But the 1960s reforms, encouraging independent investment activity by enterprises, supplemented by bank investments allocated on strict economic criteria, worked in

the opposite direction. Full employment in the absolute sense cannot therefore be said to exist in Yugoslavia.

(5) The new income law of January 1969 gave workers more autonomy in distributing incomes from the resources they created, and by 1970 differentials in Yugoslav industry had reached the level of 1 : 8 or more, compared with 1 : 4 a decade before.[16] In fact Yugoslavia classically illustrates the dilemma of avoiding bureaucratic control of society by rejection of central planning. The consequence has been a growth of inequality between enterprises as well as between individuals, and a profit ethos which extends even to differential payments of social services according to the contribution of individuals.[17] In fact, quite apart from the absence of a rich class consuming particularly imported luxury goods, a relatively high level of egalitarianism has been brought about partly by the ending of large landed estates and partly by a deliberate policy of modest wage and salary differentials in the cities.[18]

(6) The effect of Yugoslav self-management on work attitudes and job satisfaction was measured by a recent study which found that members of self-management bodies had higher general work satisfaction (except for those working with automated technology) and were more satisfied with pay, working conditions and job control.[19] However, 'work alienation' (defined as workers' inability to express their personalities and intellectual abilities in the productive process, and their inability to control work results) was also higher in self-management enterprises. Perhaps the most important finding was that participation in self-management should not be overemphasised as a source of satisfaction. Even participating members of workers' councils and boards of management ranked participation no higher than fifth in their list of desired job characteristics, that is, as less important than the issues of working conditions, wages, job interest and promotion.

Nor can the aim of replacing hierarchic and authoritarian

relations be said to have been achieved. Though workers' councils make decisions, at least formally, on all business matters, several studies have shown that workers regard them as exerting less influence on events than top management, staff, or even middle management.[20] Some have concluded that these councils have been transformed into transmission belts for line and staff instructions, losing their function as representatives of workers' interests.[21] But though hierarchical managerial organisation still dominates administrative decisions, workers' councils do exert considerable influence on matters affecting welfare.

(7) The 1960s reforms weakened the socialist principles in Yugoslavia of equality, social values and solidarity. Inequality developed in the form of exploitation of the new market conditions, the emergence of a new bureaucracy and the crude basis of current productivity for the distribution of income. Unequal opportunity in the educational, industrial and political spheres also remained, and even grew somewhat in this period. The dilemma has not yet been solved of creating a process of democratic planning which will impose socialist principles on the workings of the price mechanism without alienating the democratic aspirations of a people who do want to manage themselves. Also, Chinese criticism has alleged a gradual return to capitalism on the ground that Yugoslav economic psychology is reverting to the bourgeois outlook of profit-making rather than one of social benefit.

In summary, according to the criteria of socialism adopted in Chapter 5, Yugoslavia is a partially socialist society. The principles of political freedom, industrial democracy and significant checks on excessive inequality are largely present, and that of emphasis on worker welfare and job satisfaction (though only from participation in self-management) partly so. The criteria, however, of production for social need, real full employment and promotion of a co-operative ethic are absent or at least not strongly and deliberately promulgated.

Is Cuba Socialist?

Cuba, together with China, provides perhaps the most striking illustration of attempts to realise socialism from an underdeveloped economic base. However, its position sharply differs from that of China in that it is a very small country (population 9 million), lacking prospects of self-sufficiency, only 90 miles offshore from the US mainland, and thus thrown willy-nilly into the painful role of pawn between conflicting imperialisms, Soviet and American.

Prior to the revolution in December 1958, Cuba was the non-developing country *par excellence*. Although the per capita national income was relatively high for the Third World, it had not risen for fifty years. The economy was dominated by a small number of large firms, mainly US-owned. Thus thirteen US companies between them owned 40% of sugar production, and US firms owned the electricity and telephone systems, nickel production, oil refineries, and so on. The price paid by the Cuban people for being a raw materials adjunct of the US economy was enormous. In the countryside a huge section of the population was deliberately left unemployed much of the year so it would be available for the sugar harvest. At the same time a considerable proportion of the 60% of the land owned by the sugar producers was left fallow, to keep world prices up, not used to expand sugar production when world prices rose anyway. The beneficiaries from this situation, the large US companies and the minute local oligarchy, invested their profits either in real estate or abroad, rarely in developing local industry. How socialist has the transformation been?

(1) Following the formulation of the first economic plan in 1962, the ideological controversy began over market socialism versus centralised planning. In the former case, under the system of self-management, independent enterprises traded their products in the market, using profitability as the basic measure of success. Banks provided interest-

135

bearing credits, but loans were closely supervised so that banks played a critical role in evaluating the enterprise. Basic output and investment decisions were set by the Central Planning Agency. But managerial incentives and labour income were based primarily on material incentives.

As against this system of self-management which gained some official sanction in 1962, the alternative system of central budgeting began to emerge. Here, enterprises were not independent, but were considered part of a larger productive unit, the public sector as a whole, so that profitability played no role in assessing enterprise performance and all net income was deposited with the Treasury, which centrally allocated funds to various enterprises. Firms were directed to fulfil plan targets, and rigorous financial control was established through a central organisation that co-ordinated the accounts of firms throughout a particular industrial sector. Finally, moral rather than material incentives were stressed as the main form of motivation.[22]

Policy fluctuated between these two models until in 1966 Cuba moved decisively to adopt the latter, championed by Che Guevara, and by 1967 all enterprises were operating under radicalised versions of central budgeting. Under this system direct contractual relations involved no monetary or credit transactions; records of receipt and transfer of goods were kept, but no payments were required. The price freeze and rationing destroyed any real relationship between value and price. Moreover, the value of final goods was designed to reflect social rather than market factors. The new system led Cuban economists to experiment with a non-monetary measure of relative costs such as man-hours of labour-time. Ideologically it was argued that the full social and community implications of productive relationships would only be realised if the commodity myth were exploded and human labour were expressed in real terms rather than in money, its fetished commodity form. Certainly this radical extension from 1967 of Che's system of central budgeting can be

136

construed as meeting the first socialist principle, production for social use.

(2) Elections and freedom of the press do not exist in Cuba. Even friendly observers have noted that

> Cuba's governing system is clearly one of bureaucratic rule (in the sense that power is monopolised by officials appointed by and answerable to those above them in the chain of command). Power is concentrated in the Communist Party, within the Party in the Central Committee, and within the Central Committee in the Maximum Leader. The structure was built from the top down: first came the Leader, then the Central Committee, then the regional and local organizers, and finally the membership.[23]

Also, the channels through which other than official views could reach the public have been gradually cut off. Suppression was not confined to the 'micro-factionalists' around Anibal Escalante (the Secretary of the Communist Party). While in the mid-1960s a public debate could still take place over fundamental policy issues, albeit in muted tones and allusive style, and while then genuine differences within the government itself could still be clearly identified, thereafter the periodicals in which the debate was conducted were discontinued.

(3) Up to the change in economic organisation in 1966 bureaucratic and complicated regulations provided few possibilities for worker participation within individual enterprises. Then in 1966–7 it was decided to tie the efficiency plans to 'socialist emulation': individual workers and firms would set their own goals and try to fulfil them. Trade unions were assigned a major task in fulfilling socialist emulation goals, but their bureaucratic structure and limited function in the plant seriously undermined their effectiveness. In 1969 experiments with the Advanced Workers'

Movement, which began to replace the local trade union in some factories, were aimed partly at revitalising mass participation in the work centre. But in general these efforts were mainly directed at increasing work efficiency rather than worker participation in social and economic decisions.[24]

(4) The revolution in 1958 rapidly reversed the chronic and massive underemployment in the countryside. In 1956–7, just prior to this, a period of economic upturn, unemployment was estimated at 9% of the labour force during the sugar harvest and 20% afterwards.[25] After the revolution, by 1962 the number in employment had been increased by about a third, though some unemployment continued for a few more years. But the most significant aspect of the post-1966 radicalisation of Cuban economic organisation was that it rapidly converted the labour surplus into labour shortage. Since then, though some disguised unemployment still exists in certain sectors, it can be said that the full employment target has largely been achieved.

(5) In general, the revolution considerably reduced the glaring differences between rich and poor that existed previously. Very few new appointments were made in the early 1960s at more than US $300 a month, which compares with a minimum agricultural wage of US $60 a month and a minimum urban wage of US $85[26] (an overall ratio of only five or four to one). But a flatter distribution was not bought at the price of a lower average. In 1974 Pat Holt, chief researcher of the US Senate Committee on Foreign Relations, estimated on a visit to Cuba that GNP per capita then amounted to some US $1,587, which meant Cuba was the richest country in Latin America, with the possible exception of Venezuela (where the position was distorted by oil).

(6) As economic problems intensified, working hours increased, strikes were looked upon with disapproval, and wages remained the same though all kinds of 'voluntary' contributions had to be paid. A special campaign against absenteeism had to be started, while at the same time workers

lost rights, such as the nine days' annual sick leave, which they had enjoyed under the previous capitalist regime. None of this is to deny, however, that major advances in employment rights were achieved (for example, the new far-reaching social security system published in September 1962), but the issue of job satisfaction was necessarily relegated to a time in the future when the economic base was better secured – and the trade unions were restored to their normal role.

(7) Worker identification with the system – an essential ingredient of the Cuban model – was undermined by the fact that effective planning and economic controls were extremely weak in Cuba. Shortages and bottlenecks reduced industrial output and worker productivity, the decision-making process was plagued by bureaucracy, and managerial and administrative personnel suffered a large turnover. To a degree moral incentives fostered irrational uses of labour and capital, since administrators often regarded overtime or voluntary work as costless, waste of the precious resource of *conciencia* not being measurable.

The result was, first, resort to the military model, with command posts set up throughout the country to organise large production units and direct large units of labour. Secondly, an anti-loafing law was promulgated in 1971 to deal with absenteeism and to bring all able-bodied men between 17 and 60 into the labour force. The penalties for absenteeism ranged from working under the vigilance of other workers and revolutionary organisations to working in a rehabilitation centre for up to a year.[27] The government increasingly felt obliged to use ideological instruments (for example, the 'Revolutionary Offensive' of the mid-1960s) to develop greater expression of social commitment. Such an externalisation of revolutionary ethics, however, which relies on directives from above, can readily become just another form of repression, a substitution of the power motive for the money motive.

In summary, therefore, Cuba on this analysis is revealed

as meeting the socialist criteria of Chapter 5 only partially. It fulfils the principles of production for social use, real full employment, a high degree of equality and a determined promotion of moral values and 'socialist emulation'. However, the other factors – political democracy and individual freedom, industrial democracy and worker welfare and job satisfaction – were not, or were only partially, present. It must be doubted, however, since the basic shape of the economy was being determined by the Russians, how free the Cuban state really was to take its own decisions on some of these issues.

What Lessons?

What conclusions can be drawn from this brief survey of the degree of socialist characterisation of these five main countries so often described as 'socialist'? The most important conclusion is that not one of the five countries most frequently labelled 'socialist' matches the seven criteria in every respect. The USSR, which is often described as the prototype socialist country, meets only a single one of the seven. Yugoslavia and Cuba meet a majority of the criteria (though in different combinations), and Czechoslovakia during the 1968 reforms similarly met half the criteria without having enough time to reveal how it would have handled the other half. China, on the other hand, satisfies all the criteria except that of political democracy and individual freedom. On the basis, therefore, of the criteria delineated as key in Chapter 5, it can be seen that there is no country in the world yet which can claim to be totally socialist, as the summary in Table 6.1 shows.

There is thus no direct model for the UK, especially since none of the countries displaying some socialist characteristics to a significant degree has an economy at the level of industrialised development of the UK.

Beyond this first essential point, what specific lessons can be drawn from the political economies of these five countries? First, in the case of the USSR and its East European satellites, it can be concluded (in view of the USSR's single socialist attribute) that socialist relations of production do not simply follow from state ownership through nationalisation of the means of production. For state ownership of the productive apparatus may give rise to a ruling class deriving its power from control of the means of production. Indeed, the Russian experience offers rather a model of totalitarianism – with its single dominant political party under the command of the leader and more or less complete state control of the productive forces, the means of violence and the systems of communication. And just as property under capitalism secures the position of members of the elite by ensuring the hereditary transfer of rights to descendants,

Table 6.1 *Comparative Existence of Socialist Characteristics in Five Countries*

	USSR	China	Czechoslovakia (1968)	Yugoslavia	Cuba
Production for social use	−	+	+	−	+
Political democracy and individual freedom	−	−	+	+	−
Industrial democracy	−	+	+	+	−
Real full employment	+	+	(−)	−	+
Limitations on inequality	−	+	(−)	+	+
Worker welfare and job satisfaction	−	+	(−)	(+)	−
Promoting a co-operative ethic	−	+	(−)	−	+

Key: + characteristic is present
− characteristic is absent
( ) characteristic is partially present/absent

so it may be said that under Russian communism the party maintains the stability of the system and of itself as a ruling group by preserving its control of the *nomenklatura* (the list of positions in the administration which cannot be filled without party consent). It is clear therefore that socialist relations of production require a great deal more than simply the juridical form of state ownership of the means of production.

Secondly, if industrial democracy is one of the essential extra elements, how well does it work in practice? One view, which aspirations especially in Yugoslavia and Czechoslovakia (1968) have striven for, is that extensive decentralisation, workers' control and an atmosphere of political and social freedom can best reconcile the industrial system with individual contentment and the need for as much individual freedom as is compatible with preventing anti-social abuses of private power and privilege. But on the role of workers' control there are divergences between ideology and reality, at least as far as actual experience in Eastern Europe has so far shown. There is anyway the more pessimistic attitude to workers' control – that to give workers in the factory exclusive rights over the property and output of that factory is to make them into mini-capitalists and to encourage a bourgeois property-owning mentality. But even the more optimistic interpretation is open to doubt on practical consequences. Thus the Yugoslav approach has been that nationalisation of the means of production is a necessary though not a sufficient condition for socialism. State ownership still does not prevent workers being estranged or alienated from their product. Hence workers' control is needed as a way to equalise political and industrial participation.

Studies of the results, however, have shown that workers' councils in Yugoslavia have not been the effective source of power in enterprises. Rather they have proved that the suggestions of the director and the management are practically always accepted by the workers' council. One study of twenty Yugoslav enterprises[28] revealed that position in the organisational hierarchy was closely related to participation in company affairs, in rank order from higher management, non-supervisory staff and higher plant supervisors downwards. Further, it has been suggested that management in Yugoslavia and Sweden looks to workers' councils, not for advice on production, but as a means of gauging the impact of management policy on the workers.[29] Thus management may give a sense of participation to workers; but rather than being an actual source of decision-making, councils in practice have the real function of integrating workers into the industrial system.

It cannot, however, be assumed from these quoted studies that workers' joint control or participation, even in this particular form, necessarily entails these consequences or functions in this way. The balance of powers between the workers' council and the management could be structured increasingly to favour the former, greater training and experience as a source of confidence to workers could entrench workers' influence more deeply, and above all workers' values (such as job satisfaction and security) could increasingly prevail over management notions of efficiency. Nevertheless, experience does suggest that instruments of workers' self-management, in so far as they exist up to the present, do not yet provide an effective alternative locus of power either to market forces, as reflected in management pressures, or to state planning, as represented by centralised economic decision-making in countries like China.

Thirdly, have the 'socialist' countries, through supersession of the market, or through planned control of it, abolished class privilege and exploitation in their societies? The evidence for the USSR and Eastern Europe[30] suggests that economic inequalities have been reduced little, if at all, compared with Western societies. Careful assembly of the available data indicates that the ratio of maximum to average earned income in industry in Russia and Eastern Europe is as high as fifteen or twenty to one. Differences in skill and effort are used to justify differential rewards, and in practice workers are paid according to the amount of work done, their level of skill and their efficiency in applying their skill. One close observer of these societies argues that, as in Western countries, there is a significant break between the manual and non-manual strata in terms of a wide range of factors: incomes, availability of housing, patterns of consumption, occupational status, patterns of social interaction, access to education and opportunities for women.[31] It is further suggested that as the industrialisation process matures, the same tendency towards class rigidity becomes apparent in Eastern European societies as again is manifest in the West. Occupational strata are replenished from within (that is, children inherit their parents' social position), upward mobility continues though at a slower rate, and downward mobility from the non-manual stratum to the manual tends to cease. All this evidence implies a crystallisation of social structure – if anything the reverse of the banishment of social class inequalities.

Fourthly, then, in view of these rather sobering conclusions, what are the gains from the socialist form of society? So far the argument has been largely negative. State ownership of the means of production is no guarantee of industrial democracy or equality. Mechanisms of workers' control are no guarantee that workers are not still dominated by managerial authority and the industrial process. The existence of a market system does not necessarily produce class exploitation, nor does its absence imply freedom from class domination (albeit of a different kind). Neither does a centrally planned economy guarantee reduction of inequality or abolition of privilege; and over-riding market forces do not automatically bring about greater welfare for workers or improvements in job satisfaction. What, therefore, is the benefit from institutional reform which attempts to supersede the impersonal anarchy of market economies? Are the remedies offered by the 'socialist' states as disadvantageous as the conditions they were designed to redress?

One riposte which is certainly relevant to this challenge is that the competition and threat presented to would-be independent socialist states by American and Russian imperialism in the West and East respectively have so far distorted or even completely aborted major genuine socialist initiatives. Cuba in the Western orbit, and Yugoslavia, China and Czechoslovakia in the Russian sphere of influence, have all suffered drastically in this respect, and their societies have been profoundly perverted as a result. But despite these very real distortions of cherished ideologies – and such constraints are never likely to be absent – the question of the gains remains a genuine one and needs an answer. Nor should the answer simply be couched in terms of relative economic performance (though that is not unimportant). Comecon countries, for example, have achieved over the last two decades strikingly higher growth rates than those of West European countries, together with virtual full employment and very little or nil inflation (until the latter was imported from the West after the oil crisis of the mid-1970s) – a formidable achievement by capitalist standards, but not one wholly specifically and directly attributable to socialism as such.

Perhaps the key advantage offered by a socialist framework for society is that the question is seriously and systematically raised as to what constitute the real ultimate objectives of life, both for the individual and for society, and that the answers posed are more balanced and potentially more richly rewarding than in the monodimensional imprint of capitalist society. In a socialist framework life is not exclusively, or even mainly, about maximising economic growth or material possessions or self-interest. It is about developing all facets, not merely economic ones, of the human character, and not simply offering leisure-time for

145

such pursuits as though they were peripheral or subordinate, but installing them deeply within the productive mainstream of society's activities. Thus China and Cuba particularly have sought consciousness of their peoples as primary objectives, both to provide a degree of moral motivation to pre-empt an excessive materialism and also to provide the basis for developing the maturity and fulfilment of citizenship that comes from major decentralisation of power and real decision-sharing. Furthermore, a system in which the self-aggrandising interests of private capital are no longer dominant permits essential social objectives to become more important, notably full employment (again in China and Cuba). Economic and social equality is by and large given more emphasis, an important fact when equality of opportunity, contrary to the rhetoric of many of its proponents, actually requires a high degree of basic equality as such as a pre-condition. There is also much greater genuine pressure to make the demands of industrial work compatible with human dignity (Yugoslavia and China), or at least to prevent status hierarchies built on work-grading. Nor are these attempts in a socialist society to instil social priorities at the heart of the industrial process incompatible with a very high degree of personal and political freedoms (the Prague Spring).

But, as a fifth question, since this combination of benefits is predicated on a market socialism model rather than on Soviet-type bureaucratic centralisation, it must be asked whether the market is not in fact inherently anti-socialist. Thus it has been suggested, in the light of the short-lived 1968 Czechoslovak experiment, that three factors – the vesting of control of enterprises within the enterprises themselves, their co-ordination through the market and reliance on material incentives – do collectively push towards an economic order which, whatever it is called, functions more and more like capitalism. On the same view, any attempt at 'market socialism' leads irrevocably to the restoration of capitalism.[32] But this is to confuse the political and technical aspects of a market system, which are quite separate. The market is a device which is appropriate under conditions of scarcity for reconciling demand and supply through the formation of prices. It does not *per se* entail class exploitation. There is a clear distinction between the class nature of markets under capitalism and the technical role of markets under socialism.

In conclusion, how far the experiences of the five countries selected here are relevant both to the proponents of the socialist movement in Western Europe and to the validity of the very idea of socialism[33] is problematic. Each of these countries displays *some* of the key characteristics of a socialist society, but none displays them all, and none is quite at the same stage of advanced industrialisation or has quite the same cultural background as Britain. It is therefore unproved as to how far one society can achieve all these values jointly. But though there are potential conflicts in the desired values (for instance, freedom and equality, full industrial democracy and competent management, job security and technological progress), the experience of these countries does suggest that in each case these need not be irreconcilable differences, and that practical balances, certainly with varying success, are achievable.

Nevertheless, there is no direct prototype for a country such as Britain – far from it. The forging of socialism in Britain remains very much an indigenous task. We need to explore more closely, therefore, what are likely to be the practical problems which could face Britain in making this transition, and this is the focus of the next chapter.

NOTES: CHAPTER 6

1   R. L. Heilbroner, *An Inquiry into the Human Prospect* (London: Calder & Boyars, 1975), p. 72.
2   P. J. D. Wiles and S. Markowski, 'Income distribution under communism and capitalism', *Soviet Studies*, vol. 22, no. 4 (April 1971), p. 503, from table 27.

3   US Bureau of the Census, *Statistical Abstract of the United States, 1969*, 90th edn (Washington, DC: Government Printer, 1969), p. 321.

4   D. Lane, *Politics and Society in the USSR* (London: Weidenfeld & Nicolson, 1970), p. 332.

5   M. McAuley, *Labour Disputes in Soviet Russia 1957–65* (London: Clarendon Press, 1969), p. 123.

6   E. L. Wheelwright and B. McFarlane, *The Chinese Road to Socialism* (New York: Monthly Review Press, 1970), p. 131.

7   J. Deleyne, *The Chinese Economy* (London: Deutsch, 1973), p. 57.

8   C. Howe, *Wage Patterns and Wage Policy in Modern China, 1919–72* (Cambridge: Cambridge University Press, 1973), pp. 36, 40.

9   K. S. Karol, *China: the Other Communism* (London: Heinemann, 1967), p. 559.

10 N. Harris, 'China and world revolution', *International Socialism*, vol. 78 (May 1975), p. 20.

11 Wheelwright and McFarlane, op. cit., p. 190.

12 M. Schwartz, 'Czechoslovakia's new political model: a design for renewal', *Journal of Politics*, vol. 30 (1968), p. 978.

13 A. H. Brown, 'Political change in Czechoslovakia', *Government and Opposition*, vol. 4, no. 2 (Spring 1969), pp. 170–1.

14 G. Golan, 'The short-lived liberal experiment in Czechoslovak socialism', *Orbis*, vol. XIII, no. 4 (Winter 1970), p. 1102.

15 H. Shutt (ed.), *Worker Participation in West Germany, Sweden, Yugoslavia and the United Kingdom* (London: Economist Intelligence Unit, January 1975), p. 25.

16 R. Moore, *Self-Management in Yugoslavia* (London: Fabian Society, January 1970), p. 25.

17 P. Sweezy and L. Huberman, 'Peaceful transition from socialism to capitalism?', *Monthly Review*, vol. 15, no. 11 (March 1964), pp. 569–90.

18 B. Ward, 'Appraising Yugoslav socialism', in J. A. Zammit (ed.), *The Chilean Road to Socialism* (Brighton: Institute of Development Studies, 1972), pp. 441–55.

19 J. Obradovic, 'Participation and work attitudes in Yugoslavia', in *Industrial Relations*, vol. 9, no. 2 (February 1970), pp. 161–9.

20 *Workers' Participation in Management in Yugoslavia*, Bulletin No. 9 (Geneva: International Institute for Labour Studies, 1972), p. 164.

21 V. Rus, 'Influence structure in Yugoslav enterprise', *Industrial Relations*, vol. 9 (February 1970), pp. 148–60.

22 B. Silverman, 'Economic organization and social conscience: some dilemmas of Cuban socialism', in J. A. Zammit (ed.), *The Chilean Road to Socialism* (Brighton: Institute of Development Studies, 1972), pp. 391–418.

23 Sweezy and Huberman, op. cit., p. 219.

24 Silverman, op. cit., p. 405.

25 T. Draper, *Castroism: Theory and Practice* (London: Pall Mall Press, 1965), p. 106.

26 D. Seers, A. Bianchi, R. Jolly and M. Nolff, *Cuba: The Economic and Social Revolution* (Chapel Hill, NC: University of North Carolina Press, 1964), p. 29.

27 Silverman, op. cit., p. 414.

28 Cited by M. Warner, 'Bureaucracy, participation and self-government in

organisations', *Participation and Self-Management*, Vol. 2 (Zagreb: First International Sociological Conference on Participation and Self-Management, 1972), p. 195.

29 G. Strauss and E. Rosenstein, 'Workers' participation in management: a central view', *Industrial Relations*, vol. 9, no. 2 (February 1970), pp. 197–214.

30 M. Matthews, *Class and Society in Soviet Russia* (London: Allen Lane, 1972), pp. 90–3; D. Lane, *The End of Inequality? Stratification under State Socialism* (Harmondsworth: Penguin, 1971), pp. 71–9; S. M. Lipset and R. B. Dobson, 'Social stratification and sociology in the Soviet Union', *Survey*, vol. 19 (Summer 1973), pp. 126–7.

31 D. Lane, *The Socialist Industrial State* (London: Allen & Unwin, 1976), p. 197.

32 P. M. Sweezy and C. Bettelheim, 'On the transition to socialism', *Monthly Review*, vol. 22, no. 1 (May 1971), p. 4.

33 L. Kolakowski and S. Hampshire (eds), *The Socialist Ideal* (London: Weidenfeld & Nicolson, 1974), p. 12.

7

But Is It Realistic?

The conclusion of the last chapter, that there exists no ready-made model of socialism anywhere in the world along the lines prescribed in Chapter 5, must now raise one awkward question. Though the characterisation of a socialist system deployed here may yield theoretical redress to fundamental contemporary problems, is such an economic framework really practicable in the modern Western world? Quite apart from the difficulties of transition, which are undoubtedly great, what new conflicts are likely to be inherent in a system of this kind, once realised and operating? Even if one set of fundamental human problems is resolved, or the means for their resolution is much more readily made available, is a new set opened up or are previous aspirations or satisfactions relegated? This chapter attempts a critical assessment of socialism in answer to these issues.

Power of Decision over Production Questions

Perhaps the most basic question in any modern economy is who decides what is to be produced and how is this decision taken. Now societies described as socialist have historically frequently taken authoritarian forms, either because of the difficulties of capital accumulation in underdeveloped nations, or because of war or external economic threats, or because of the legacy of feudal traditions. But the structure of classical so-called state socialism itself also seems to have inherent tendencies towards hierarchy, away from participation and democracy. To the extent that nationalisation centralises decision-making to achieve the planned allocation of resources, the problem of alienation reappears. Indeed, nationalisation has historically largely precluded the emergence of a network of local power groups rooted in control of independent resources and thus able to retain some control over the central authority.

One notable attempt to organise economic power away from the centralised state is reflected in the Yugoslav argument for workers' self-management, namely, decentralisation of economic power to the social and organisational unit of workers in a firm. But this model raises several difficult problems. It has not been able to prevent such (partial) groups developing special interests ('workers' capitalism') which run counter to the interests of the broader community. Over-reliance on the market has failed to close major inequalities between communities, and has led to commercialism and exploitation. An ethic of individual gain and profit has often taken precedence over the ideal of co-operation. As competitive tendencies have emerged between worker-controlled industries, the accompanying need for some central co-ordination has generated other anomalies. Thus the banks now control many nationwide investment decisions, several reducing local economic power, and the Yugoslav Communist Party has played an often arbitrary role in both national and local decisions. In recalling the historic themes of both guild socialism and syndicalism, the Yugoslav model demonstrates how difficult it is for a political economy based primarily on the organisation of groups by function to achieve a just society since such a structure inherently tends towards the self-aggrandisement of each functional group against the rest of the community.

This suggests that workers' control should be set firmly in

151

the broader context of, and subordinate to, the entire community. The social unit at the heart of a socialist system should, as far as possible, embrace all the people – minorities, the elderly, women, youth, as well as paid workers who at any time number only some 40% of the population and perhaps 60% of the adult citizens. Now the only social unit which includes all the people is one based on geographical proximity; in a territorially defined local community a variety of functional groups must coexist alongside each other. Long-term relationships can be developed, and conflicts must inevitably be mediated directly by people who have to live with the decisions they take. Moreover, when territorially defined communities own capital socially (as in the Israeli kibbutzim and the Chinese communes), there is no built-in contradiction between the interests of owners and beneficiaries of industry as against the community as a whole. The problem of 'externalities' is dealt with because the local community, as the controller of productive wealth, can decide rationally whether to pay the costs of eliminating the pollution which its own industry causes for its own people. Furthermore, the community as a whole can decide how to divide work equitably among all its citizens.

However, though local ownership of capital might resolve some problems, it raises others. As in the case of the conservative view that individuals should control capital, or the Yugoslav view that workers should (both of which agree with the socialist view propounded here that political power must somehow be related to decentralised economic power), the socialist argument in favour of local communities does not avoid the danger that they, like any other economic units, may function to protect – and out of insecurity, to extend – their own special, status quo interest, even though that may conflict with the broader interests of the national community. This necessarily poses the issue of the relative distribution of power between small units and large frameworks, and of precisely which functions can be decentralised and which cannot. Now if the socialist vision is not of a streamlined, planned state but rather of an organic, diversified distribution of power, then a community, as the basis for a larger framework of regional and national co-ordinating institutions, would hold several important advantages as the unit for exercising a whole range of independent social decisions – initiating new investments, experimenting with new training approaches and various worker–management schemes, locating jobs, homes and schools so as to maximise community interaction, and for other similar purposes. But the problem remains of creating a larger, perhaps confederate framework which can deal with the economic insecurity of competing community industry and can obviate the self-aggrandising expansionist logic of market systems.

A governing continental-scale state would be far too large for any hope of democratic management by localities, and unnecessary even for technical efficiency, given co-operation between areas for purposes such as cross-continental transportation and some forms of power exploitation. This suggests a key role for regional units intermediate between local communities and nation,[1] and capable of taking many of the decisions at present monopolised by the largest industrial corporations. But again the question arises as to how within the larger unit decisions should reflect the needs of real (that is, local) communities. Here it is relevant that control by the appropriate unit of a local market through its direct receipt of some surpluses and its control of some capital can offer economic leverage, while its organisational principles permit political leverage. The goal, utopian, but in a positive sense, is that the larger unit must have enough independent power to balance the pressures from the strongest community, but not so much as to overwhelm them. Essentially, the principle would be to leave as many functions as possible to localities, elevating only what is absolutely essential to the higher unit.

On this model, social priorities would be developed first

153

in each community and then subsequently in regional and national politics directed out of local experience. Planning might proceed in a manner akin to the Chinese 'two ups and two downs' process. Thus information, priorities and criteria would be generated at local levels, then these would be integrated at a higher-order 'planning stage' and the implications calculated, then the proposals would be returned to the smaller units for reconsideration, and finally in this more finished form they would be returned back up again.[2] Though such decentralised, democratic planning might seem inefficient in consuming too much time, it might be expected to more than compensate by gains in released energies, in enriching the quality of life and not least in ensuring with greater reliability that plans are actually fulfilled.

Thus power over production decisions is firmly located at plant level, though this is constrained both vertically by the necessary minimum co-ordination for planning purposes at the centre and horizontally by joint ownership of capital vested partly in the local community. The model thus combines both a certain form of market exchange and planning. It is a capitalist market (one based purely on profit criteria) that is rejected as exploitative, not market exchange as such. If the social system is to overcome its origins in capitalism, trade-offs between competition and co-operation must inevitably be attempted at different stages of development within socialism, as larger national political possibilities open up.

Rational Pricing

Pricing so as to secure optimal allocation of resources has often been regarded as the Achilles' heel of socialist planning. Yet leaving aside the fact that rational pricing is anyway already severely diluted under existing conditions of semi-monopoly capitalism, in fact decentralised or market socialism should have no more difficulty than competitive private enterprise in allocating resources rationally.[3] For irrespective of the form of ownership of firms, provided that each firm acts as an independent unit, its management can still set prices and output so as to meet given objectives, whether maximising the firm's profit (as under capitalism) or maximising output at a predetermined price fixed by politico–social criteria.

Moreover, as Lange indicated in his answer to Hayek's strictures on the impracticability of socialist planning, a socialist model can also be posited of intermediate decentralisation whereby planners set prices, but plant managers still control production. Thus if the planners began by setting arbitrary prices, prices could still be rational guides for managers provided the central planners reacted promptly to any shortage of supply by raising prices and to an excess of supply by lowering prices. The planners could thus simulate market prices by trial and error, and thereby induce managers (rather on the Eastern European pattern) to increase or reduce outputs respectively.

In the rather more fully decentralised model posited earlier, however, prices would be fixed at plant level, but with constraints against price inflation imposed from various sources. First, because production would not be undertaken by monopolies but by a range of independent producers (with strengthened anti-monopoly and anti-cartel legislative safeguards), upward price pressures would be limited partly by competition. Secondly, to the extent that local communities jointly own industrial capital with employees in each plant, workers' interests also as consumers would be reflected, indirectly but effectively if necessary, in the price-setting process. Thirdly, price excesses could be checked by the central planning agency responsible for economic co-ordination, either by delegated legislative controls or by threats of, or the reality of, foreign import competition (licensing of imports being a function of the central planning body which would regard the planning of participation in international trade as an inseparable part of its responsibility for overall domestic economic planning).

Pricing thus remains a decentralised function based on marginal cost criteria (or for specific social grounds on below-cost criteria subsidised by central government funding) plus a surplus for the purpose of future investment, R and D, and so on. There remains therefore a strong motive to pursue efficiency, subject only to the 100% full employment constraint.

Inflation, on the other hand, is likely to be minimised for several reasons under the model of socialism set out in Chapter 5. One is that greater self-sufficiency should insulate the national economy from the more violent inflationary and deflationary ebb and flow of international fluctuations. Another is that the steadier growth flowing from much fuller utilisation of plant and from real full employment of manpower would obviate the current need for regular massive and inflationary expansions of domestic credit to counter the inherent stagnating tendencies of capitalism and the growing rise of chronic unemployment. A third reason for believing that inflation should be well controlled within such a system is that, with the advantage of a more autonomous and less internationally dependent economy, the reserve price control powers of the central planning agency should be fully effective.

How Efficient?

A third objection traditionally put forward against the idea of a socialist economy is that it tends to be rigid and inefficient and fails to respond either quickly or adequately to demand. However, in the decentralised or liberal (as opposed to authoritarian) socialist model proposed here, flexibility is in fact preserved because production, pricing, manpower and investment decisions are all firmly located at company level, subject only to limited central supervision to ensure re-conciliation with over-riding national requirements.

The fundamental difference between capitalism and this type of market socialism, apart from the identity of the local decision-makers, is that the trade-off between profit and employment is pitched differently. Whereas within the capitalist firm the level of employment is a variable, dependent on the level of production required to equalise marginal cost with marginal revenue, within the socialist economy on the other hand the attainment of real full employment is paramount and firms as a last resort are allocated extra labour (in a manner designed to preserve fair competitive balance) which is not absorbed by training pro-grammes or alternative job-creating projects. In other words, while capitalism aims to provide as many jobs as are com-patible with organising production and pricing to maximise profits, socialism seeks to achieve the most efficient pro-duction of goods and services as is compatible with ensuring that all adults seeking employment are indeed offered a job (or retraining between jobs).

Again, there are in fact sound reasons for regarding the type of socialist economy envisaged here as productive of a high degree of efficiency. Quite apart from the fact that firms can be put out of business as a penalty for competitive inefficiency or failure to innovate (though without quite the panache of private enterprise capitalism and without the callous disregard for the human consequences), there are three separate and positive incentives to efficiency under-written by a socialist economic system which are missing from a capitalist framework. One is that if the firm's capital is vested partly in the employees jointly and partly in the local community (through its representative organs, embracing particularly the consumer interest), then because employees share in the profits, either as workers or con-sumers, they have a strong incentive to maximise pro-duction at least cost. A second factor here is that greater

157

decentralisation of economic decision-making and democratic involvement of workers at plant level might be expected to release energies now repressed and should increase productivity. Thirdly, if a job or retraining is guaranteed, then the pressure to protect existing jobs by over-manning or other restrictive practices disappears.

Individual Freedom

A fourth traditional objection against the concept of socialism is that it erodes individual liberty. Not only is it said that state planning undermines individual independence, but even that trade unions are robbed of their central function of free collective bargaining on pay and conditions of work on the specious grounds that 'the supremacy of a workers' state' makes such activities outdated.

In fact, in the model outlined in this chapter individual freedom will actually be strengthened because of the restructuring of powers and rights envisaged. First, since jobs are to workers what property is to the middle class, real full employment entrenches for all the fundamental freedom of livelihood without which citizenship is an empty concept. Secondly, a much greater equality of income and wealth would widen the basic economic freedom of control over resources. And thirdly, by decentralising economic decision-making and by making industrial democracy a reality at the workplace level, the freedom and power entailed by control over corporate resources would also be much more widely disseminated than it is with its present restricted concentration on certain small elite groups.

As to the relevance of the trade union role in a socialist economy, there can be no question but that the unions would retain their function as independent organisations representing workers' interests. However local or central management is recruited, and in whatever form economic control is exercised, there will always remain a need for shopfloor workers, and salaried and technical grades in addition, to be organised in autonomous groups, lest accountability of management becomes unenforceable. Collective bargaining with external owners or controllers of the enterprise would be replaced by income allocation determined jointly between all the employees, but each main grade of worker would require separate representation for this process. Similarly, the division of corporate surplus income would involve joint determination by representatives of each of the main employee grades.

A Lower Standard of Living?

Another conventional criticism of socialism from the right is that by substituting as central goals other objectives than straightforward corporate maximisation of profit, the socialist economy yields, whatever its other social effects, a lower overall standard of living for the nation. This is based on the assumption that imposing politico-social constraints such as the full employment condition must so undermine the ruthless and constant search for efficiency that industry loses its competitive edge, unit costs rise, production is cut back, unemployment mounts and the rise in living standards slows.

There are several fallacies about this application of classical market theory to late twentieth-century Western economies. First, it is by no means self-evident that an economy which oscillates between boom and slump, between labour scarcity and heavy unemployment, creates more wealth than one which aims at steadier growth, with full employment maintained throughout the same period. Certainly there is no guarantee that the former rather than the latter will produce a higher increment in the standard of living of the average worker, as opposed to a skewed distribution of incremental

159

wealth or income in favour of capital-holders and higher earners.

Secondly, the slump costs of a market economy in under-utilisation of plant and manpower are enormous: in the UK in 1976–8, for example, when 1½ million were registered unemployed, the Exchequer cost in social security benefits and loss of taxes forgone was estimated at some £4·5 billion a year, while the shortfall of actual output below a posited 'full employment' output (arbitrarily defined as maintaining unemployment at a level no higher than 650,000) has been calculated for the period 1970–5 in the UK at some £7 billion.[4] Of course, it may be argued that against this must be set the inefficiency in the use of resources implied by virtual-100% full employment in terms of excessive over-manning. But quite apart from the fact that over-manning exists in the UK anyway by international standards even at high levels of unemployment, the full employment objective need by no means entail intensified over-manning. For clearly it would have to be associated with a steady growth in public and private investment in both new plant and services reflecting both technical change and the develop-ment of social and economic needs.

Thirdly, the *laissez-faire* market economy prescription may succeed for countries in the 'virtuous' phase of domestic capitalist expansion (for example, Japan and West Germany in the 1950s and 1960s), but by definition their trade surplus has as its obverse other countries' deficits (for example, the EEC or USA in respect of Japan, or the UK and Italy in respect of West Germany). The latter countries may then be exposed to evolution over successive cycles through a 'vicious' phase of stagnation and decline where beyond a notional point (as in the case of the UK from the 1960s to 1970s onwards) resuscitation of the private market mechanism, far from increasing the creation of wealth, tends rather to intensify dependence on imports and weaken the economic base yet further.

But the fourth and perhaps central argument against the view that socialism involves a lower increase in living standards is that the national psychology of economic growth is as much a matter of politico-social values as of type of economic system. Thus 100% full employment can be combined with a powerful ethic of hard work and self-denying commitment (as in China), while quite a significant level of unemployment can be associated with the persistence of restrictive practices which markedly undermine efficiency.

Apocalypse or Planned Evolution?

One rather different facet to the critique of the socialist economic model outlined here should be added. This is the view, usually expressed by the left, that socialism will not be achieved by establishing in advance a series of target objectives like the seven principles enunciated here. It is an arid approach, it is said, to try to construct 'building blocks' to socialism in isolation of the vitality of real events which it is designed to meet. Rather the advent of socialism is not registered by the appearance of a precisely blueprinted series of institutions methodically planned for, but as a moment ('revolutionary', though not in the barricade sense) when political and social consciousness has reached the point where people begin to act quite differently towards their political and social institutions and towards each other. It is like a crossing of the Rubicon. When one enters uncharted territory, one does not appeal for a map.

But this is wholly to misunderstand the function of seeking to outline the key features of socialism as attempted here. It is not meant to pre-empt blueprints, but to provide a vision of what might be, in the light of which the challenge of the present order can be tackled better. It is based on the assumption that people need a vision if they are to form a judgement of what is possible as an alternative system,

161

against which they can more effectively formulate their demands in the context of actual events as they evolve. It is also an attempt to establish some measure by which the outcome of the transformation, however it is in practice fashioned by events, can be tested against aspirations. There is, of course, nothing definitive about these aspirations, and objectives have to be marked out beforehand for discussion and hopefully agreement as guidelines to assess the real movement of events. The pressure of events remains the central engine of change, but man's own value judgements equally remain, and must remain, the ultimate arbiter for the assessment of that change.

Problems of Transition

A final aspect of the critique of socialism concerns the tactical issue of transition. Even if action directed towards these ends came about in Britain, which would require a higher and more widely based level of political consciousness and a stronger and more strategic leadership than yet exists, is it possible to conceive of a British transition to an avowedly socialist society without harsh economic disruption and profound political resistance overseas? Or is it possible that the people of Britain could be sufficiently inspired by a new ideal that they would willingly bear the possibility of temporary economic dislocations and determinedly outface political antagonisms abroad? Would security of supply for Britain's unavoidable imports of food and essential raw materials not available domestically be put at risk? What sanctions might the USA, the EEC, or other foreign powers seek to interpose, and how readily could they be resisted or deflected?

These questions are all very real, though the answers to them can only be conjectural. But it is essential to examine such evidence as is available, so that consequences are foreseen as clearly as possible of the main strategic options for change. In particular, since the economic strategy advocated here does not involve any reduction of imports below current levels, indeed perhaps a small increase, there seems no obvious reason why countries abroad should have any economic grounds for retaliation. But this general question is pursued in more depth in the next chapter, as we now turn in Part Four to the detailed implications of implementing the socialist strategy outlined in Part Three.

NOTES: CHAPTER 7

1 Organised along the principles of a 'pluralist commonwealth' ('pluralist' to emphasise decentralisation and diversity, and 'commonwealth' to emphasise that wealth should co-operatively benefit all), as described by G. Alperovitz, 'Visions of a socialist alternative', in R. G. Edwards, M. Reich and T. E. Weisskopf (eds), *The Capitalist System* (Englewood Cliffs, NJ: Prentice-Hall, 1973), p. 530.
2 Compare too some large US corporations' sophisticated linear programming models for their decentralised internal management which resemble this process.
3 See O. Lange, *On the Economic Theory of Socialism* (Minneapolis, Minn.: University of Minneapolis Press, 1938); and A. Lerner, *Economics of Control* (New York: Macmillan, 1944).
4 Department of Applied Economics, University of Cambridge, *Economic Policy Review*, no. 2 (March 1976), p. 4, table 1.3.

Part Four
What Socialism Would Mean in Britain

8

Socialist Economic Strategy

The essence of any acceptable economic strategy for Britain, socialist or otherwise, must be escape from stagnation and long-term decline. It must involve expansion, at least to meet the aspirations of people for a regular real improvement in living standards, even if the degree of such expansion is constrained by over-riding social or environmental considerations (as is indicated later on pp. 183–96). To achieve this target of expansion there are broadly three models available, and only three (with variants).

Economic Models for Sustained Expansion of the British Economy

(1) THE TRADITIONAL CONSENSUS APPROACH

The first of these models is the one that dominated the economic thinking of the British Establishment for three and a half decades after the Second World War. It is the characteristic 'mixed economy' approach, emphasising investment incentives, wage restraint, constant exhortations to increase productivity, and some limited state intervention to curb excesses of the market or to fill gaps left by it. It is an approach that has constantly ricocheted from one economic fad to another – a floating pound, devaluation, indicative planning, dashes for growth, incomes guidelines or statutory

167

wage controls, NEDC forums, and the rest – but overall has presided over a quarter-century, some would say a much longer period, of economic decline. At each successive trough in the trade-cycle (1955, 1958, 1963, 1968, 1972, 1976–7) the size of the balance-of-payments deficit has grown, the total of unemployed has risen, output and growth have increasingly stagnated and declined relative to other countries abroad, our share of world trade has continued to fall, and manufacturing investment has diminished relative to our main competitors and even in absolute terms since 1970.

Now, after so much failure, the British economic Establishment looks to North Sea oil as a way out. Its hope is based on the assumption that the removal of the balance-of-payments constraint on sustained expansion will end the era of British stop-go deflation/devaluation. However, North Sea oil, which probably has a lifespan of only some twenty to thirty years, will only regenerate British industry if the profits accruing from it are actually expended on massive investment in UK plant and machinery. Even if governments determinedly channel the oil wealth into cutting taxes and increasing public expenditure on industrial incentives in order to stimulate a higher rate of economic activity, the marginal propensity to import then becomes the critical consideration from the point of view of major investment revival in Britain. For if the UK marginal propensity to import rises sharply (fed by the keenness of foreign countries' export drives when still gripped by world recession), even more sharply than the steady rise during the earlier 1970s, then any investment recovery will be choked off in its infancy. Moreover, if the British authorities let the sterling exchange rate rise steadily as the oil flood reaches peak, as the new Tory government did in 1979, then a petro-currency market approach, by making imports cheaper, must again greatly discourage any large-scale UK domestic investment upturn.

It is therefore highly unlikely that *laissez-faire* market forces will of their own accord generate the switch on the scale required (up to a doubling of current levels in real terms within, say, a ten-year period) from this new source of wealth into productive investment. Of course, a certain degree of fresh investment (though not necessarily new *net* investment) is bound to be generated through normal market mechanisms. But the problem for the British authorities is that a grace period of sustained high investment for perhaps ten to fifteen years is necessary before the related accumulated problems of chronic low productivity, poor industrial relations and economic stagnation are likely to be cured. This will not be achieved by the traditional market approach.

(2) LARGE-SCALE DEVALUATION TO BOOST GROWTH

A variant on this free trade approach has been to draw attention to the acceleration of Britain's decline which must accompany the import-led recession with manufactured imports rising in 1979–80 three times as fast as exports. It is also right that this can only be made much worse by the economic policies pursued at the end of the 1970s of a high exchange rate (with the pound reaching US $2·35 in July 1979, no less than 57% higher than three years ago) and of tighter monetary and fiscal restraints when the oil price rise is already sharply deflating the international economy.

But it is wrong to suggest that 'keeping the exchange rate down to keep exports competitive',[1] even with an expanding money supply, would alone be sufficient to reverse Britain's decline. A managed devaluation is certainly needed, given the artificial boosting provided by North Sea oil, but it cannot by itself meet the scale of the problem that confronts the country.

To sustain growth in the British economy sufficient to prevent unemployment rising above its present (already far too high) level would require UK cost competitiveness to improve by about 4% per year from now on. But to achieve this by means of devaluation, the exchange rate would have to fall from its 1979 level to about US $1 to the pound by 1985 and to around a mere 65 cents by 1990. Moreover, to make such a policy work, pay settlements would have to be held down to about 10% a year, regardless of soaring price inflation. At the same time post-tax profits, as a result of the continuous devaluation pressure on wages and in favour of profits, would almost double their share of national income. Is such a policy remotely practicable?

(3) IMPORT-CONTAINED EXPANSION

The only other way now left to obtain growth in the British economy is by faster domestic reflation combined with the planned growth of imports. Growth of about 4% per year from 1980 on would bring unemployment below 1 million by 1985. To avoid the balance-of-payments constraint, this would require holding the growth of imports to about half the degree of increase they would otherwise achieve. But other countries would not lose, in fact would gain, because they would increase their exports to Britain compared with what they can hope to achieve while the government's present highly deflationary policies remain in force.

Higher growth made possible by this policy, and by this alone, would make it easier to bring down inflation, because it would enable a faster growth of real earnings to be sustained. Similarly it would enable public expenditure to increase again at an annual rate of about the average for the postwar period.

Such a policy, it is claimed by the Cambridge Economic Policy Group, offers a genuine break-out from the current regime of beggar-my-neighbour deflation and accelerated decline. The next section therefore examines in detail the impact such proposals might be expected to have on the main indices of Britain's deteriorating economic performance.

170

How a Planned Trade Economy Could Secure Higher Growth – the So-Called 'Alternative Economic Strategy'

The axiom from which this policy prescription starts is that the attempts of successive governments of both parties to counter low profitability and poor competitiveness in industry, particularly in the export sector, as well as steadily growing unemployment by an expansion of consumption (for example, by cutting taxes or increasing government expenditure) have all foundered after relatively short-lived periods of stimulated growth. The aim of promoting the profitability of domestic industry and stimulating investment led in practice simply to sucking in large quantities of imports, thus worsening the balance of payments. On the other hand, attempts at direct stimulation of investment by grants, subsidies, or tax relief have not been successful because businessmen are more concerned with the prospects of their markets than with the cost of investment. They will not invest in new plant and equipment if they consider sales prospects to be poor, more or less regardless of how much the actual cost of the investment is reduced by government grants. Thus any British government wishing to stimulate growth and reduce unemployment has faced a very serious dilemma. Only an expansion of the market has stimulated industry but the only ways the government could find to stimulate the market have resulted in a balance-of-payments crisis.

Against this background it might be said that the solution for the UK was to devalue the pound so as to try to emulate the success of Japan and Germany. However, the devaluation of 1967 was at best only a temporary success – possibly because of inappropriate economic policies in the UK and possibly because sales were not so sensitive to price as had been hoped. It is difficult to repeat a devaluation, partly for international reasons and partly because workers become

171

more aware of the fact that a devaluation reduces their real income in the short term and thus more willing to press for higher wage increases. For these reasons, and for those stated a little earlier, import controls are to be preferred as a more appropriate policy measure.

(1) PLANNING OF IMPORTS AS A PRE-CONDITION OF INVESTMENT EXPANSION

At first sight it might appear that controls on imports would do little to help the industry of a country which relies so heavily on exports and has suffered from a lack of competitiveness in export markets which has resulted in a sharp decline in its share of world trade. This is not to deny that ultimately the only hope for British industry is to become competitive with foreign industry on equal terms. However, it is argued that the key to becoming competitive is to have a period of high profits and investment which would result in industry having the modern efficient equipment of its competitors. Eventually industry would therefore be able to do without import controls.

Equally it may be said that this ignores the wider international implications of protectionist policies. However, contrary to the received wisdom, it would be more logical to argue that widespread import controls would be beneficial to the international economy as a whole. For if countries are only forced to adopt deflationary policies because of deficits in the balance of payments if they try to achieve full employment, then any reform of the international economy which would eliminate the chronic balance-of-payments deficits would allow those countries to expand their economies and reduce unemployment. The purpose of import controls is not to reduce the absolute level of imports but to allow an economy to operate at a higher level of activity (that is, with lower unemployment) for a given quantity of imports. Therefore those countries which export to the UK would not lose by the UK adopting import controls since the volume of UK imports would not fall. All that would happen is that the UK would benefit.

This benefit to the UK is absolutely crucial. Even as late as 1970 its exports of all manufactures were nearly 50% greater than its imports of manufactures, yet by as soon as 1974 the excess of exports over imports had shrunk to only 15%. To put it another way, the trend growth during the decade to 1975 in the volume of imports relative to exports meant that the net balance of exports less the 'full employment' volume of imports declined from a surplus of nearly £1 billion (1975 prices) in 1965 to zero in 1970 and then to a deficit of £2·5 billion in 1975.

Given on these grounds an over-riding need for at least temporary industrial protection, how wide-ranging should such a policy be? At present quota or 'voluntary' restraints are largely confined to a few industries (textiles, footwear, cars, TV sets, ballbearings) and to certain trade blocs only (developing countries, Eastern Europe and Japan). This means in effect very limited selectivity in both product and geographical terms. Moreover, it is not so much in the case of sensitive industrial sectors (cars, TV sets and tubes, radios, electronic components, domestic appliances, textiles and clothing, footwear, paper and board) nor in the case of countries already restricted (where the UK is largely hitting the weaker, underdeveloped economies) that the real damage to the UK is done. For it is in the key manufacturing sectors of our economy that imports have over recent years achieved their biggest inroads. Thus the import penetration levels have risen during 1970–5 in the case, for example, of electrical engineering from 17 to 27%, in instrument engineering from 30 to 54%, in mechanical engineering from 17 to 25%, in motor vehicles from 11 to 36% (by mid-1977 the latter figure had passed 50%) and in steel from 9 to 21%. An extension of selective import controls on the existing pattern will not, therefore, achieve the strategic objectives posed

173

here nor offer much more than political cosmeticising.

If then there is no alternative to a more generalised form of import restraint, a number of tactical options are available. One is the fixing of import penetration ceilings for each of the key sectors of manufacturing industry, as the TUC recommended in its *Economic Review* for 1976.[2] In that year it was estimated the plan might save £1·35 billion a year on the balance of payments and create at least a quarter of a million more jobs. Another option is an import standstill scheme. Thus it has been estimated, again at 1976 prices, that if imports, particularly of consumer goods and semi-finished manufactures, had been held at their 1975–6 levels wherever domestic substitution was possible, this should have improved the balance of payments by 1980 by some £1·5–2 billion, reduced unemployment by up to a quarter of a million, and increased manufacturing output overall by some 3–4%. It would, however, also have tended to maximise international opposition through adherence to a zero increase where possible, and it might therefore have increased the likelihood of retaliation.

A third possibility, therefore, is a policy of restricting imports to match foreign exchange available from export earnings and other sources (for instance, income from abroad and capital flows). This would be much more flexible. It would also accord closely with TUC proposals for an absolute growth of imports in line with the growth of GDP. On this basis, given the incentive for import substitution, the target for growth of domestic demand would have to be set in relation to the feasible expansion of domestic supply. On the other hand, where damaging bottlenecks in supply did occur, it would be possible, because of the large UK surplus of export earnings over minimum import requirements, to release foreign exchange to import particular goods to fill the gap.

(2) THE FRAMEWORK FOR SECURING FASTER INTERNAL GROWTH

Providing the means through import restraints for achieving a sustainable faster reflation of the domestic economy, however, is only to lay the groundwork for the so-called 'alternative economic strategy' (that is, the alternative to the traditional economic consensus of the Establishment). How is faster growth actually to be brought about in the UK?

The main instrument for this purpose in the private sector is the 'planning agreement'. The essence of a planning agreement has been described as

> a deal negotiated between a large firm and the Government – with the appropriate trade unions deeply involved – which sets out what the firm needs to do to help the Government meet certain clearly defined objectives (e.g. to get extra investment in a key sector) and what, for its part, the Government is prepared to do to help the firm fulfil those objectives (e.g. by providing selective financial assistance).[3]

However, it is clear that the widespread implementation of planning agreements will only come about if they are made compulsory or at least an offer is made by the government which the companies cannot refuse, for example, no price increases to be awarded under a renewed price code for selected major companies till a planning agreement is made.

Planning agreements would be negotiated with each of the largest manufacturing firms, given the fact that the 100 largest manufacturing companies now account for more than half of total manufacturing output. The purpose of the system is, first, to get up-to-date information from major companies concerning past performance and advance programmes in such areas as investment, prices, product development, marketing, exports, regional development

175

and import needs. Secondly, the information should be used to help clarify planning objectives and to help government to back up its macroeconomic policies with appropriate measures at the level of the large firms. Thirdly, the aim is to get agreement with these firms that they will help to meet the planning objectives, for example, an increase in output and investment consistent with a 4% overall growth rate for the economy. And fourthly, it should provide a means of channelling selective government assistance directly to the major firms which need it, and to do this as part of the planning agreements system.

At present the government has no clear indication of what the major firms in the economy are intending. The companies too do not know how the government sees its plans for the future. Planning agreements were designed to bring about a closer working relationship between government and the private sector, and wherever possible such agreements should be administered with maximum flexibility. But in order to ensure firms keep to the agreement once entered into, the relevant ministry would have the power, as well as that of giving or withholding grants of aid to these companies, to give or refuse permission to a company for price increases, either on particular products, or as a ceiling across the board. Only as a last resort would the government be empowered to put public trustees on the board.

(3) THE ROLE OF THE PUBLIC SECTOR – THE NATIONAL ENTERPRISE BOARD

Having thus secured some guarantee of the implementation of a growth strategy at the big-company microeconomic level, the government would still have to confront several important issues in pushing home such a strategy. For example, how could a lead be given in investment, pricing policies and regional expansion to influence other major manufacturing companies through a competitive stimulus?

How could unwanted foreign takeovers be staved off, when already no less than 20% of UK manufacturing assets are in foreign hands? How could countervailing bargaining power be restored to government in relation to multinational corporations, especially over the siting of new investments? How could monopoly be reduced where the entry of new firms in the private sector might require an excessive initial capital outlay? How could national employment objectives be underwritten in the face of the massive labour rundown of the new computer-controlled capital-intensive industries? How could a strong external management back-up be provided where an ailing firm jeopardised an important sector of the economy?

Such questions point strongly to the need for a major new role for public enterprise in manufacturing. Hitherto the mixed economy has been unbalanced by the restriction of the public sector to basic utilities and often declining industries dependent for their growth on private manufacturing demand and further hamstrung by discriminatory pricing policies imposed against them. Now, when these questions demand a more positive instrument of intervention to supplement the planning agreements in order to create a more dynamic economy as well as a socially more accountable one, that new role is the purpose of the National Enterprise Board (NEB).

The central role of the NEB would be to counter the current power of the big-league monopolistic market leaders to determine in their own interest the direction and pace of development in the economy. For the concentration of industry has led to a position where one firm can affect the actions of the whole of its sector. The top companies set the scene for the remainder. If the government had control of one of these companies in each sector, then it would be able to set a pattern of investment, job creation, pricing policy, import substitution, and so on. Other companies in the sector would have to follow suit or live with the danger of having their markets eroded. The threat of competition could thus be used to galvanise industry, and the government's strategy secured while still leaving the tactics to individual firms.

To establish public participation in key sectors of industry, the NEB would hold all the existing government shares in joint public and private firms and in companies that were wholly government-owned. However, this in itself would not be a sufficient base for it to carry out the role envisaged, so it would be provided with a suitable base by the public acquisition of a controlling share in firms in lead sectors of the economy. The firms affected need not be the largest in their sectors, but they must be one of the leaders. There would be no intention of taking over whole industries but the companies concerned must be profitable ones, otherwise the strategy could not work if it were simply confined to taking over lame ducks.

The NEB would thus be able to challenge the multinationals in the home market. The NEB companies producing at a true cost would be able to uncover the inflated import costs brought about by transfer pricing. They would also gain the knowledge of the markets essential to the government if it is to have effective control over profit margins, pricing policy and the quality of goods produced. NEB companies could also take advantage of export incentives, and thus challenge the multinationals in their overseas markets. They would, moreover, be encouraged to produce substitute goods to avoid unnecessary imports, thus again helping the trade balance. Above all, provided the NEB had a sufficiently large base to be able to stand up to the multinationals, it could if necessary take over plant if the multinationals threatened to leave. For the NEB could acquire the UK portion of a multinational in the same way that it could acquire a domestic company.

Another of the main tasks of the firms under the control of the NEB would be to assist in regional policy and help to create jobs. A sufficiently large number of firms within its ambit would enable the government to change the present inequalities by investing in the hard-hit regions on the scale required.

(4) WORKER INVOLVEMENT – THE DYNAMICS OF WIDER INDUSTRIAL DEMOCRACY

Not only do planning agreements and the NEB offer a direct means to promote desperately needed investment in manufacturing where private enterprise has so badly failed; they also offer new challenges for democracy. For otherwise these initiatives become largely paper-pushing exercises between big business and Whitehall, two arms of the same ruling elite. Also, to the extent that planning agreements with leading companies in the private sector are backed up by a parallel expansion of public sector investment, the same stricture about close worker and union involvement applies. Otherwise public ownership simply means a transfer from private capitalists to, in effect, state officials working hand-in-hand with a new set of managers drawn from the same capitalist class, with minimal parliamentary and wider public accountability and with very little change in industrial relations.

The relevance of planning agreements for the workforce is that it extends joint decision-making into areas traditionally beyond the scope of collective bargaining. Alongside the need for management to secure agreement with its workforce before being in a position to enter into a planning agreement with the government, there must be a systematic and comprehensive development of information-sharing within the firm. Key information about the firm's activities, hitherto reserved for management, would have to be made available to workers too. Such information would certainly include disclosure regarding investment, the company's capital expenditure, fixed capital assets, any disposal or acquisition of such assets, and the company's current

179

employment and manpower planning, output, productivity and exports.

But conversely, where management had agreed on corporate targets with its workforce representatives under this system, planning agreements would then also represent a means whereby the co-operation of the shopfloor could be harnessed in support of positive goals, and not simply used negatively (as so often at present) where unacceptable management decisions have been taken unilaterally. Since planning agreements can only work effectively if they have won trade union and worker co-operation, they represent both a highly significant extension of the industrial franchise and also perhaps the best means of breaking out of the institutionalised trench warfare that has sapped the strength of British industry for decades.

(5) OBJECTIONS RAISED AGAINST THE 'ALTERNATIVE ECONOMIC STRATEGY'

Several objections have been made by opponents of such a strategy. The commonest concerns the likelihood of retaliation by other countries because of the import restraints imposed. However, the use of import controls with fiscal expansion to raise the level of activity need not be a 'beggar-my-neighbour' policy. The total volume of other countries' trade will not be diminished provided that there is no retaliation, that the country introducing import controls does not use them to secure a larger trade surplus or smaller deficit than it would otherwise have done, and that the composition of its imports does not shift in favour of 'surplus' countries. Indeed if the composition of its imports is shifted against 'surplus' countries and the latter do not retaliate, the total volume of world trade will rise, enabling the rest of the world to expand production. 'Surplus' countries will regain elsewhere trade which they have lost in the country which discriminates against them and therefore will have no valid reason for retaliation.

Secondly, it is objected that import control restricts consumer choice. But consumers are bound to gain overall from fiscal expansion with import controls, whatever the size of the enforced reduction in the proportion of imports in total consumption, because there would be a large absolute addition to the quantity of consumption of domestic goods and services and only a minor reduction in the absolute volume of consumption of imported manufactures and services (as compared with what would otherwise happen). It seems inconceivable that the net gain to consumers in aggregate would not be positive. Nor is there any necessity for the emergence of black markets on a significant scale since imports could be restricted by tariffs or auctioning of quotas, and profits attributable to scarcity would accrue to the government.

Thirdly, it is objected that import control would 'featherbed' inefficiency. The relevant aspects of the environment in which domestic firms operate include the general level of domestic activity as well as the severity of overseas competition (measured in terms of relative prices and costs) in home and overseas markets. The level of activity is raised by import control (or devaluation) relative to what would occur with deflation and all historical evidence, whether cross-section or time-series, suggests that a higher level of activity has a beneficial net effect on productivity and innovation.

Fourthly, it is said that such a strategy would be incompatible with Britain's adherence since 1973 to the Treaty of Rome. But international agreements are made for the benefit of all their signatories. If they are harmful to some and neutral to others, they can and should be amended. For example, the EEC already radically altered its own rules on one of the fundamental ideas of the Community – that there should be free trade in food between member states – as soon as it became clear that this was to the advantage of none of them. If the same holds for EEC rules on industrial trade, these also should be changed.

A fifth objection asserts that the imposition of import controls would result in increased domestic inflation. However, it can be argued – and there is statistical evidence to support this view – that domestic prices are not influenced by the prices of competing imports, but that they are set by adding a constant mark-up to costs. Thus any policy which increases industrial costs will cause inflation, but a policy which does not increase costs will not cause inflation. This argument is relevant to the preference for import controls over devaluation. Since the import controls can be imposed on items which are not part of industrial input, they will not increase costs. Devaluation, on the other hand, will normally increase the prices of all imported goods, whether raw materials, semi-finished manufactures, or consumer goods, and this will therefore be inflationary.

A sixth objection is based on the assumption that such a strategy would lead, not to an overall growth in output, but simply to a considerable amount of switching of sales from exports to the home market in the short term. However, it can be argued that the short term is completely unimportant compared to the long term. Although British firms would not necessarily initially have the capacity to expand output immediately, they would have the confidence to invest in new plant and equipment because of the protected home market. Even in the long term, though, the critics[4] would argue that the effect will be an expansion of import-competing industries at the expense of export industries. The import-competing industries will become more profitable and therefore be able to offer higher wages and rewards to capital. But this argument depends for its validity upon the assumption that output as a whole cannot be much increased. Otherwise it is clearly possible for both export industries and import-competing industries to grow at the same time. And it would be the role of the planning agreements system precisely to bring this about.

The Socialist Economic Implications of a Planned Use of Resources

So far the case, essentially that of the Cambridge school,[5] has been put for a policy which could offer Britain the sure prospect of faster economic growth which would be sustainable. How would such a policy relate to the socialist principles outlined in Chapter 5?

In the last analysis socialism in Britain means using resources in a planned way to serve the needs of the people. For this to be possible Britain must become more self-reliant, and must make better use of its own not inconsiderable resources. The need is outstanding for more home production of food, to reduce the need to import half Britain's food, and the more it can dispense with imports of things it is well able to make for itself, the less the need to make exports to pay for such imports. In this way foreign trade which, taking imports and exports together, accounts at present for about half of Britain's national income, could be reduced to a smaller proportion. There would be more scope for planning production to meet the needs of the British people without risk to this planning from foreign uncertainties and ups and downs which are outside British control.

Two-way exchanges of very similar manufactured goods (Britain sending cars to foreigners and receiving comparable cars back) may be profitable to the powerful interests which prosper by doing this, but are they not largely meaningless to the British people in terms of real economic values? In foreign trade Britain's emphasis should be on exchanges with countries able to supply items and materials which cannot be produced at home, in return for British manufactures which these countries require. Britain should strive to build up two-way trade exchanges, particularly with the Third World countries where the majority of mankind lives. These countries today are poor and their trading capacity is limited, but their people will not permanently accept their

183

poverty. Complementary trade with them would be the most durable kind of foreign trade for a country like Britain.

By contrast, in reality Britain has had for two centuries, and still in essence retains, an imperialist-structural economy. For about seventy years up to the Second World War imports of goods were on average 30% higher than exports (with the gap reaching a peak of 49% in the 1930s). Income from foreign investments and from services covered the difference. A large proportion of British exports were moreover 'tied' (capital equipment for British-financed overseas investment) or were fostered by British imperialist control of overseas economies. The whole position and outlook derived from Britain's past has made for investment outflows together with supporting government foreign expenditures, to the detriment of the development of the domestic economy. As this putting of the City's interests first steadily weakened the domestic industrial base in relation to that of other countries, this itself further stimulated British investment abroad, with the attraction of higher profits than those expected at home. It increased the importance attached to the City's earnings from financial and other services and intensified the efforts to restrain British living standards in order to increase the resources available for overseas use. But these efforts to keep the home market in check only reinforced the propensity to limit investment. Hence there is a self-feeding process of British decline.

If, then, the central economic choice, as explained above, is really seriously to avoid succumbing to further decline, an entirely different outlook is required, one that cannot be built on present foundations. If Britain is to change its current imperialist-structured economy and build a sustainable industrial economy, then the necessary key economic changes must include increasing self-sufficiency, particularly in food supply and by finding alternatives for finite resources; cutting down the import of goods which could perfectly well be produced at home, thus reducing the need to fight for exports; linking the planning of production with planned requirements both in domestic consumption and in foreign trade, via stable agreements with countries abroad which produce goods Britain must import and which need the kind of goods Britain can supply; and reducing overseas investment and controlling the City's financial operations. Each of these is now examined in detail.

(1) INCREASING SELF-RELIANCE

At present, just under half of UK imports are food and raw materials. The goal would not be complete self-sufficiency, but a substantial reduction of dependence in the most crucial areas, especially in finished and semi-finished manufactures, but also in other sectors where feasible.

(a) Reducing external dependence

Quite apart from the role of the 'alternative economic strategy' in containing the import of manufactures, ways need to be thoroughly examined of easing export pressures by lessening Britain's dependence on external sources for current major import requirements. Two of the chief areas for investigation are food and raw materials. The UK can at present provide enough food for only 30 million people. The total land area is 21 million hectares (52 million acres), 9 million hectares (22 million acres) of which permit arable farming; 2 million are urban, the rest are suitable (at best) for grazing. The country is practically self-sufficient in eggs, milk, poultry, potatoes and most meat, but only half the wheat flour, one-third of the sugar and one-sixth of the fats are home-produced. In addition most of the feeding stuffs for the animals and poultry have to be imported and 80% of the fertilisers. In 1974/5 52·6% of total food supplies and 65·1% of indigenous food were home-produced.[6]

On the demand side steps towards greater self-sufficiency in food could include taxes on certain foods where the

185

nutritional value is low and import cost high, plus a large-scale study of the influence of different factors on diet and patterns of food consumption, where little is known at present. Equally, on the supply side, policy measures would include a halt to the reclassification of agricultural land for other uses, conserving as large a land area for farming as possible,[7] together with grants to halve barley acreage in favour of wheat, aiming at complete self-sufficiency in wheat production.

A further top priority is to reduce energy demand which has been increasing in the UK during the past thirty years at a rate of 1·87% per annum, a doubling-time of thirty-seven years.[8] By projecting this trend forward a big energy gap looms in the 1990s – just when oil production from the North Sea may be starting to decline. The present solution of the energy industry is nuclear power. But Britain's self-sufficiency in coal (reserves will last 300 years at present rates of consumption), oil and natural gas could be used to avoid the hazards and costs of a major nuclear programme (forty 20,000 megawatt reactors would be needed by the year 2000 at a cost of £3 billions),[9] provided that a major programme is launched now to conserve energy and reduce demand, and also that part of the oil fund is used to search for viable alternatives.

A comprehensive policy for all finite resources is required. Successful energy conservation, if it releases income to be spent on other energy-intensive products, may mean that there is no overall check to the growth of demand. What is needed, therefore, for such a comprehensive policy is an Energy Conservation Commission. The political problem is at the heart of the ecological dilemma, because although the ecological constraints on human behaviour will in the end prove far more inflexible than the economic and political constraints, in the short run the latter rule and rational persuasion will not melt them. Like St Augustine, the Western nations would like to be made chaste, but not yet.

No programme of political ecology will succeed unless the workings of present political systems, the manner in which conflicts are resolved and consensus achieved, are taken into account.

The Energy Conservation Commission would have the power, for example, co-operating with the Treasury, to impose taxes related to the use of certain finite resources and to place restrictions on certain activities and commodities, even in opposition to the fiat of other government departments. In particular, the tax system should be reformed to allow the present VAT (value added tax) to be replaced by RAT (resource added tax), through which the full finite resource and environmental costs of all goods and services would be reflected in their prices. It would apply to imported and home-produced manufactured goods equally. Since it would encourage a move away from energy-intensive towards labour-intensive production techniques, exemption might have to be given to industries whose exports were still essential to pay for necessary imports (otherwise they could not compete internationally). These exemptions would be phased out when the containment strategy began to show results and when RAT agreements were concluded with other nations. RAT would be introduced in progressive stages. In the meantime special subsidies could be given from the oil fund for products that conserve resources. [10]

On the supply side, the single most beneficial use of an oil fund would be to invest it in the search for sustainable energy sources and alternative technologies that would prevent Britain's ever again becoming so dependent on imports of energy and raw materials. In the late 1970s the government spent £60 million per year on nuclear research, less than £1 million on research into solar and wave power. [11] Support on a large scale should be given by the Commission to alternative energy research and the development of an industry around it. Examples of projects that could be included involve tidal power, wave power, solar power, R and D on recycling raw materials, and improved technologies for extracting and using finite resources (for example, improving on the present 30% recovery rate of oil deposits and coal liquefaction).

(*b*) *Reducing internal dependence*

At present the cultural, political and economic systems of industrial societies all sustain growth and steadily increase the dependence of individuals on a growth-oriented economy. The Energy Conservation Commission's work would therefore be judged not only by how far it succeeded in making Britain self-sufficient, but also by how well it encouraged the development of institutions and individual aspirations that would sustain an industrial society that was not dependent on maximising the growth of material consumption.

Some broad goals can be identified. For the cultural system the central values would include living within material limits, personal independence and non-material growth. For the political system the objective would be to seek the creation of institutions that promoted a stable economy, conservation of the environment and devolution of much centralised decision-making to local communities. One must then ask how far the containment strategy is in harmony with these long-term goals of transformation and how quickly support for the Commission might build up.

In this task the Commission would have four main weapons. First, it would require publicity – drawing attention to the targets of the containment strategy. Secondly, its fiscal and administrative measures would help alter attitudes and patterns of consumption. Thirdly, it would promote policies that allowed more individuals to escape the trap of dependence on centralised agencies and to choose a more sustainable future for themselves and their families, such as the grants from the oil fund for local energy supplies and small-scale alternative technologies. Fourthly, it would build on existing cultural preferences for leisure, quality of life,[12] more satisfying and meaningful work and self-help activities, by sponsoring creative leisure – sports, arts, education – where the resource cost was low and where future growth in human societies will be focused.

(2) PLANNING DOMESTIC PRODUCTION AND FOREIGN TRADE

Increasing self-reliance is only part of what is required to break the millstone of external and internal dependence (as described in Chapter 1) which is remorselessly dragging Britain down and to establish an alternative way of running Britain's economic affairs which is not foredoomed to decline. What would be the basic principles, under this alternative approach, for organising both the domestic economy and foreign trade? The best long-term trade partners are countries which can enter into a complementary relationship, supplying Britain with things it cannot produce and taking from it things they need which Britain can supply. On this basis, bearing in mind long-term historical trends, the Third World countries, with their possibilities of acting as complementary trade partners, should merit major attention. They should be seen, not one-sidedly, either as suppliers of materials or as market outlets, but as capable of acting as partners in assured two-way trade exchanges. Both Britain and these countries would benefit from a reliable relationship which reduced ups and downs in the volume and price of their supplies, with reciprocal benefit to Britain in their demand for the goods it supplied in return.

It will, of course, be argued against this approach that modern technical factors make it uneconomic for a country of the size of Britain to enter into certain branches of production unless large foreign markets (such as the EEC) can be added to the domestic market. It is true, for example, that Britain is at a great disadvantage against the USA, with its much greater domestic market, in the production of large civil aeroplanes. There are such cases. But if satisfying people's needs is seen as the purpose of production, the British economy is large enough for most requirements to be produced economically. We should be cautious about accepting technical arguments relating to specific cases as justification for general policies which arise instead from the economic laws of the present capitalist market. Britain's resources should be utilised for maximising domestic production of all the items where these technical problems do not genuinely arise.

Where, however, these problems do arise, and Britain needs the items concerned, then it either imports them (as with foodstuffs or minerals which can never be produced in the UK) or enters into collaborative ventures with selected countries abroad. In other words, this does not invalidate the general principles being enunciated here, namely, that Britain does not need participation in a large free trade zone like the EEC for its economic prosperity (indeed, on the contrary, its decline can almost certainly now be reversed only on a basis directly inconsistent with the Treaty of Rome); that foreign trade should be regulated to fit the needs of domestic industry rather than left to private business decisions which merely steadily increase the overall propensity to import; and that while some multilateral trade is bound to continue for the UK, there should be greater resort to bilateral deals to prevent the pushes and pulls of the world capitalist market from becoming the sole or even main determinant of trade operations.

Of course two-way trade exchanges have, self-evidently, to command the support of both sides through yielding mutual benefits. In conditions of depression, as now, when business is precarious and has to be fought for, there would be clear benefit to both sides in reliability of trade exchanges. Britain's need for food and materials makes it possible for it to consider a firm programme of purchasing commitments spread over appropriate sources of supply. The classic argument against doing this is that it would tie its hands and prevent its taking advantage of shifts in the market to secure the lowest possible prices. But since food and material exporters need Britain's market, would they not be interested in offering assured supplies on acceptable terms (that is, lower than current market prices) and taking in return their requirements of manufactures which Britain could supply? Two-way trade which helped these countries to develop faster and further should bring more employment, rising standards and increased domestic consumption. Not that this approach envisages 'freezing' trade with Third World countries simply in the form of exchanges of food and materials against manufactures. It accepts that the majority of mankind who live in these countries do need a 'new economic order', and time will gradually change the nature of these exchanges.

How could trade actually be organised on this basis?

The great businesses already have close links with government. Exchanges of information and of ideas on policy go on continuously with officials and politicians, as part of the process by which business influences government in its interests. These relationships should be utilised to inform firms of what would be expected from them if a given trade agreement were concluded. Where the agreement included buying and selling that in any event would be undertaken, there should be no problems. But could firms be involved in arrangements which, however useful from an overall national point of view, they might consider as either of no interest or even detrimental to themselves? Why should not tax devices, already used to encourage investment and employment in selected regions of the country, be utilised in connection with foreign trade policy, using both carrot and stick? On both current profits and investment outlays, firms could be given rewards for co-operation and penalties for non-co-operation. This is not a new fiscal principle, but applying it to foreign trade would nevertheless give rise to much business clamour. Fiscal devices hitherto have mainly been government attempts to meet the wishes of business. What is suggested here is government use of such devices, negative and positive, to make business work to the plans of government. At bottom the question of power is involved. But trade agreements are merely declarations of mutual hopes unless they embody firm commitments on quantities and, within limits, prices.

In sum, these proposals involve a fundamental new direction of policy for Britain, a turning away from the market ideas of capitalism to socialist ideas of trade as support for production for use. They are based on the concept of strengthening British self-reliance, although they do not envisage British self-sufficiency. They are not ideas for a 'siege economy' (the fashionable phrase used to deride criticism of multilateral free trading) but are ideas for ending Britain's present role as a 'surrender economy'. But there are truly enormous political obstacles to be overcome if these ideas are to be implemented: deeply rooted traditional attitudes and ideas which are widespread among the British people; the propaganda and activity of very powerful interests which want to continue on the existing basis; difficulties in negotiating suitable arrangements with overseas countries which, like Britain, are also gripped by ideas of the past, and which are subject to financial, economic, political and military pressures from the forces which now dominate the world; and, in particular, the explicit commitments made by Britain's rulers to the IMF, GATT and the EEC, and the no less important unofficial commitments which result from the close influential connections of the great firms and banks and the ruling political establishments in the major Western countries. Almost everything would seem to bar these new ideas – except for the one thing that is decisive, that they express realities and meet the needs of the British people. If the will to change to this new basis is established, it must, even if slowly and by roundabout ways, prevail. All policies are tested by events. As present policies fail, alternatives now ruled out will look different.

(3) REDUCING FOREIGN INVESTMENT AND CONTROLLING THE CITY

There can be no serious change in Britain's economy without simultaneous or preceding change affecting finance and the City. Whereas Britain today is a society where capital uses labour, if Britain changed from production for the market to production for use, labour would use capital. Money would cease to be the master of the economy and would become its servant. But what, pragmatically, would be involved in such a fundamental change?

At present, because of the City's predominant influence over the orthodox wisdom, the main lessons drawn in the 1960s and 1970s have been that it is essential to preserve financial stability. Three specific policies have been adopted, under the City's guidance, to cope with this problem. First, the balance of payments must not be in deficit; otherwise sterling falls, financial confidence evaporates, import costs rise and inflation is made worse. The main technique for preventing balance-of-payments deficits is to restrict the public sector's budget deficit. Although exact calculations are complex and arguable, the essential point is that the government must not pump too much money into the economy, because otherwise spending will rise, drawing in imports in excess of exports. The public sector borrowing rate has to be kept down, if necessary with the consequence of low employment and output. In the past governments, whether Labour or Tory, varied the budget deficit from 'stop' to 'go' as they worried alternately about the balance of payments and unemployment. But in the end, events since

1974 – particularly the sterling crisis in 1976 – forced the government to give priority to the balance of payments.

Secondly, money wage settlements must be restrained. The scope for raising wages by cutting profits is small. The scope for raising wages by increased economic growth is non-existent under orthodox policies. Wage restraint is therefore the chief mechanism for containing inflation.

Thirdly, public expenditure must be limited to keep taxes down. Again calculations are complicated: cuts in public spending often do not save much money owing to consequential loss of tax revenue, as well as costs of the dole and of propping up industries. Nevertheless, without strict limits on public spending, in a recession tax rates have to be high, bearing on families with average or below-average incomes as well as on the rich.

These three orthodox City-oriented policies of restraint are supposedly guaranteed (if they are accepted) to procure a balance-of-payments surplus, a strong pound sterling, low inflation and general financial stability. But they do not permit the government to have targets for employment, living standards, or public services. Nor are they constructive internationally. A balance-of-payments surplus means importing less than Britain exports; if the imports come largely from other surplus countries, this is a true 'beggar-my-neighbour' policy.

Under orthodox City-determined policies the trends have worsened to the point where without North Sea oil, growth of national output would have to be zero because the rate of import penetration is about equal to the growth of exports. Up to the early 1980s rising North Sea oil production lifts this constraint enough to permit modest expansion at about 3% a year. But when oil production levels off in the early 1980s, growth will again have to come to a halt. When oil production eventually declines, growth might actually have to be negative. The range of uncertainty is not very great. With a fast recovery of world trade, the UK growth rate could be about 1% higher; with accelerated import penetration it could be 0·5% lower.

The essential starting point for Labour must be repudiation of this disastrous City domination of state decision-making. It must be replaced by policies to make full use of existing production facilities so as to produce immediate increases in employment and income which will finance investment, public services and better living standards. This can only be done if the balance of payments is regulated to lift the constraint on home spending. The essential instruments for this have already been outlined earlier in this chapter.

Above all it needs to be said, in the face of all the current pervading pessimism, that the possibilities for expansion of national output are now very large because unemployment is high and productivity has been held down. If the essential reforms needed to restart growth are introduced, national income and output could expand by 4·5% a year for at least a decade, raising average income by 50% in ten years' time and reducing unemployment to a very low level. But the problems of introducing import planning and the industrial policies advocated here are formidable. They include extensive mobilisation of public opinion, a realignment of Whitehall attitudes and a major training programme for the trade unions in a new role. Yet without both these policies, little can be achieved.

Nevertheless, it would be very dangerous to underestimate the strong opposition by the USA and others (including many powerful interests within Britain) to British retreat from these commitments to uninhibited private trading and financial flows. All manner of pressures would be used – not least pressures against sterling – to make Britain toe their line. It is precisely because struggles over the introduction of import restraints will be so intense that the issue has its political importance for workers.

Finally, and most fundamentally of all, none of these

changes will occur in Britain (or indeed anywhere else) without a decisive change in the balance of class power in society in favour of workers. That is why in the last analysis Britain's economic strategy is not a matter of economic theory, of whether one model is right and another wrong, but a class question and a power question. To secure the recovery strategy is not therefore simply a problem of rational communication, but of countering the ceaseless propaganda of Establishment ideas and values that saturate social life, culture and political thinking in Britain. For this reason, at least as important as constructing an alternative economic strategy is the launching of a counter-ideology to facilitate the transfer of power that must come if Britain is to recover. This is the issue examined in the next two chapters.

NOTES: CHAPTER 8

1   J. Mills, 'Alternatives', *Guardian*, 4 July 1979.
2   TUC, *Economic Review* (London: TUC, 1976).
3   Labour Party, *Labour's Programme 1976* (London: Labour Party, 1976), p. 22.
4   W. M. Corden, *Trade Policy and Economic Welfare* (Oxford: Clarendon Press, 1974).
5   T. F. Cripps and W. A. H. Godley, 'A formal analysis of the Cambridge Economic Policy Group model', *Economica*, vol. 43 (November 1976), pp. 335–48.
6   *Annual Abstract of Statistics 1976* (London, HMSO, 1977), table 266.
7   M. Allaby, 'Can we feed ourselves?' *Ecologist*, vol. 5, no. 6 (July 1975), pp. 190–5.
8   P. Chapman, *Fuel's Paradise: Energy Options for Britain* (Harmondsworth: Penguin, 1975).
9   W. Patterson, *Nuclear Power* (Harmondsworth: Penguin, 1976).
10   Compare the detailed proposals in NEDO, *Energy Conservation in the UK* (London: HMSO, 1974).
11   I. Fells, 'North Sea oil – a limited resource', *Ecologist*, vol. 6, no. 3 (March 1976), pp. 102–3.
12   'Survey on expectations', *New Society*, 28 April 1977.

9

Socialist Democracy

While the City of London/top companies/state bureaucracy nexus may traditionally have been suited to a regime of competitive growth designed to maximise capital accumulation and material goods production, it is not at all appropriate to an economy determined more by concepts of work as a means to human fulfilment, ecological and environmental constraints, quality-of-life goals, distributional equity in rewards and democratic accountability in decision-making. What kind of power structure, then, is appropriate to these purposes?

Whose State under Socialism?

Is the implication that one dominant class, whose power is based on ownership of industrial property, is dispossessed and replaced by another class, whose strength lies in its labour power? Is socialism to be ushered in by the nationalisation of all or most major industrial plants and the removal from power of their owners (shareholders) and controllers (managers)? Clearly it will not be on the basis of the existing principles and practices of nationalisation: nationalisation plus Lord Robens clearly does not equal and has not equalled socialism. Public ownership plus top management drawn from the private sector has proved all too compatible with state capitalism; indeed, it has been one of its central props.

How otherwise, then, is power to be taken from its present excessive concentration on the dominant City/top companies/Whitehall elite and disseminated instead in a much more democratic fashion?

There are broadly three answers which have been given to this question. One is favoured by those who insist that the power of a dominant class in any society can only be broken by another class organised to overthrow it, if necessary by force through revolutionary means, so that trained political cadres need to be prepared who would represent the vanguard or spearhead of working-class political struggle. The danger of this course is that a counter-elite of this kind, even if successful, replaces one kind of autocratic domination by another, and the dissemination and accountability of power is not necessarily much advanced. On the other hand, allegations of the arbitrary abuse of power, once obtained, can be and often are greatly exaggerated (as illustrated by precedents such as Cuba, 1958, China, 1949, and even Russia in the period immediately after 1917).

The question is rather whether such a traumatic and violent overthrow of the established order – even if feasible, which seems extremely unlikely in present-day Britain – could be justified. It could only be justified if, as in South Africa, the avenues to fundamental political change, of the kind postulated here, were blocked by any other means. In Britain today it is not self-evident that they are: appearances are all to the contrary. It is not obvious that the power structure is inflexibly insulated against change, but rather that a movement to locate power on a different basis and around a different ideology to the prevailing one has never been systematically organised. However toughly established interests might be expected to resist – and that can be taken to be very toughly indeed – that is still not the major obstacle, which is rather clarity of vision about an alternative order.

A second answer to the question of where power should

198

lie under a socialist system of control has been the bureaucratic centralist counter-check on large-scale agglomerations
of private economic power. Stuart Holland in particular has
drawn attention to the 'meso-economic sector' of multinational enterprise,[1] characterised *par excellence* by the 100
largest manufacturing companies which account for no less
than half of total UK manufacturing output, and propounded a countervailing strategy via widespread public
ownership, detailed planning agreements for leverage
through a Whitehall planning unit in the Department of
Industry, and a huge new public sector National Enterprise
Board to remedy private sector gaps and weaknesses by
takeover and competition.

The fallacy of this approach – however useful any of these
instruments may in practice be in specific circumstances – is
that it assumes a theory of the state which is not in fact valid.
For it assumes that a political party, the Labour Party, on
winning a general election, wins state power, in that the
main institutions of the state, both ideologically and for
practical purposes, become subject to its control. This is far
from being the case. Civil servants in Whitehall are steeped
in the principles of capitalism, regard their main function as
the defence and consolidation of the existing (capitalist)
order and view the boardroom spokesmen of the large
multinational companies not only as their main source of
industrial information, on which they are greatly dependent,
but as their natural allies in the running of the country. To
orient them instead towards the role of public monitor and
regulator of these companies requires, given their class
affinities and close identity of philosophy with the directors
of these companies, a great deal more than the winning of an
election, as indeed the fate of *Labour's Programme 1973* in
the ensuing five years showed. The answer to the question
'whose state?' at present is that it is the civil servants' state,
and any idea that Labour could use state power 'to bring
about a fundamental and irreversible shift in the balance of

power and wealth in favour of working people' (in the opening words of *Labour Programme 1973* and *1976*) is altogether illusory.

But there is a third option to the vexed question of the location of power in a socialist society where this is characterised (as Chapter 5 insists) by decentralisation and genuine democratic accountability. This is that all the main institutions of society should be ruthlessly made subject to a real democratic structure of decision-making, in place of the present sham that passes for democracy in so many aspects of British public life, in order to shift the operative centre of gravity of power from the top, the elite of society, to the base, the mass of workers. Of course, this does require determined visionary and committed political leadership, and the arousal of political consciousness through mobilisation of mass opinion; and it requires too the waging of a fierce struggle against the traditional established wielders of power at state level. To that extent this third approach incorporates essential elements of the other two. But it differs from them in stressing ends rather than means, without in any way minimising the scale and severity of the confrontation that is necessary to achieve them, or the bitterness of the opposition.

The answer to the question 'whose state under socialism?' is not a sectarian or factional one, nor a bureaucratic centralist one, but a universalist, decentralised, wholly democratic one. The state is not controlled by, nor is power concentrated on, one particular group or class; control and power are widely disseminated, varyingly in each different context, throughout the broad mass of the population. It is an ideal that has often been expressed and frequently still informs the propaganda that acts as a facade for notoriously repressive regimes. So how can the ideal be made real? How can Michel's iron law of oligarchy be resisted, or Pareto's circulation of elites be avoided?

Socialist Accountability of Power: Industry

Because of the power structure in a state and a society based on private property and market relationships between people, nationalisation measures in Britain (and elsewhere in the West) have been transmuted into forms of businessmen's syndicalism. Hence public ownership is not enough in itself, and never will be, without a shift in the balance of class power. Nor are Bullock-type proposals for penetration of the boardroom by workpeople sufficient either, except under certain strict conditions – including that the worker representatives should be held closely accountable to their electors, that they should not be constrained by unreasonable claims about confidentiality into preserving board secrets from their constituents, and that all should be subject to the direct power of recall from below.

Ultimately the question of industrial democracy is about where economic power should lie. Just as political democracy is about redistributing power away from autocracy and oligarchies, so industrial democracy is about redistributing power away from a narrow circle of largely self-appointed and self-perpetuating directors to the whole of a company's workforce. Running British industry like the British army is no longer acceptable to workers, but neither does it make for high productivity or efficiency.

DIVERSIONS – EXCLUDING A SHIFT OF POWER

Given that the aim is securing genuine accountability of power in industry, several proposals have been made in recent years which, attractive as they seem at first sight, are essentially diversionary. The first is the idea of co-ownership under which workers hold a few shares in the companies in which they work. But this does not resolve the basic conflict of interest that exists in industry, nor does it give to worker-shareholders any real share in the power of the firm.

It could also put their savings and their pensions at risk, as well as their jobs, as happened with Rolls Royce. Secondly, there is the proposal of the worker on the board. This proposal, adopted, for example, in the British Steel Corporation worker-director scheme, does not enlarge the power of the workforce in that the worker-director is not elected by, or accountable to, the workers as a whole. He may indeed become a captive of the board and a permanent minority voice on it.

Thirdly, there is the EEC fifth directive proposal for a supervisory board of which one-third would be workers' representatives. But this actually entrenches workers in a permanent minority position and also isolates them from executive management decisions. Fourthly, emphasis has sometimes been put on works councils as the key democratic element. But elected works councils separated from the organised trade union movement can only weaken that movement without providing a representative system of comparable strength, and this too is unacceptable to the trade union movement. Fifthly, some bodies, including some members of the CBI, have drawn attention to management communication programmes. The most enlightened management is now waking up to the need for programmes of job enrichment, better company communications, extended consultation, and so on. But however successful these may be in themselves, they do not constitute any shift towards democratic control.

RECENT DEVELOPMENTS TOWARDS GENUINE
POWER-SHARING

However, apart from these limited devices which might sidetrack workers into ineffective participation giving an appearance of power without reality, a number of recent developments point to the way in which industrial democracy is coming to be seen by those who are actually seeking a fairer distribution of power for themselves as employees. One example is the 'right to information' demands. The TUC in its *Guide to Good Industrial Relations* set out a list of information requirements which it believed negotiators needed to do their job properly. This list would certainly increase the power of employees substantially, alert them to any future threats to jobs and stimulate further pressure for a transfer of power from management to labour. Secondly, workers have begun to go beyond protest about job loss and begun to think out, as in the case of Fisher-Bendix (IPD/KME), how they would actually organise and run their own enterprise if it were funded to achieve long-term viability. New initiatives can also be expected under the Industrial Common Ownership Act 1976. Thirdly, some groups of workers have undertaken detailed studies on the application of industrial democracy in their own firms. Thus the British Aircraft Corporation shop stewards at Bristol, triggered by fears about the future of their industry, published a plan for 100% workers' control under which a workers' representative council, elected through the trade union organisation, would actually employ the executive management, leaving the trade unions to negotiate with that management in the normal way. This model is, of course, based on the accepted pattern of municipal democracy.

Fourthly, the development of joint shop stewards' committees in factories and combines connecting different plants in a single firm, or a whole industry, has been growing apace and even extending internationally in response to multinational companies. In 1975 the Lucas Aerospace Combine Committee shop stewards used this structure to challenge the strategy of their company with an alternative, detailed, full-length corporate plan involving new products and techniques. Because their company was forecasting redundancies due to falling demand for the goods they traditionally produced, the workers brought forward their

203

own carefully researched prototypes in the sectors of health, safety and transport as alternative requirements for production. Now this very significant development is being emulated by workers in other companies in other areas of the economy (for example, Vickers, British Aerospace).

Then, in addition to these various separate and developing strands, the Bullock Committee of Inquiry on Industrial Democracy reported with a majority recommendation that employees should have the right to be represented on the top policy boards of the largest companies in the private sector. The committee proposed that legislation to provide for employee representation should be introduced for enterprises employing 2,000 or more people in the UK, that is, in an estimated 738 enterprises employing about 7 million people, more than a quarter of the total workforce. It would be for recognised trade unions, with bargaining rights on behalf of at least 20% of all employees in the company, to make a formal request. There would then be a secret ballot of all employees and if a majority, comprising not less than one-third of all employees eligible to vote, was for representation the process of reconstituting the board would begin. The board would be reformulated to include an equal number of employees and shareholder representatives with a smaller third group of co-opted directors who would be mutually agreed (the so-called $2x+y$ formula).

SOCIALIST REQUIREMENTS FOR ACCOUNTABILITY OF POWER IN INDUSTRY

Bullock sharply highlighted the historical fact that the struggle for industrial democracy has been beset by the twin dangers of ambiguity of programme and incorporation within corporatism. On the one hand it has been diverted, since Whitleyism introduced consultation in 1919, by the idea of participation in management as a substitute for power. On the other, workers' representatives can become absorbed at local level, as under the German *Mitbestimmung* (co-determination) system, in the routines of management and thence constitute a privileged and isolated grouping, quite alienated from their constituents. To avoid these dual diversions it is necessary to translate general objectives into actual plans and detailed programmes for particular industries. This is not to suggest that overall demands – such as for opening the books or for the right of recall of workers' representatives, and so on – are not critically important, but rather that if these slogans remain disembodied they do not carry full weight as representing real, serious possibilities.

Furthermore, specific industrial democracy demands have a vital role in the struggle to create a consciously socialist mass movement. They cut through the respect and awe with which working people have been led to view the existing institutions of capitalist management, and they reveal, however dimly and provisionally, that a socialist way of running industry is at least conceivable. For converting the experience of alienation and the feel of exploitation into a clearly formulated idea of a non-exploitive free society is a major pre-condition of any socialist transformation of the balance of power in society.

Obviously it is necessary to be severely realistic. As Coates and Topham have argued,[2]

it would be utopian in a predominantly capitalist economy, to demand laws giving full self-management powers. What is needed is to mark out those areas in which workers' councils can have unfettered democratic authority, and other areas where the appropriate demand should be for rights of supervision and access to accounts: this approach both stimulates the workers' appetite for control and awakens an understanding of the need for wider socialist reforms; at the same time it defends, by extension, trade union freedom and thus husbands the essential power upon which the drive to socialist structural reforms is based.

205

As an illustration of these principles, the 'Voice' document on the steel industry, produced by the Sheffield and Scunthorpe steelworkers, rejected the 'Clegg' thesis that the trade unions should remain a permanent opposition and insisted that 'so long as they retain their freedom of action to defend their members' interests and in the last resort to pull out from a framework of action in which the cards are stacked against them, then there might seem no reason why they should not actually begin to take part in government'.[3] The 'Voice' statement then elaborates proposals for a national board including 50% trade union nominees, the ratification of regional management appointments by workers' councils, and extended powers of ratification at local and plant level for workers' councils over the appointment of shop managers, deployment of labour, promotion, hiring and firing, safety, welfare and disciplinary matters. What is important here is less the precise detail of the proposals than the principle of a programme of control to be tested against the experience of workers, to be tempered in the face of conflict, and to be modified in the light of new requirements. What is needed urgently is the extension of such plans to all key growth points of the economy – electronics, the petrochemical industry, and so on – as well as to the other basic industries like engineering and building, and to the public industry sector, particularly transport.

Other specific preparations need to be set in hand too. One concerns training and facilities for worker-directors. Training should be partly under the control of the trade unions, but provided jointly by them and public sector education. Training should involve release for courses comparable with those for senior management. Public sector colleges should be set up, or at least special courses at adult colleges, to produce a cadre of public sector managers as business schools produce cadres of private sector bosses. Also, extra courses should be provided by the trade unions, perhaps in co-operation with management colleges or courses. Furthermore, individual unions could establish a list of cadres of acceptable candidates for worker-directorships. Management training will not, of course, by some strange alchemy turn worker-directors into bosses' men. Rather it will enable them to understand the terms in which the bosses take decisions and this is a first requirement for any attempt to influence and change decisions at the very heart of industrial decision-making.

Another relevant area that needs to be developed on a large scale is the systematic provision of information about key matters for decision in firms. Thus under part IV of the Industry Act 1975 the Secretary of State for Industry could designate any significant manufacturing company and require it to supply information on any of the topics there listed – persons employed in the undertaking (including subsidiaries), capital expenditure, fixed capital assets, intended disposal or acquisition of assets, output and productivity, product sales, exports and sales of industrial property. Similarly, under section 17 of the Employment Act 1975 the employer is required to disclose to representatives of independent trade unions on request all such relevant information as he possesses and that of any associated employer provided it is necessary for collective bargaining purposes and without it the union representatives would be materially impeded, and provided that it is in accordance with good industrial relations practice to disclose the information. Such information disclosure, which has hitherto been almost wholly neglected, would probably contribute more in the long run to the goals of industrial democracy than changes in the constitutional structure of the boardroom.

Socialist Accountability of Power: Finance

A second main focus of power lies in control of the leading finance institutions. In capitalist Britain the power of the

City is based on three main tenets. Exchange control policy permits freedom of movement for capital and preserves the relatively unfettered openness of the London financial markets. Exchange rate policy determines the level of the currency according to supply and demand for sterling, rather than on the basis of internal full employment desiderata or similar social objectives. And monetary policy determines the level of activity throughout the economy, and again has been used primarily for anti-inflation and wage restraint purposes, despite the deflationary consequences, rather than for maximising job opportunities or related aims. In a socialist economy these priorities would be reversed in order to ensure that capital served the interests of the mass of the working population rather than the reverse.

THE NEED FOR A NEW ORGANISATIONAL STRUCTURE

General accountability of financial power in Britain must involve much closer public supervision of financial institutions than exists at present. The need for this was most dramatically illustrated in late 1974 when some £1,200 million was recycled by the Bank of England and big banks 'lifeboat' scheme to prop up twenty-six collapsing secondary banks (including, notoriously, London and County Securities, Slater Walker Securities, First National Finance Corporation, Keyser Ullmann, Edward Bates, and many others). Altogether, probably not less than £2,000 million was deployed during the crisis from late 1973 to bolster the liquidity of secondary banks and property companies which the banking system had so heavily, and so imprudently, financed. As a minimum requirement of real financial accountability, such statutory underpinning is needed to an improved system of surveillance as would prevent any recurrence of the 1973–5 crisis.

Without necessarily following the form or the detailed

procedures of the US Securities Exchange Commission, much greater reliance should be placed on statutory regulation of the securities industry than the powers vested in the Council for the Securities Industry currently permit, though in a manner suited to the British context. Further, on the model of tripartite planning agreements in the manufacturing field, a tripartite Bank of England policy board is required, with wide-ranging powers of banking supervision, to ensure that workers' interests as well as the government's interest are effectively represented in City affairs and to ensure that strategic financial decisions are made according to national priorities, not those of private profiteering. A committee of the board should be responsible for bank licensing, and a more representative deposit protection board is also required.

Arrangements are also needed to ensure that the rapidly growing building societies become more publicly accountable in terms both of their lending policies and of their structure and organisation. And to help the institutions participate in investment in industry without compromising their duty to depositors, a new lending facility needs to be created, jointly funded by the assurance companies and pension funds and the government, under the control of a tripartite steering committee, which would be able to replace existing institutional shareholdings with its own money. An institution could then withdraw from a company, if it needed to protect the interests of savers and depositors, without threatening the interests of the company.

A SOCIALIST ROLE FOR THE NEW SUPERVISORY BODIES

Devising a different organisational structure is one thing: but clarifying alternative objectives and roles is quite another, and the real key to securing accountability of financial power. How, then, would the new supervisory bodies achieve the central socialist objective of full employment? It requires changes both in policy and in working practice: externally, in exchange rate policy and regulation of overseas investment, and internally, in the channelling of domestic funds into industrial investment.

Exchange rate policy and full employment

What would be involved in systematically operating exchange rate policy in the interests of full employment and growth? Experience has shown that throughout the postwar era sterling has not depreciated to anywhere near a sufficient extent to create an efficient manufacturing sector in terms of providing sufficient exports to pay for the nation's imports at full employment. Indeed, the case that the pound has been overvalued for a century has been clearly established.[4] On the other hand, it may be argued that within present constraints an exchange rate policy aimed at full employment is not politically practicable. Foreign exchange markets, to put it simply, reflect relative money supply growth, relative inflation rates and the state of the balance of payments. If the government tries to bring down the exchange rate, as it tried to do in November 1977, below this 'market' rate which is inflated by North Sea oil, there are immense pressures to revalue again: such a massive inflow of reserves occurs as foreign exchange dealers buy sterling, expecting it to rise again, that the money supply soars and threatens the monetary targets.

However, it is possible for an exchange rate policy geared to a full employment parity to be made compatible with international monetary flows, without the drastic expedient of closing foreign exchange markets or suspending dealings, through the device of negative interest rates. One illustration of such a strategy of priority for full employment has been provided by Jeremy Bray, using the Treasury model of the British economy.[5] Reworking this model, but feeding in full employment as the central required objective, he produced a set of policy guidelines which would fundamentally alter the direction of economic policy. Starting from the conditions of 1978 and aiming to reduce unemployment by a million (to 400,000) in four years, the reworked model pointed to a managed devaluation of 10%, a simultaneous cut of £1 billion in income tax, and increases phased over four years of £5 billion in public authorities' current expenditure, plus a temporary increase in corporation tax while profits rose rapidly after devaluation.

Channelling funds into industrial investment

Complementing a very different role for exchange rate policy is the question of the internal flow of funds. At present the position of the banks and other financial institutions as intermediaries – channelling funds from savers and depositors to borrowers and investors – has put into their hands a vast concentration of private power, and there are good grounds for charging the City under the present capitalist order with abusing this power to seek its own enrichment at the expense of the national interest. First, in their search for maximising profit, the controllers of financial capital have been ready to resort to indefensible priorities. The notorious property boom of 1972–3 was fuelled not only by insurance and pension funds, but most notably by a massive increase in bank lending. In the year following the August 1972 explicit request from the Governor of the Bank of England for banks to restrain their lending to property companies, their lending to manufacturing industry rose by 19%, while their loans to property companies soared by 75%. The real total of property borrowings from the banks may have reached more than £5,000 million at the peak (twice the level of investment in manufacturing industry), with the sharpest increase in lending coming from the secondary or so-called 'fringe' banks.

Secondly, the role of the Stock Exchange must be called in question, both in its primary function as a source of new risk

211

capital and in its secondary function as a market in existing securities. In recent years it has degenerated to barely even a marginal source of new funds. Indeed, the City has still to answer the charge that an over-active secondary market is actually holding industry back, by forcing companies to justify their share price every single day in conditions of increasingly extreme cycles in average share prices, thereby compelling industrialists to restrict their horizons to projects with relatively short pay-off terms.

It is against this background that the objective must be asserted that if a full-scale and sustained recovery in UK manufacturing is to be achieved maybe a target of doubling manufacturing investment (from £4 billion to £8 billion per year) is not out of scale. How can this social control over funding flows be achieved? Perhaps the most important mechanism needed is an investment reserve fund, into which large companies would be expected to plough a proportion of their funds. Releases from this fund would be supervised by a reformed Bank of England and conditional upon being devoted to productive investment. Based on the Swedish model, this would embrace the category of the largest companies with sizeable 'blocked balances' at the Bank of England, earning no interest at all and available only for investment agreed through the planning agreements system. By earmarking a proportion of firms' pre-tax profits in this way, and by reducing the 'opportunity cost' of investment (such as the high interest rates which the 'blocked' funds could otherwise attract in the money market), the attraction of investment projects at the margin could be enhanced sufficiently for them to be given the go-ahead. Favourable treatment could perhaps be given to participating companies in access to external funds, possibly in the form of subsidised interest rates.

A further mechanism for securing social control over internal funding flows, which would be a hallmark of a socialist economy, lies in the channelling of insurance companies' and private pension funds' portfolio investment into priority industrial sectors. There are indeed plenty of overseas precedents for this. In France insurance companies are subject to a list of permitted investments (cash, mortgages, public debt, quoted securities and urban property), and fixed-interest securities must amount to half of assets, while property must not account for more than 40%. Investment trusts are required to put 90% of their capital in quoted securities, with not more than a 5% holding in any one company, and 30% of investments in bonds or liquid assets. In Germany the insurance sector is closely controlled, and companies are not allowed to invest more than 20% of their funds in equities. In the Netherlands the share of total funds going to the public sector remains very high in the case of institutions subject to the Investment Act. In Sweden at least two-thirds of the increase in assets of insurance companies and the National Insurance Pension Fund must be invested in so-called priority assets, that is, cash, net claims on domestic banks, government securities, and long-term and short-term loans and bonds financing residential construction. Even in the USA there have been severe investment restrictions on lending for property and limits on the overall proportion of a bank's assets which are permitted in property.

By comparison, UK controls are at present largely concerned with liquidity safety margins and money supply constraints. A determination to assert social priorities over short-term private profit-making considerations would require a framework for disposing of institutional funds in accordance with certain agreed socioeconomic criteria. For illustration, it might be decided that a high proportion, perhaps up to three-quarters, of these funds should be channelled into a list of specified priority assets which should include, apart from government securities, a selected group of key industrial sectors for equity investment. Conversely, property, land and associated investment should not repre-

213

sent more than 5% of their total portfolios. Such an arrangement would offer several important economic and industrial gains. In the face of the long-term decline in net real profits, it would provide an alternative secure source of company funds when no government can adequately promote corporate profitability by such regular fixed measures as stock relief, even on the scale laid down in 1974–5. Also, the use of institutional funds as an alternative to undistributed profits as a main source of industrial and commercial financing is likely to be far more compatible with any economic policy concept of the social contract and with trade union power to reduce corporate investible surpluses.

Regulating overseas investment and inward investment in the national interest

Complementary to channelling a desired target level of domestic funds into priorities for industrial and especially manufacturing investment is the need to ensure that access to overseas investment does not undermine the recovery and strengthening of the home industrial base. UK private direct investment overseas amounted to (at current prices) £2·1 billion in 1976, £1·9 billion in 1977 and about £1·8 billion in 1978, which compared with gross domestic fixed capital formation in manufacturing over this same period of (again at current prices) £3·9 billion, £4·9 billion and about £5·4 billion respectively.[6] Thus overseas direct investment was equal to no less than a third to a half of domestic manufacturing investment. Furthermore, the growth of British direct investment overseas during the decade to 1976 amounted to as much as 579%,[7] a growth of no less than 21% per annum in money terms – a much higher rate of growth than that of British exports, or British domestic investment, or the inflow of foreign direct investment into Britain. Thirdly, it seems significant that many more successful economies undertook foreign investment on a much smaller scale than did the UK, not only with no apparent deleterious effects but perhaps with considerable domestic gain. Thus French overseas direct investment in 1976 amounted to US $1·2 billion, Japanese to US $2·0 billion, West German to US $2·5 billion, but British to as much as US $3·4 billion.[8] Yet each of the other countries had a higher level of domestic growth and investment than the UK over the last decade.

Of course, this strong orientation of British direct investment overseas would not damage the domestic economy if it were complementary rather than substitutive. On the assumption that manufacturing investment abroad is entirely defensive (that is, in the absence of a UK subsidiary a similar foreign-owned company would have been set up), the Reddaway Report in 1967 concluded that on average the effect on UK exports had been favourable, though to the extent of only 0·8% of the production of overseas subsidiaries.[9] Yet even on this very questionable assumption of complementarity, official Treasury analysis concedes that up to 35% of UK overseas investment (equivalent to 16% of gross domestic fixed capital formation) might lead to operations which displace UK exports, or up to 45% for investment within the EEC. But what this analysis ignores is the effect of the displacement of investment from the UK, which weakens the home manufacturing base as well as losing the jobs which would have been involved in undertaking the investment itself. In general, the effect on jobs, on productive capacity at home, on exports, on the dissemination of technology and on similar areas of vital public concern is not at present taken into account from a balanced national point of view. Nor are voluntary guidelines adequate when a firm's interest may conflict sharply with the national interest.

Similarly, there is no regular or systematic monitoring of inward investment. The proportion of British industrial assets controlled from abroad reached 14·7% in 1970, including 16% in manufacturing, and has been rising since then at a rate of rather more than 0·5% per year. The

215

proportion is much higher in some industries than others, including some of the most technologically advanced and rapidly growing, amounting to 25% in chemicals, 29% in mechanical engineering and 36% in vehicles (which includes aircraft manufacture). American companies control over half the British motor industry and proportions rising to 80% of sectors of engineering and other industries. Yet at present surveillance of inward investment is limited to the Whitehall interdepartment Foreign Exchange Control Committee, which is entirely unconcerned with the all-important industrial criteria.

There is no body in Britain which compares with the Foreign Investment Review Agency set up by the Canadians in 1974 to assess 'significant benefit' to Canada in all foreign takeovers, including the likely impact on employment, exports, domestic processing of raw materials, development of local suppliers, industrial efficiency and competition, technological development, and participation by Canadians as shareholders, directors, managers and technical personnel. Similarly a US Bill in 1974 (as also, for example, in Japan and Sweden) sought to establish a Foreign Investment Review Administration (FIRA) to review continuously foreign investment even though it accounts for less than 1% of total investment in the USA.

The benefit of a British FIRA would be chiefly that the present exclusive concern over the foreign exchange implications of the transaction would be supplemented by the much more important consideration of industrial cost-benefit. In assessing the UK national interest, the FIRA would examine whether the advantages of such investment could only be obtained by a foreign bid. It would seek maximum benefit for the UK via joint ventures, licensing agreements or state shareholdings. It would seek to identify through successive reviews significant gaps or weaknesses in British competitive strength which could best be met by injections of foreign-recruited expertise and technology. And it would recommend, where necessary, divestment of a UK subsidary by its foreign owners where transfer to UK ownership (subject to fair compensation) would benefit the national interest.

Similarly, on the outward investment side, the FIRA would for the first time ensure that industrial criteria are taken into account in assessing whether overseas investment would be in the national interest. At present exchange control merely ensures that investments by UK-based multinationals in their overseas subsidiaries do not, on balance, draw on official reserves. Certain other countries, such as Sweden, seek to monitor and control outward investment on the basis, not of operating standards in the host country, but of damage to the home economy. In Britain the FIRA would vet the industrial arguments for and against locating new investment abroad within the framework of the planning agreements system.

Socialist Accountability of Power: Government

The third part of the power nexus identified in Chapter 1 is the Whitehall-Westminster machine. How would this be transformed within a socialist framework of accountability?

MAKING THE GOVERNMENT MACHINE RESPONSIVE

At present Britain has not so much a democratic government as a parliamentary bureaucracy. The problem of accountability of the civil service machine arises for several reasons, including the sheer size of government administration, the permanence of civil servants compared with the transience of individual ministers, the way civil servants filter information to ministers, the network of contacts that civil servants build up, particularly with senior management at home and with Brussels officialdom in the EEC, and so on. Moreover, many commentators with intimate experience of the ways of

217

Whitehall have noted in recent years how public officials act independently of ministers. They have asserted that each department has its own policy of which it seeks to persuade the minister (Richard Crossman), that permanent secretaries can stop a minister's policy (Sir Anthony Part), that Treasury officials worked against the Labour manifesto when the Labour Party was in government (Fred Hirsch and Peter Jenkins), that the Treasury sought to impose a statutory incomes policy by trickery (Joe Haines), that the Treasury, Defence, Foreign Office and Environment particularly had their own policies (Joe Haines), and that departments come to represent the bodies they sponsor (Joe Haines).[10] Above all, it is officialdom rather than ministers which sets the wider framework incorporating broader strategy, priorities and implicit values within which policy decisions fall.

To counter this entrenched bureaucratic traditionalism, several reforms urgently need to be implemented. A Freedom of Information Bill, which is further discussed below, is required to ensure that all information on public issues, save that covered by genuine considerations of national security, commercial confidentiality, or other proper grounds for restriction, should be made available for public discussion. The House of Commons committee system should be reformed to make both ministers and civil servants genuinely susceptible to detailed scrutiny. A minister on accepting office should have the right to confirm or not confirm a permanent secretary and other top officials in their posts, to seek their transfer later where he feels it right, and to approve or veto all appointments in his department at under-secretary level and above. A minister should also have his own political office which would include several (perhaps a dozen) specialist and political advisers, and these would act as his personal 'eyes and ears' in the department, especially by serving on official committees. Junior ministers should chair important departmental and interdepartmental committees which are at present confined to permanent officials. New selection procedures, including perhaps a selective quota system, should be introduced for recruitment to the higher civil service in order to erode the bias in favour of applicants from public schools, Oxbridge and arts backgrounds. And to reverse the discrimination in the internal career structure against those with technical/ professional backgrounds as opposed to the generalist administrator, a new unified grading structure should be implemented, bringing in more outsiders with experience in industry and elsewhere and reducing the 'mandarin' ethos.

OPENING UP THE BOOKS OF THE STATE

No socialist democracy can exist without enabling citizens to be involved in all the processes of government through full disclosure of all relevant information. People must be given sufficient information to know who is really wielding power (there is currently very extensive ignorance about this), and in whose interest they are governing. Public authorities need to disclose to the citizen not only what their policies are and how they can be assessed, but what are the intentions, motives and values behind them. Secrecy may suit weak ministers and strong bureaucracies, but it is the enemy of ministers and public servants dedicated to strong, vigorous democracy.

A Freedom of Information Act, modelled on the US and Swedish precedents, would be an essential bulwark against bureaucratic centralisation. A code of practice for disclosure of official information, to be administered by the Parliamentary Commissioner for Administration, as proposed by the organisation Justice in 1978, offers no adequate substitute. What is needed is comprehensive legislation requiring public authorities – government departments, nationalised industries, local and public authorities and very many other public bodies – to make available to the public all information not specifically exempted. Clearly the confidentiality of personal files should be protected, and public bodies in competition with both domestic and international companies must not be commercially disadvantaged. For obvious reasons, certain information relating to foreign relations, defence and criminal investigations should also be protected. But all other material dealt with by public bodies should be open to public scrutiny.

REFORMING PARLIAMENT

Systematically extending the flow of information underlying public issues is an essential prerequisite for the workings of socialist democracy, but it is not enough *per se*. It is equally important that procedures should be implemented to ensure that, given this access to information, the House of Commons as the elected chamber should be able to subject the executive (i.e. the Cabinet and the civil service) to genuine accountability to the people. Perhaps the most necessary reform is the establishment of new, powerful investigatory committees by the House of Commons which would cover the work of each government department and would hold televised sessions – rather on the model of the US congressional hearings – which both ministers and senior civil servants as well as relevant outside witnesses could be subpoenaed to attend. These committees would have full research and administrative support, including tapping the best possible advice from the universities, both sides of industry and elsewhere.

Another requirement would be to replace the present time-consuming and often ludicrously inappropriate legislative process by a new procedure which makes the legislature into a genuinely searching instrument of scrutiny. Thus when a Bill is published it should be accompanied by a document setting out the history of the proposal, the need for the Bill, the purpose of each clause and the reasons for selecting the particular means adopted to achieve that purpose, and also appendices containing relevant statistical and other background material, so that MPs and others were as well informed as the minister himself. The Bill would then go to a select committee which would call witnesses to assist its examination if it chose and would decide on its own timetable in discussing the issues and amending the legislation. A revision committee would then take a second look to see if any flaws or drafting mistakes remained, and effectively these 'second thoughts' would be performing the only useful role which the House of Lords now performs. On this basis, instead of acting as a blocking restraint on the Commons as it often does in practice, the second chamber should be abolished, with its role as a Court of Appeal continued outside the Palace of Westminster.

ACHIEVING AN ACCOUNTABLE POLITICAL LEADERSHIP

But whilst procedural reforms should not be neglected, the essence of democratising political power lies in the means of obtaining a political leadership that is systematically accountable.

Corporate irresponsibility – the uncertainty where power ultimately lies within the complex machinery of the corporate state and the suffocating hierarchies of government administration – is a central fact of life in the modern industrial nation. As the level of education and social amenities is raised, more people are equipped with those skills which provide the basis for responsibility. Yet the nature of our institutions is such that fewer people are in a position to take decisions which govern the lives of the total community. On one level the problem is that, in a class society, wealth and function are the guarantees of power and status. So long as ownership and control of the means of producing wealth is exercised by one group whilst labour is sold by another, so long as labour and capital are separate, the society is divided and class-bound. And no measures of simple redistribution and no amount of joint consultation councils can undermine this central fact. An essential concomitant, therefore, of a socialist democratisation of power is a socialist attack on the class roots of capitalist society.

NOTES: CHAPTER 9

1 S. Holland, *The Socialist Challenge* (London: Quartet, 1975), p. 28.
2 K. Coates and T. Topham, 'Participation or control?', in K. Coates (ed.), *Can the Workers Run Industry?* (London: Sphere, 1968), p. 238.
3 Proceedings of the 'Voice' Conference of Sheffield and Scunthorpe Steelworkers, 1968.
4 B. Gould, J. Mills and M. Stewart, *A Competitive Pound* (London: Fabian Society, 1978).
5 J. Bray, 'Cracking open the secrets of the Treasury's black box', *New Statesman*, 14 July 1978, p. 42.
6 Central Statistical Office, *Monthly Digest of Statistics* (London: HMSO, various dates).
7 Central Statistical Office, *Balance of Payments 1966–76* (the 'Pink Book') (London: HMSO, August 1977).
8 OECD, *Main Economic Indicators* (Paris: OECD, 1976).
9 W. B. Reddaway, *Effects of UK Direct Investment Overseas*, Occasional Paper No. 12 (Cambridge: University of Cambridge, Department of Applied Economics, 1967).
10 Labour Party, *NEC Statement on Reform of the Civil Service* (London: Labour Party, 1978).

10

A Socialist Ideology

Now these profound economic changes will not come about without *pari passu*, or perhaps prior, transformation of the ideological climate and of the pattern of power relations in Britain. For what binds Britain to the current economic orthodoxy is obviously not the clear and demonstrable success of these policies, but the fact that they reflect the interests, in both ideological and power terms, of the dominant economic elite. Nor will these policies be changed unless a clear, practicable alternative ideology is presented to the British people.

Without vision there can be no sense of purpose and direction. Without a clear ideology there can be no real political vision – no driving force for change. In this light, of all the criticisms that can be levelled against the Labour movement in its present plight, perhaps the most devastating indictment is that it is rudderless, without any distinct ideology (judging by its actions, whatever its rhetoric), and equipped with a level of political consciousness so low that it succumbs easily, almost painlessly, to the constant Establishment propaganda backlash. In this state a set of economic policies, such as that described in Chapter 5, is of little relevance if, in the absence of a determined political movement bound together by a cohesive and dynamic ideology, the will is lacking to implement them. This is the more so when the economic reforms outlined here require a decisive shift in the focus of power in Britain, away from an old and discredited regime to a new one, and the forces to effect such a shift will only mobilise sufficiently round a commitment to a distinctive ideology.

Why a Socialist Ideology Is Currently Lacking

Four quite separate elements can be distinguished in the formation of a dynamic socialist working-class consciousness. First, there is a distinct *class identity* – the definition by a worker of himself as working class, as playing a specific role together with other workers in the productive process. A second element is *class opposition*, the perception that the capitalist and his agents constitute an enduring opponent to oneself as a worker and to fellow workers. These two elements tend to strengthen one another in that opposition itself tends to reinforce identity. A third aspect is *class totality*, that is, the acceptance of the two previous elements as providing the defining characteristics of one's total social situation and of the whole society in which one lives. The final, and essential, element is the conception of an *alternative society*, a goal to which workers move through struggle with the opponent.[1] The question then is whether in mature capitalist society the capital–labour conflict is sufficient to generate all four elements of working-class consciousness.

If workers possessed full class-consciousness, they would seek worker control of industry and society. In fact, historical experience in the West has shown that industrial action has tended to be separated from political action, and that the former has itself divided into two distinct areas – the struggle for economic gains as opposed to the issue of job control (that is, workers' attempts to gain a measure of creativity and control within the work process). As between these two objectives, industrial conflict has institutionalised around an aggressive economism in conjunction with a defensive line over control. To the extent that unions pursue economic and job control goals separately and the latter defensively, and so long as they do not pursue wider issues of work control, they serve to weaken workers' class-consciousness. Facing employers also who will normally concede on economic though not on control issues, workers settle for what can be readily secured and try to reduce the salience of what is denied them. This leaves them partially alienated, though not to the point of being relegated 'outside' capitalist society, but rather compromised by it. Nor is any counterpoise provided by such radical elements as exist in workers' consciousness, since these tend to be populist in nature (for example, that the poor have always been exploited by the rich) rather than of a class or political type. With little appreciation, therefore, of alternative political structures, workers comply with the authority structure of liberal democracy because they pragmatically accept a lower position in society.[2]

It is sometimes said that workers in the advanced technologies represent a new working class who are characterised by their concern with an alternative system of industrial control, precisely what is lacking among traditional workers. They are seen as reacting against the antiquated system of control based on private property and reflecting the new industrial forces against the traditional capitalist relations of production. But the other elements of consciousness are lacking. Whilst a sense of class identity is usually well developed among traditional workers, it is relatively weak among technical and scientific workers. Any notion of their own identity among the latter has tended to be as a middle class, between workers and management, and this ambivalence has impeded any unqualified working-class self-identification. As to opposition, it is participation rather than conflict which attracts most concern, and where conflict does nevertheless arise it is sectional rather than class conflict. Nor does the 'new' working class see its social situation as defined by its productive situation, so that the element of totality is also weak, partly because workers in advanced industries are unlikely to reside in exclusively working-class communities. For these reasons the 'new' workers, while the opposite of the traditional working class which was strong on identity and opposition but weak on totality and alternatives, seem no more likely to be able to translate a mixed consciousness into a consistent programme of radical actions.

The key missing element among traditional manual workers is thus a realistic appraisal of alternative structures, even among the most class-conscious workers in the most explosive situations. Even though objectively they may be in a potential position to adopt the role as bearers of a new principle of social structure – socialism – they themselves either do not perceive this or do not know how to turn it into practical action. So often collectivism means no more than collective identity. Socialism is not a philosophy which suddenly and spontaneously explodes within the working class. It has to be learned, evolving from the continuous experience of workers in their lives at work and from the interpretation of this experience by organised groups over a considerable timespan. Moreover, both the experience itself and the actions of the organisations transmitting this experience must be consistent and mutually reinforcing; otherwise the thrust of working-class protest towards the creation of a new society is blunted or diverted. Thus the mediation of industrial experience through the revolutionary traditions of France and Italy has at key moments in this century been neutralised by the pressure towards compromise generated by existing collective organisations. Furthermore, another major obstacle against the cumulative development of class-consciousness towards socialism as a specific philosophy is that in the West those hardest hit by recession are disproportionately drawn from distinct ethnic (blacks), religious (Catholics), or cultural subgroups whose plight may not activate the working class as a whole.

What hope then for a specifically British socialist ideology to emerge? An adequate, comprehensive and satisfying ideology has to meet several criteria. It must outline a social order which meets men's ideals in a practicable manner that can be achieved. It must point the way to a system of values and culture which dignifies relationships and releases individual aspirations towards the wider ideals of society. Yet at the same time it must accord with the economic and power realities of the country and present a viable path for the nation to follow. It must also take full account of fundamental ecological constraints.

An Ideology for a Socialist Democracy

The struggle for socialism revolves round certain key ideas which express not simply different values but an entirely different way of running society. Capitalism's version of society can only be the market, since its purpose is profit in particular activities rather than any general conception of social use. At the heart of socialism, on the other hand, is sharing and social co-operation.

The social psychology of capitalism is intensely selfish. The epitome of the system is aggressive individualism and the unequivocal pursuit of self-interest, and whilst the forces of humanitarianism and charitable organisation have softened some of the crueller harshnesses of unfettered economic self-aggrandisement, capitalism as a system can never permit such forces more than a limited remedial role.

As against this the ideology of social democracy of the Croslandite reformist period of the 1950s to 1960s[3] propounded three main principles – that the 'mixed economy' was a success and had solved the problems of unemployment and depression, that the keymark of the socialist was a commitment to high public expenditure and thus to high-quality public and social services, and that the only main

227

requirements outstanding were an extension of social welfare and social equality. Recent history, however, has ruthlessly invalidated all three prescriptions. On the first, it cannot be held today that capital accumulation is no longer anarchic, that the concentration of private economic power is reduced to the point of effective control, that the role of profit has been drastically altered and business increasingly socialised, and that a major redistribution of income has been achieved, let alone that the disaster of high unemployment and deep recession has been resolved – quite the reverse. On the second point, public expenditure was in 1976–8 for the first time since the war cut back, not only below planned levels of increase, but absolutely in real terms, and this process was taken still further by the Thatcher government in 1979–80. On the third point, an unprecedented backlash has been launched against the welfare state in the 1970s, and despite the spread of comprehensive schooling advances in social equality have not been striking.

With the philosophy of social democracy so cruelly discredited by events, what is the alternative ideology of socialism which can satisfy the changed economic and moral world of the 1980s? The essence of socialism lies in *putting people before property*, with all that this prodigious prescription implies. At present this notion is a subordinate one in the Western scale of values, only introduced at a time of crisis for the sake of convenience and appeasement. Thus, for example, the system of wage-labour inherent in capitalism necessarily tends to the reduction of the meaning of work to its wages alone. But whenever there is an important strike, business leaders and the whole panoply of propaganda in the media react by defining a totally different conception of work, namely, service to the community, responsibility to others, pulling together. Certainly work ought to mean these things, but it is hypocritical to smuggle in surreptitiously when under pressure such a concept entirely foreign to the notion of a 'labour market' and the behaviour appropriate to such a work system.

How can the ideal of co-operation, of putting people first, be realised in general and not merely in crisis out of convenience? One recent writer has envisaged the objective thus:

> The co-operative ethic differs markedly from the aggrandizing ethic that underlies the dominant model in the minds of business people and economists today, which is to pursue a single objective – such as the maximization of profit or economic growth – subject to meeting various other constraints. It also differs from the competitive ethic underlying the adversary model prevalent in the minds of most politicians, trade unionists and lawyers – according to which the right conclusions will be reached in politics, collective bargaining and the law by a process of confrontation between two sides. Following from this, the public interest should not be conceived in terms of maximizing welfare, utility, social benefit or any similar construct in the minds of economists, philosophers and public officials. It should be concerned with helping to develop and maintain a framework of functions, rights and duties in society – a framework which will hold the balance between differing interests, from which social justice will emerge, and within which people will have scope to fulfil themselves – a framework which will itself be continually evolved by the participative process of collective learning and collective change.[4]

SHARING, ALTRUISM AND CO-OPERATION *VERSUS* ELITISM, MATERIALISM AND EXCESS COMPETITIVENESS

But how? How can we secure a society that provides such a balance and does away with exploitation of man by man? Paradoxically the growth process of market capitalism is

229

itself a propellant to a new ideology. For while the extension of middle-class material and cultural values is itself an impetus to individual economic advance and is a natural consequence of the principle of universal participation to which the liberal order is committed by the demands of political legitimation, the same process also spreads what are essentially minority facilities beyond the minority that can use them without mutual damage. It entices additional demands for goods and facilities which of their nature are attainable only by a minority. Thus Fred Hirsch has identified two factors as qualifying both the priority and promise of economic growth. One is the paradox of affluence, namely, that the growth process runs into social scarcity. The other he calls reluctant collectivism, in that continuation of the growth process itself depends on certain moral preconditions (the traditional middle-class values of ambition, thrift, and so on) which its own success has jeopardised through its individualistic ethos.[5] For, paradoxically, the assimilation through embourgeoisement of manual workers to the goals of the market system poses threats to its economic stability because the normal channel of self-improvement for workers in occupations with no career structures is through collective bargaining which, if widespread and unrestrained, can undermine the harmony and anonymity of the market system.

The crude but classical case for giving priority to growth rather than to distribution has always been that the growth process over a relatively short period of compounding would raise the consumption of the lower-income groups to levels higher than would result from redistribution of all the excess resources currently accruing to top-income groups. Thus the growth objective dominated the distributional objective in the USA and Western Europe for the quarter-century after the Second World War. But it has become increasingly undermined because each group of workers, so long as the individualistic calculus of values has prevailed, have refused rationally to take into account the social repercussions of their actions. In a society where individuals and groups exploit as best they can their positions within a generally unprincipled structure of power and advantage, shopfloor workers can scarcely be expected to hold back their power to secure piecemeal advantages for the general welfare.

Apart from this central dilemma over the growth objective, public concern and sensitivity has sharpened over the assault on the environment, the challenge to civil liberties, the breakdown in standards of public services and the deterioration of inner city ghettos, and the succession of financial scandals exposing a seamy morality in private business (Slater Walker, Lonrho). The late 1960s also saw developing support for individualist philosophies in deliberate and strong opposition to what they regarded as the institutions of remote and cynically manipulated power. Not merely reacting against commercialisation, mechanisation, bureaucracy, car culture, hygienic and work ethic obsessions of current affluent society, it was also positively a critique of the whole established industrial order.

Besides such philosophic repudiation of grosser materialism, there are at least two other important signs of growing public concern for social as opposed to economic maximisation goals. One is the mounting pressure for higher quality of life, particularly in amenity and environmental terms. Partly this is a reaction to the diminishing returns of growth beyond a certain level of industrialism, as Hirsch particularly has emphasised. Thus a rich man in a semi-developed country has servants, high status, a car with unblocked roads on which to use it and no commuter problems; a rich man in the richest country in the world, America, has no servants, relatively lower status, severe traffic jams to contend with, and he lives perhaps two hours from work. However, when confronted with the advertising machine and the massive Galbraithian artificial generation of needs, it is unlikely that qualitative consumerism will do more than channel the forces of growth in particular directions; it will not counter them.

Another sign has been the growing discussion about increasing gross national welfare as opposed to gross national product. In May 1970 the draft report of an OECD working party on long-term growth broke new ground by urging that economic policy in the 1970s be directed, not merely at achieving a particular rate of growth, but at securing certain goals, including the prevention of urban congestion and pollution, the elimination of poverty, and the provision of adequate health services and social security. Even the CBI in its public relations has felt obliged to lay approving emphasis on the 'social responsibilities' of business.

Not that any of this is to suggest that a desire for achievement, for higher living standards, or for success in struggle against others are pejorative and should, or indeed can, be eliminated in any society; but rather that elitism, materialism and competitiveness can sometimes be gross and excessive. In Britain and other Western capitalist societies they are all too often gross and excessive. Thus there is abundant and persisting evidence of deep-rooted elitism and defence of entrenched privilege.

The essence of the alternative ideology of socialism lies in the values of sharing, altruism and co-operation. How practicable is it to propose that they should become the dominant ethos in a society that is economically dynamic as well as socially compassionate? What mutual support on the side of *social* institutions is needed to reciprocate the development of more social goals for economic institutions? How does one inculcate 'a concept of power, not as the capacity to dominate or impose, but as the capacity to develop and draw out potential that is clearly there – like the power of Michelangelo to liberate the living forms imprisoned in the marble rock'?[6] Above all there is the central issue of how man can become more self-fulfilled as a sharing animal. In other words, how can we construct a society which imbues service to a cause and to the wider community as the prime motivation above self-advancement?

It is important to realise that a commitment to advance social or community ends as the essential motive and criterion of an individual's thought and action – a society where public concern dominates private interest and where self-sacrifice, comradeship, generosity and loyalty to the cause become internalised norms – does not in any way imply an authoritarian or centralised, let alone totalitarian, state. Far from it. It implies rather that major decisions in every sphere of work and leisure should be reached and implemented democratically, in order to prevent individual resentment and psychological withdrawal from the community. Voluntary acceptance by the overwhelming majority of leaders and of the people must be a prerequisite for any workable system of moral incentives.

There are two ways to introduce moral incentives in genuine socialist democracies. A weaker method to resolve this problem is to emphasise material incentives in the primary areas of work, and moral incentives in the expanding free goods and service sectors. A stronger thesis was the Chinese attempt (under Mao at least) to build moral incentives into the very structure of public life. The most significant instrument for this was the *hsia fang* (transfer to lower levels) system. By requiring systematic participation in physical labour on the part of administrative workers for specified periods of time, it was aimed to narrow the inherited inegalitarian conditions which subvert moral incentives.[7] At one level it challenges fundamental Western notions of rationality which determine the organisation and management of modern production, as well as providing the principal justification for hierarchy, authority, power, status, wealth and privilege. But at another level it erodes the divisions, which are the price of this rationality, within and between mental and manual labour; it is these that fragment workers into atomised parts governed mainly by mechanistic concepts of efficiency in factory or office.

So how can moral incentives, which are at the heart of socialism, be evolved and implemented in practice? First, the merits of co-operation and the severe drawbacks of excessive competitiveness could be much more strongly voiced by political leaders and other opinion-formers. These include resentment and compensatory retaliation by the losers, such as restrictive practices, lack of commitment to organisational goals when monetary differentials reinforce rather than balance inequalities in status and power, social divisiveness including reinforcement of class divisions, and development of anti-social and delinquent subcultures like vandalism. Instead of solely lauding its economic effects in enforcing improved performance, they should acknowledge more realistically the heavy social cost of over-competitiveness as being wasteful, destructive and alienating. After all, in the last analysis, what is life for? Man, even capitalist man, cannot live by material things alone. Yet at present he is severely starved of moral or spiritual values by the sheer unbalanced weight of materialistic propaganda grossly distorting the value system of society in the economic interests of the capitalist Establishment. Both the religious side of man and the secular construct of the welfare state, each of them motivated by aspirations which transcend the self, have been downplayed by the selfish forces of materialism, and a counter-revolution is urgently needed if Western man is to rise above the distortion of his present unidimensional mould.

Secondly, co-operativeness as an ethic demands both real participation in all major social and economic decisions and a sharing-out of rewards (and responsibilities) which is broadly accepted throughout society as being fair and equitable. On both counts contemporary British society sadly fails, both in lack of genuine accountability over political and industrial decision-making, and in gross inegalitarianism that cannot be justified by the known facts of the distribution of ability. Each of these facets is explored more deeply in its own right below. But it needs to be said here that a real ethic of sharing involves more than mere institutional changes like election of the managerial board, discussion meetings on corporate strategy, full disclosure of information on company policy, regular re-selection of MPs, Cabinet and party leader, or incomes engineering.

It involves too, *par excellence*, much more thorough and comprehensive efforts at job enrichment than have yet been made (limited at present to such isolated experiments as those at the Swedish car plants at Kalmar and Södertälje and at the Philips electronic assembly plant at Eindhoven). More important still, it involves at least a limited degree of job-sharing, in a world where intrinsic job interest is limited to a small minority of jobs, yet the known distribution of ability suggests that very many more persons could do these jobs than is ever possible under the existing system of territorial claims to jobs virtually registered for life, with initial access, moreover, often determined more by social than merit criteria. Equally, unpleasant jobs do have to be done; but why should they not be shared, to prevent a highly undesirable ossification of status differentials and a dangerous lack of understanding arising from distinct and unmixing social and economic strata which scarcely ever share any mutual experience? Why should managers, professionals, white-collar workers, MPs and all such privileged groups not spend, say, two or three months on the factory shopfloor, in public service manual jobs, or on a farm every five years or so? Would not the gains in social cohesion, breakdown in industrial barriers, and enhancement of a much more just allocation of opportunities between individuals far outweigh the losses in economic 'rationality' from extreme specialisation in employment?

Thirdly, the values of a sharing philosophy need to be asserted much more strongly in such key areas as education and housing. These are not sectors where maximising economic competition is appropriate. Schools, colleges and universities are not, or should not be, obstacle courses to pre-select their intake for slotting into a suitable niche in the hierarchy of positions in business or the economy. They are institutions to develop individuals towards a much broader and more self-fulfilling concept of adulthood and a more varied understanding of service to the wider community. Similarly, housing is not, or should not be, a status symbol, an object of conspicuous consumption, or a source of market power and wealth like the competitive accumulation of industrial assets. It is a place rather where individuals and families should be able to live and interrelate in mutual happiness without restrictions imposed by lack of adequate income. Yet at present too many people have second homes or too-large homes for their needs, whilst too many others are homeless or badly overcrowded or lacking even basic facilities. A greater commitment to real sharing and a playing down of the ethic of personal aggrandisement in housing is necessary as a first step for the political mobilisation of the will to end what is perhaps the biggest single indictment of current British society.

DEMOCRATIC ACCOUNTABILITY *VERSUS* CONCENTRATION OF POWER

If sharing and co-operation are one key part of the concept of socialist democracy, accountability is the other. Concern about a lack of accountability is now expressing itself in many spheres in our society in what can be regarded as a series of parallel power struggles. These power struggles all have a democratic theme running through them. They are in part an expression of concern about and frustration with the failure of those who have taken office to assume power and introduce the fundamental reforms that appear in political manifestos. They appear in various forms, including:

the unelected House of Lords *v.* the elected House of Commons
the executive *v.* the bureaucracy
Parliament *v.* the executive
party representatives *v.* party workers and supporters
trade union officials *v.* shop stewards and combine committees
workers and managers *v.* shareholders[8]

At present political power is not accountable in British society for several reasons. We have prime ministerial government based on patronage, the system of Cabinet government and the operation of the whips. It is both sustained and held in check by the growth of civil service power, some of it formally accountable to the Prime Minister, some of it formally accountable to other ministers, much of it unaccountable save in a strictly nominal and theoretical sense. Furthermore, prime ministerial and bureaucratic power is being enhanced through the institutions and practices of the EEC and through the growth of corporatism at the expense of parliamentary democracy.

Corporatism is defined here as a system of government in which, first, the leaders of the big institutions in our society see their role as that of bringing or keeping their members in line with government policy rather than necessarily expressing the views of these members and, secondly, those leaders, in return for carrying out the role which has been assigned to them, whether tacitly or overtly, and through a variety of pressures and inducements, are given a say in, or more likely a veto over, certain impending governmental decisions. Thus the CBI and the City have successfully persuaded politicians (some of them may not have needed much persuasion) to veto trade planning, industrial democracy, the introduction of a wealth tax and the extension of public ownership. Trade unions, who have a veto over industrial legislation, may find to their cost that as the corporate state develops the vetos of the CBI and the City may prove stronger than their own veto. All prime ministers during the 1970s have been corporatist.

Furthermore, we have corporatist government where values are determined more by those who make up what we have referred to traditionally as the Establishment – leaders from the CBI, the City, the press, the professions and the church in conjunction with the civil service – than by working people as represented through their trade unions. We have government that relies for its popular support on an appeal to experience and trust rather than on reason and argument; and relies further on the press to project corporate state images and Establishment values. All modern governments are able to rely on a number of journalists prepared to prostitute themselves on the Establishment's behalf whilst protesting their independence of it. And we have closed and secretive government that pays lip service to openness.

Industrial democracy and workers' control are perhaps the final expression of the desire for democracy in each of these main spheres. Economic growth, public expenditure, the quality of the environment may all spring from this one life force. Yet already the corporatists are exercising their veto. But neither is trade union democracy to be neglected when one of the greatest challenges to the trade union movement in the last quarter of the twentieth century will be the power of multinational corporations. One of the critical problems for a large part of the trade union movement is to ensure that its branch, district and area structures can meet the aspirations of its members at plant, factory and company level. The growth of combine committees is one indication of strains developing here. It has many deep implications. The struggle for real accountability as a dominant value in society is only just beginning; this would need to be fully developed in a socialist society. It implies that those who represent others can be replaced by democratic processes, including and especially elections; that those who elect others to represent them know what problems are under discussion by their representatives before decisions are taken; that there are arrangements by which people can make their views known to their representatives before decisions are taken; and that those who wish to contribute to the decision-taking process should have access to all the information they need to enable them to put forward their arguments. In short, a genuine socialist democracy is a continuous process and not a system of government based exclusively on trust where people go to sleep or are forgotten between elections.

EQUALITY, CLASSLESSNESS AND SELF-DETERMINATION *VERSUS* ESTABLISHMENT DOMINANCE AND CLASS EXPLOITATION

The third essential component of a socialist ideology must lie in the assertion of freedom and the right to self-determination that can only flow from confronting class privilege and the dominant elite whose power supports it. The present industrial order is based not only on gross inequality but also on gross inequality of opportunity, yet it is preserved against attack from its victims by a series of beliefs skilfully propagated to justify inequalities of power and rewards. Myths are created, with the prime object of legitimating the right of rulers to rule, of owners to own, of managers to manage. These myths, however, can only succeed in their prime object, of holding a subject class in thrall, if they achieve a secondary effect, namely, under-mining the self-confidence, critical judgement and independent initiative of all those over whom rule is exercised. A central requirement of a socialist ideology therefore is to expose the mythical nature of these purported legitimations of the supremacy of the established elites, not only for its own sake, but as an essential pre-condition to root out the implanted sense of inadequacy among the ruled which is more a cause of their being dominated than any force at the disposal of authority. In the same way, the Black Consciousness movement and Women's Liberation have been necessary in order to free these groups from the complex attitudes of inferiority – held by themselves – contributing to their own subordination.

What are these myths? One is that people in subordinate roles occupy them because they are inadequate in intelligence, and could not do otherwise than they are doing. In fact, while all kinds of characteristics can be inherited, most people who are not mentally handicapped are capable of learning up to the highest standards, provided that the learning starts early enough, that the teaching is effective, and that the process is not subject to counter-influences from the labour market which discourage the learner and distort the role of the teacher.[9] Because it is a social development and highly influenced by motivation, intelligence can in fact be drastically affected by changes in the social environment. It is more true that people in subordinate roles occupy them because people who are not in them like to keep things that way.

Another myth is that property is the whole basis for a free society. Even if once true in the Middle Ages, it is now the opposite of the truth. Unless ownership of the vast, modern, complex manufacturing plant is communal and hence truly social, it restricts the freedom of all those who have to work it, rather than advancing it. Yet another myth is that everyone today has an equal chance in society, so class warfare is outdated and huge differentials in rewards simply reflect proper recompense for hard work, perseverance and ambition. This conveniently ignores the role of inheritance of wealth, the huge variations in aspirations between individuals according to class which very largely predetermine performance, the severe restriction on opportunities in line with social stratum, and so on.

How are these myths created and how do they gain currency? They reflect, as does the prevailing ideology in any society, the interests of the dominant elite in the boardrooms of the leading companies, in the City and in Whitehall. The British Establishment, like every other power elite in history, acts exclusively in its own interest (whatever concessions may be extracted from it from time to time), but it does so with skill and sophistication behind a smokescreen of soothing assurances that its sole concern is 'the national interest'. Hence a key part of the role of a socialist ideology is to expose this dichotomy between the Establishment's self-interest and the wider national interest of the general community. For as the British crisis deepens, the Establishment continues, no less than before, to sell out Britain's interests and to use its almost total control over the country's communication networks to persuade workers that it has their interests at heart. The central theme of a socialist counter-ideology must therefore be a restoration of our control over our own affairs. The first step to this end is to detach workers' interests from those of the ruling capitalist Establishment, and for this to be seen to be done. That is one reason why the Lucas Aerospace Shop Stewards' Combine's alternative strategy remains so important, including the persisting campaign that has flowed from it. It is also why the Benn industrial co-operatives of 1974–5 and the trade union involvement in the company reconstructions of that period were so significant, in that they aroused workers' political consciousness.

The accent must be on workers' control, not as an instrument to secure the dominance of one class over another (which would simply repeat the authoritarianism of the present situation, only the other way round), but rather as the natural and purest expression of democracy in the exercise of power. The aim must rather be classlessness, greater self-determination. It must be acknowledged that whilst this is easy to advocate, it is singularly hard in practice to fulfil. It requires workers, organised in trade unions or political parties that are themselves responsive to pressures from below, to elaborate strategies to erode prerogatives over decision-making and monopolies of information, and to create powers of representation, veto and supervision over political and industrial decisions. Reporting back procedures, and the right of members of power organisations to call their delegates and representatives to account, and to dismiss them if necessary, are all vital insurances against the dangers of rank-and-file incorporation into their leaders' ethos.

The other crucial requirement for advance is that national and local trade union centres/political parties gear themselves to give effective services to shopfloor/grassroots initiatives. The whole strategy of progressively extending group self-determination requires a huge expansion in trade union and political education, and of research and financial services being both available to workers through their organisations and at the same time accountable to them. All this presupposes the need for both workers and their leaders to acquire self-confidence in handling a whole new range of ideas and facts. As Ken Coates has observed, all the experience of adult education confirms that workers are perfectly capable of acquiring this self-confidence once given the opportunities to do so.[10]

However, self-determination means much more than imposing restraints on the exercise of autocratic authority in industry or public affairs. It raises more positive issues of new forms of social ownership and democratic administration. 'No man is good enough to be another man's master', as the English socialist William Morris said. But models for self-management in such a new society, if masters are not once again all too readily to dominate, require several principles which are by no means necessarily operative in present-day Britain – an end to secretiveness in public affairs and provision for systematic access to official information, the widest freedom of criticism (untrammelled by the present bias inherent in the class ownership of the press), genuine openness of the press and communications media and freedom of political association.

The essence of this aspect of socialist ideology is taking power to regain control over our own future. In so many ways, both in its international relations and in its disposition of the country's domestic resources, the Establishment has been selling out the real national interests of Britain. To change this requires both an ideology to infuse confidence in workers and to transform their psychology of acquiescence, and in addition understanding of a structure of democratic authority whereby a whole new system of different values could be put into effect in society. Britain run genuinely by the British people and for the British people remains still as yet an unachieved goal, the more so as this fact remains largely unrecognised by a considerable majority of working people.

The Politics of a Counter-Ideology

In the face of the power of this propaganda machine constantly reinforcing the ideology and established position of the dominant class in capitalist society, how far have alternative value systems survived and flourished in this climate, and how far are they capable of so doing? Several general social trends are relevant here. First, there has been a decline of homogeneous working-class communities which nourished a corporate working-class culture which in turn encouraged positive attitudes to socialist tenets. Secondly, there has been gradual transformation of the social outlook or value system of this working-class constituency. It is associated with certain attitudes becoming more prevalent, including an instrumental orientation to work and to trade unions; a decline in instinctive working-class solidarity and in class-consciousness; an even smaller interest in political activities, together with growing indifference or cynicism towards political parties and towards politics as a meaningful pursuit; and a more calculating attachment to the Labour

Party, increasingly conditional on its ability to 'deliver the goods' as fairly narrowly defined.

How can the sway of the dominant ideology be countered? Only by a mass socialist party intent on disseminating socialist values and ideas. As one observer has said:

> Once established among the subordinate class, the radical mass party is able to provide its supporters with political cues, signals, and information of a very different kind from those made available by the dominant culture. To a considerable degree workers may look to their party for political guidance in the attempt to make sense of their social world. They themselves have relatively little access to knowledge, so that the political cues provided by their own mass party are of key importance to their general perception of events and issues.[11]

This is what the Labour Party has signally failed to do. It either makes no attempt to compete with orthodox definitions of political matters, or actually colludes in transmitting them. Far from radicalising its supporters, it usually prefers to tranquillise them. Ignoring the fact that the roots of Labour's support lies in its identification as the party of the working class, its spokesmen regularly disown all 'sectional', class-based, 'divisive' politics, and preen themselves as the firmest upholders of the national interest. Indeed, by endorsing and relaying orthodox definitions and evaluations, Labour leaders help confer legitimacy on the existing social order among Labour's constituency. To take one example: instead of demystifying the concept of 'confidence' (of the business community, the financial markets, and so on), Labour spokesmen regularly invoke the need for it as a constraint on their policies.

One of the results of this is that politics has become increasingly marginalised. Political action has, in the minds of many, come to be equated with casting a vote. Political change is understood as the alternation in government of two, not dissimilar, sets of politicians. Political debate has shrivelled into disputes over the best means to achieve broadly similar ends. Political conflict is looked upon as little more than the squabbling of quarrelsome politicians, or petty partisan bickering. Yet so long as the attitudes of instrumentally minded workers are fragmentary, inconsistent and relatively malleable in character,[12] one can conclude that this provides opportunities for a dedicated political leadership, equipped with radical policies, to generate much greater support for socialist policies. While these opportunities may have been disregarded hitherto, it remains entirely open for radical leaders, first, to combat the belief that the social system cannot be transformed by human effort, and secondly, to present a vision of a radically different type of society without gross disparities in the distribution of power, wealth and access to education. At present little is being done to educate and mobilise socialists in Britain, as is illustrated most strikingly perhaps by the virtual absence of a socialist press. Until much more is done, it is certain that the grip of the dominant value system will strengthen further still, and the ideological supremacy of the Establishment will be even more firmly consolidated.

NOTES: CHAPTER 10

1 M. Mann, *Consciousness and Action among the Western Working Class* (London: Macmillan, 1973), p. 13.
2 M. Mann, 'The social cohesion of liberal democracy', *American Sociological Review*, vol. 35 (1970).
3 C. A. R. Crosland, *The Future of Socialism* (London: Cape, 1956), p. 517.
4 J. Robertson, *Power, Money and Sex* (London: M. Boyars, 1976), pp. 82–3.
5 F. Hirsch, *Social Limits to Growth* (London: Routledge & Kegan Paul, 1977), p. 175.
6 Robertson, op. cit., p. 87.
7 P. Clecak, 'Moral and material incentives', in R. Miliband and J. Saville eds, *The Socialist Register, 1969* (London: Merlin Press, 1969), pp. 114–15.
8 B. Sedgemore, paper on accountability, June 1978. Private paper, unpublished, to Labour Coordinating Committee.

9   K. Coates, *Beyond Wage Slavery* (Nottingham: Spokesman, 1977), p. 43.
10   ibid., p. 39.
11   F. Parkin, *Class, Inequality and Social Order* (London: MacGibbon & Kee, 1971).
12   J. Goldthorpe etc., *The Affluent Worker in the Class Structure* (Cambridge: Cambridge University Press, 1970).

11

Socialism as a Society Free of Exploitation

The deep and persisting inequalities in economic command over resources, status, opportunities and power that constitute the class divisions that continue to stain British society are well understood. The essence of socialism, as it is defined and elaborated in Chapter 5, lies in sharing, altruism, the co-operative ethic, the ending of exploitation of man by man – the antithesis of the class society. Socialism as a philosophy is therefore highly relevant to combating the class-ridden disfigurements of British social life. But while these goals have in theory unfailingly united socialists over the centuries against the evil of class exploitation, it is necessary to ask the much harder question as to how these ideals can be brought about in practice in the particular conditions of modern Britain. We must also ask whether, even if achievable, these ideals simply reflect philosophically desirable principles or whether, much more important, they are also intimately related to the moral, psychological and economic regeneration of Britain.

Social Justice and the Spread of Income and Wealth

Inequalities in command over money, and the power it confers, are still very great in Britain today, have diminished

247

remarkably little during this century and are still closely aligned with class divisions. The Diamond Royal Commission on the Distribution of Income and Wealth was charged in 1974 with seeking information 'to help secure a fairer distribution of income and wealth in the community'. But of course this begs the crucial question of what is meant by a 'fairer distribution' and what the differentials ought to be. What is known is what they are: for the post-tax ratio between top and bottom incomes is at least 20:1. Is it possible to reconcile the classical supply-demand view of scarce skills, that persons need compensating for longer training, with the social equity view that persons need compensating for enduring boring, soul-destroying, dangerous jobs?

The capitalist response, especially in the face of inflationary pressures and leap-frogging wage claims, is synchronisation of pay settlements so that existing differentials can be largely preserved within the sum of the global increase fixed by the rise in productivity and growth of the economy. This approach, which is instinctively corporate statist, makes little or no concession to remedying the gross injustices inherent in the present distribution of income.

The socialist response, on the other hand, would focus on pay bargaining at plant level and would require representatives of all occupation groups – managerial and white collar as well as manual – jointly round a table to determine between themselves on an annual bargaining basis what should be the appropriate differentials. Each representative of each occupational grade would have a vote on the pay increase merited by each of the other occupational grades but not on the increase for his own grade. In the light of this, pay increases permitted by the organisation's economic position (as revealed by disclosure of the financial situation as an element of industrial democracy) could be varied by agreement between employee grades. This approach, by contrast, is decentralist in nature and emphasises individual and group accountability in justifying increases in pay (which for this purpose would include fringe benefits and all quasi-income rewards).

There can, of course, be no claim that such a relatively simple change in the procedures for negotiating pay would resolve the deep differences of attitude and value that under-lie much of the social conflict over incomes. All that is asserted here is that this approach, which is essentially a socialist one, would at least enable the underlying conflicts to be faced overtly and thus the possibility of resolving them to be opened up. The present system, on the other hand, of compartmentalisation of pay negotiations between different occupational groups and of self-defeating competition at national level, cannot solve the latent conflicts which, what-ever the temporary successes of incomes policies, regularly become explosive.

The epitaph of the present system lies in the pay statistics consequent on the 1973 Barber gross inflation of the money supply – pay rose 1974 to mid-1978 by 108%, but prices by 103%, and productivity and real growth were almost stagnant. In net terms, therefore, workers gained hardly at all, despite the huge cost in loss of British competitiveness. Yet it was not a situation in which any particular occupa-tional group could, by their own restraint and self-sacrifice, affect the national outcome more than marginally, given the structuring of the present system of negotiating pay rises. That is why, against the background of the persisting impact of wage inflation, this socialist approach to the whole issue of income differentials, both socially as the bastion of class and economically as a key foundation of competitiveness, is so crucially relevant to Britain's recovery.

But changing the process of pay bargaining, in order to seek maximum consensus about income allocation, is clearly by itself not enough. As a corollary it is necessary positively to teach the morality of socialism as an alternative to the morality of the market, as the basis for the system of public values underlying policy on incomes. This is a much more deliberate policy than simply presiding over what redistribution happens to take place contingent on high inflation, the exigencies of wage control and the balance of organised labour power (though in point of fact executive surveys in 1978 showed that the professional-managerial grades increased the differentials – contrary to much received wisdom – during stages 1–3 in 1975–8 as a result of phoney promotions or job changes or by enlargement of fringe benefits).[1]

What is needed is a much more powerful, eloquent and sustained campaign on the merits of greater equality than has yet been attempted by the political leadership. This is in no sense the propagation of absolute equality, which is no doubt impossible to achieve and perhaps not even desirable either. It is rather a considered and outright repudiation of the present huge and indefensible inequalities in command over resources between the richest and poorest in Britain. It is not a rejection of diversity, even less of liberty. It is rather the vast inequalities in control over resources which massively reduce or even eliminate the potential diversity of British society and the potential liberty of millions of individuals.

A campaign on public values, on the justification of income relativities, is critically important. Otherwise economic engineering will be broken every time on the rock of market traditionalism. For in the absence of determined counter-pressures the resistances against redistribution are strong and the force of market norms against increasing equality is very pervasive, even though the structure of income inequalities cannot be justified by the distribution of ability (when a large majority of classes I and V have the same IQ distribution scatter) nor by the balance between monetary and non-monetary attractions (when in fact prestige, job satisfaction, authority, security and pleasant working conditions all tend to be concentrated on the higher-paid).

But the most massive pillar of indefensible disparities of

income consists, still today as it has always done, of inherited wealth. But what should be the target for a positive socialist policy on wealth distribution? It is first necessary to distinguish between wealth which is inherited and wealth which is built up by individuals over their lifetime. Regarding the former, it might be reasonable, in order to provide for equality of opportunity and to create a fair spread of incentives, to restrict inherited capital or property (other than to the spouse) to some £30,000 per individual. In other words, an accessions tax, or progressive capital transfer tax levied on the donee, would reach 100% at about £30,000. This would eliminate the fantastic inequalities in opportunity, security and power which derive from very large-scale inheritances (or *inter vivos* transfers) which cannot be justified by capitalist meritocratic canons of reasonable equality of opportunity, let alone by socialist canons of equality and social justice.

This would, of course, still leave existing extreme inequalities in wealth-holdings in their present hands. For this purpose, two further fiscal measures are needed for a socialist policy on incomes and wealth. One would be an annual wealth tax at, say, 5% on holdings above £0·5 million (1980 prices); this would have a limited selective impact on the most excessive disparities of wealth, when Inland Revenue figures reveal that, even among the richest 1% of the UK population, the members of this group with the average (i.e. mean) wealth-holding had about £109,000 in 1975.[2] The second requirement, in the form of a tax on the income from wealth, is one of horizontal equity (that persons with the same taxable capacity should pay the same amount of tax). In terms of progressive taxable capacity and in the light of relative tax equity between those with low incomes and no wealth (a substantial part of the population) and those with both high incomes and large wealth (a tiny elite), a tax should be imposed on the imputed incomes from wealth-holdings above the threshold (say £30,000) at the

251

wealth-holder's marginal rate on his earned income, or at a minimum 50% where the wealth-holder has little or no earned income.

A major economic advantage of this latter proposal is that it would compel wealth-holders to seek out high-yielding assets, especially in industrial investment, rather than let their capital stagnate in property, land, works of art, and so on, which offer a high rate of appreciation in capital value, but a low annual yield. Another economic advantage is that the increased tax on unearned income could be used to reduce the standard rate of income tax, so as to produce a direct redistribution from the rich to the average- and low-paid. On the other hand, in order not to penalise the high-paid by an unearned income tax pitched at artificial marginal rates, the structure of income tax should be altered to incorporate the present range of tax allowances (on mortgage interest, life assurance, occupational pension scheme contributions, and so on), on the basis of averaging, within the basic rates. In other words, these non-personal tax allowances would be abolished, but the tax rates would be correspondingly reduced so that the average recipient of these allowances was no worse off. This would avoid the deterrent effect of the false impression of marginal rates at significantly higher levels than they in practice are, and also eliminate a highly anti-progressive element in the tax system.

Social Justice and the Pecking Order of Status

A second facet of class divisions, and one by which Britain in particular is diseased, lies in rigid status hierarchies between different social strata. Of course, any given society will inevitably accord differential status to varying occupational grades, but the relevant questions are whether the status differences are made large or small, obtrusive or minor; what are the criteria for allocating status; and whether these criteria are mutually cumulative or mutual alternatives. In the case of present-day Britain, status differences are large and obtrusive, they are allotted largely on traditional, inherited and non-functional criteria rather than on the basis of the agreed value of contribution to the community, and these status ascriptions are limited in coverage and concentrated on a small elite. In a socialist society the reverse would hold on each count. How would this be brought about?

The most important requirement is the launching of a sustained public debate, preferably by the political leadership, regarding job relativities, not only in terms of income comparisons but of general value or worth to the wider community. The effect of this would be not so much to downgrade any particular occupations as to upvalue many others whose contribution is surely, by any objective standards, under-recognised. This must lead to some slimming down of the status hierarchy, and probably also to a more variegated structure of status, given a wider and deeper public understanding of the multiple supports of community life.

But public exhortation and public debate cannot, of course, by themselves be enough. They need to be buttressed by policies which more directly confront artificial and harmful status distinctions. One such approach has already been proposed in Chapter 5, namely, requiring each individual to spend a period of, say, two years at the start of working life undertaking some form of community service. Nor need this be a compulsory requirement: the Manpower Services Commission reported a survey in 1977 of 3,000 young people who were asked if they would be prepared, for example, to run local community projects and services, or work alongside staff in existing departments and institutions providing services for various client groups, and two-thirds said they would, even though the questioner said the work would be paid at the level of unemployment benefit.[3] But such an innovation should not be simply an exercise in youthful idealism. It would be much more important that it should be repeated at least once later in working life. Nothing is likely to telescope artificial status differentials so sharply as the knowledge, and experience, of those in senior positions that they will be undertaking in the future, at least for a period, a relatively menial job. Nothing is likely to break down so effectively the barriers that still so starkly divide off the Two Nations in Britain. Nothing is likely so positively to build up genuine community understanding and solidarity, in contrast to the Them and Us divisiveness which fatally weakens British drive.

Other institutional changes are relevant here. If industrial democracy involves representatives at board level for each of the main occupational grades in a plant, and especially if collective bargaining of pay and conditions at work were shifted to a plant focus and vertically structured to embrace all occupational groups (as proposed earlier), then questions of status and allocations of material benefits at particular job levels would certainly be brought within the ambit of democratic discussion and decision. Separate facilities like private lavatories, size of rooms, depth of carpet pile, quality of upholstery and varied expensiveness of furnishings, as well as the carefully calibrated range of so-called 'fringe' benefits, would doubtless no longer be permitted to generate the shameless and arbitrary demarcations between individuals that disfigure the life of so many organisations.

Other relevant institutional reforms that should serve to diminish artificial status distinctions lie in the educational and housing spheres. Comprehensive schools prevent segregation between schools on what purport to be academic, but so often turn out in practice to be social, criteria. They also permit, though do not always achieve, greater social mixing between the classes; but it may be that this reform will never be complete whilst streaming remains, since, as Julienne Ford's research has indicated, 'this form of selection has all

254

the implications and all the consequences of segregation into separate schools.'[4]

In the housing field the postwar New Towns philosophy was aimed consciously at reducing class segregation, and at least till the mid-1950s they did achieve an overall social balance. But neighbourhood class balance was never properly achieved because private houses were specifically located and not diffused, and social segregation was increased by the better-off going to live in towns and villages around the New Towns.[5] A policy of reducing artificial status divisions in housing must aim therefore at deliberate inter-penetration of council and private housing estates by significant numbers of units of the other type, and some local authorities' efforts in this direction need to be taken a great deal further. And of course those prime embodiments of status artificialities – the honours system, inherited peerages and other aspects of patronage – should be done away with for the baubles of social divisiveness (as well as the levers of power and influence) that they are.

Social Justice and Genuine Opportunity for All

Perhaps the most serious vice of class society, both from the point of view of obstruction of individual self-fulfilment and wastage of the national pool of ability, is the hamstringing of opportunity because of social class barriers. The essence of classlessness, and an important facet of socialism itself, lies in a genuine and meaningful equality of opportunity for all citizens. But how can this be brought about when social engineering through educational reform has received such enormous attention in the last few decades, yet been so conspicuously unsuccessful?

This liberal package, whereby educational equality was viewed as the avenue to social change by proxy, failed on several counts. First, equality of access to education did not guarantee equality of outcome. Spending more money on education turned out to mean, because of 'the iron law of social class', spending more money on the already advantaged. The effect of expanding higher education in the twenty years after the war was to get an extra 1½% of unskilled working class children into the universities, compared with an extra 13% of upper-middle-class children.[6] Such extra social mobility as has been achieved in Britain over the postwar years almost entirely derives from changes in the occupational structure. Where more working-class persons have attained professional and white-collar jobs, it is because the number of such jobs has increased. There has in fact been no significant increase in the social 'openness' of elite groups this century, in Britain or any other Western country, and there has been no decrease in the correlation between the occupational status of fathers and sons.

The second failure of the liberal package is that it is now apparent that meritocracy does not and cannot legitimise the social structure. Inequality was not made more palatable by the comprehensive school. Whilst educational or social failure may be bearable when it is thought to be the result of accident of birth, it is much less so if it is seen as the consequence of personal shortcomings. The third failure of the liberal package on education reform is that the connection between increased education and higher rates of economic growth remains obstinately unproved. The 'human capital' argument lost its previous conviction. And fourthly, even the contemporary fashion after Bernstein with compensatory education has been disconcertingly ineffective in equalising opportunity. For there has proved to be little evidence at the main variables in school environments, such as expenditure, teacher qualifications and class size, have any consistent effect on attainment. Educational underachievement has increasingly come to be seen as merely one manifestation of several social and economic disparities experienced by disadvantaged groups. Yet on the other side, genetically, the correlation between IQ and educational attainment is rather poor; even if the most extreme estimates of the genetic contribution to IQ were accepted, it appears that inherited ability still accounts for rather less than half educational attainment.

Education has therefore turned out to be a disappointing form of social engineering. Above all, it should be seen in its proper context and not invested with political potential beyond its realistic means. Thus it is not to be taken as an indirect political redistributor of wealth and power in society; for that, more direct political instruments need to be employed. Nor is it an agent of modernisation, or a legitimator of the inequalities of advanced industrialism.[7] Nor should it be regarded as a means of redistributing the national cake, but rather as part of the cake itself.

How, then, can equality of opportunity be made into a genuinely practicable prospect and what role must education play in this? In an egalitarian society education should be distributed according to egalitarian principles. It is necessary to distinguish between education for specific skills and occupations and education of a more general nature. There is no reason why the former should not be distributed unequally according to the need to ensure competence among qualified practitioners, whether engineering craftsmen, doctors, or the like, and the distribution would have little connection with customary notions of social status.

All other forms of education, including, for example, that leading to most university degrees, would be made available on demand. Every person should be entitled to three years of university education (or two years or one if that is all the nation can afford at a given time) whenever he or she chooses. If applications exceed available places, access could be limited by lottery, perhaps with quotas for various social, regional and ethnic groups. Nor is this without precedent: the Open University, with over 60,000 students, imposes no selection and handles excess demand by a system of lottery and quota. Those rejected in this way one year get another chance next year.

Of course, it will be said that universal open entry to higher and further education is inimical to national economic efficiency. However, Japan, for example, certainly does not in any sense limit top education to the most talented, yet its economic efficiency can hardly be said to suffer. It is not self-evident that three extra years of education for the highly intelligent yield greater national economic returns than, say, one extra year for the average or below-average intelligent – indeed, the contrary may well be true. Secondly, it may be said that the middle class would make more use of open access than the working class. But this is only an obstacle so long as education is still viewed as a form *par excellence* of social engineering. Higher education as an avenue of opportunity would at least have been genuinely universalised, however skewed in practice the take-up continued to be, and more explicit egalitarian goals could still be pursued through more direct political means.

Social Justice and the Balance of Power in Society

Lastly, how would a socialist society handle the question of power relations, not only regarding the great institutional foci of power (as discussed in Chapter 9), but in terms of the individual authority-compliance dimension of class relations? Almost all the socialist criteria proposed in Chapter 5 would militate against the exploitative aspects of capitalist class society.

Thus production for social use rather than to maximise private profit-making would remove the pressure on the employer to extract maximum output for least feasible pay, as well as conversely on the employee to seek maximum obtainable pay for minimum reasonable effort. Near-full employment would prevent the employing class using mass unemployment, or the threat of it, to seize the whiphand over the employed population in general, and the manual working class in particular, especially in the face of any signs of class militancy. Again, an employment ethos primarily emphasising worker welfare and job satisfaction would mean that labour ceased to be treated, as in the capitalist economy, merely as a factor of production. Differential relations to the productive process, which are essentially class relations, would cease to be hierarchic and authoritarian in the traditional sense of the dominance of one class over another, and would be exercised solely in the functional interests of organisational efficiency and accountability. And promotion of a co-operative ethic by its very nature emphasises rejection of competitive pressures to dominate and of any institutionalisation of authoritarian inter-group or inter-class relations.

Above all, the key socialist principles of industrial democracy and economic equality, if implemented in any deep and meaningful sense, must dramatically reverse the Them/Us, bosses versus workers, mentality of the institutionalised trench warfare of capitalist class relations in industry. The essence of industrial democracy, whatever precise mould it is clothed in at any particular time – and it is capable of almost limitless development – is that the traditional class pattern of power in industry is transformed. Instead of capital hiring labour in accordance with capitalist power relations, labour in a very real sense hires capital. This is not, of course, to suggest that expert and professional management of the highest order is not still needed within a socialist industrial regime; only that the pyramid of ultimate accountability has been turned on its head.

The other socialist principle which would reduce the power divide between the classes is economic equality or, more realistically, a marked diminution in the present huge disparities in control over resources. Under capitalism, power is built on money, especially large-scale holdings of property and wealth, sometimes directly but more often indirectly through the manifold avenues for exercising influence which high income or substantial wealth conveys. The removal under socialism of the stark injustice of major wealth inheritance (skill at choosing one's parents is not specially a capitalist virtue) plus a flattening of the spread of earned income in recognition of the multivariate nature of individuals' functional contribution to society would very significantly reduce the capacity for institutionalised dominance by one class over another.

Class-Consciousness and the Achievement of Social Change

The last two chapters have sought to show the meaning and relevance of socialism in meeting and overcoming the fundamental defects in British society identified in Part One, in terms of respectively economic decline, class ideology, overconcentration of power and social injustice. Of course, there can be no blueprint about so complex a vision, but that does not remove the over-riding need to clothe the vision with some degree of concrete detail if it is to inspire application to reality. Socialist theory and theoretical struggle remain an essential part of economic and political struggle.

Allied to the need for a clear vision, and fed by it, is the need for a heightened working-class political consciousness and self-confidence. The conditions for radical political change in the socialist canon are a new self-conscious class, related in a new way to the developing productive forces of society, and the failure of the old ruling class, related to the earlier productive forces, to manage the new forces. The failure of the traditional capitalist order to deal effectively with the new forces emerging so destructively in the 1970s has been documented in Part One. But why has the level of class-consciousness remained so persistently low in Britain?

The conditions for the arousal of class-consciousness are, respectively, consciousness of a division of interest between employer and employee, consciousness of a community of interest among employees and mobilisation of individual alienations into collective solidarity, a belief that change is possible and that things could be different, and that they cannot go on in the old way, and a strong and pervading sense that things should be fundamentally different. The key elements here are a powerful sense of deprivation relative to expectations plus the capacity for mobilisation. The sense of deprivation may even be greater at a time of boom, if enough people feel they are deprived of their rightful stake in growing prosperity, than at a time of slump, if people feel conditions could well be worse still. But historically these requirements for arousal of class-consciousness have not been met.

Over the course of the present century history has amply demonstrated that the scope and tempo of reform has simply reflected the concessions necessary to placate the sporadic stirrings of class struggle. Parliamentary reform has been highly circumscribed and largely reactive to immediate economic and social pressure. Ostensible control of the legislature was not used (at any rate, not by the left), nor was it intended to be used, as a direct instrument in class struggle or as a means of fundamental reversal of class imbalance of power. It is designed essentially to maintain the existing power structure, not to transform it, with adjustments and concessions made sufficient to preserve existing authority patterns as intact as possible and to head off more fundamental reform. To this extent even the Labour Party is a party of capitalism, and one indeed that is positively favoured by the dominant class at times of economic crisis (as in 1974–6, for example) since it provides more plausible ideological cover for policies of working-class restraint. For even though Labour Party and trade union leaders have never achieved (nor in most cases shown much inclination to

261

achieve) more than limited incursions into the domination of Britain's traditional ruling groups, deference to their authority remains strong, and indeed the best protection available for big business-finance interests when under severe stress.

When class-consciousness has developed it has been sidetracked – by war in 1914, by defeat in 1925–6 and by a sense of affluence in the 1950s and 1960s. More generally classconsciousness has remained latent because the trade union and Labour Party leadership have usually quickly become institutionalised, and class politics has been deliberately played down. No attempt has been made, for example, to establish a working- and middle-class alliance against the monopolies, or on the international plane a patriotic alliance. Little or no attempt has been made to spell out in concrete situations, as and when they arise, how the national interest diverges from the interest of the ruling elites, or to explain what, even where these interests converge, are the limits of their compatibility. The key question 'in whose interest?' is not systematically explored in public. As a result, political consciousness and understanding have remained at a low ebb and there has been little diminution in the pervasive ignorance about how the power structure really operates.

Against this background of relatively successful postwar containment of working-class aspirations – against all the odds of inequality and exploitation as outlined – it is possible to posit certain conditions whose satisfaction would seem to be necessary if this policy of incorporation is to continue to succeed in future. One is that the opportunity shall persist for securing a steadily rising standard of living. Another is that society shall be open enough to offer a reasonably free avenue for social and occupational mobility. A third is that there should be acceptance of working-class social and power aspirations which match economic gains. On both these last two counts the foregoing analysis has suggested that these conditions are absent, whilst on the first criterion recent history suggests that the present economic system can no longer consistently guarantee a sufficient annual rise in the standard of living to satisfy the expectations of its wage-earning majority, and indeed the survival of the system itself seems dependent precisely on the downgrading of this objective.

Yet it still remains true that the arousal of class-consciousness sufficient to generate radical political change would require, in combination, four conditions: a crisis in society (which the persisting deterioration of Britain's relative economic position foreshadows), a crisis of self-confidence in the governing group (of which there are definite signs), a sense of self-identification in a new class (dissipated in the 1950s, now returning via Upper Clyde Shipbuilders and other work-ins, but under strain in the mid-1970s world slump) and a new vanguard capable of providing leadership. It is this last condition which it is the fundamental task of class politics to provide, but which at present shows little sign of real development.

NOTES: CHAPTER 11

1   T. Forester and J. Mack, 'Whose pay policy?', *New Society*, 12 October 1978, pp. 76–7.
2   Calculated from *Report of the Royal Commission on the Distribution of Income and Wealth*, Cmnd 6999 (London: HMSO, November 1977), p. 70.
3   Manpower Services Commission, *Young People and Work* (London: HMSO, May 1977), p. 37.
4   J. Ford, 'Comprehensives as social dividers', *New Society*, 10 October 1968, pp. 515–17.
5   B. J. Heraud, 'New Towns: the end of a dream', *New Society*, 11 July 1968, pp. 46–9.
6   P. Wilby, 'Education and equality', *New Statesman*, 16 September 1977, pp. 358–61.
7   W. Tyler, *The Sociology of Educational Inequality* (London: Methuen, 1977).

12

A Socialist Policy towards the Wider World

Democratic socialism is not an insular concept, but an international one. If British democratic socialism represents a redistribution of wealth and power within Britain, it would be myopic not to consider its contribution to the redistribution of wealth and power in the world outside too. This chapter therefore concludes the agenda for socialism by spelling out the international dimension of the task facing British socialists.

The Tightening Grip of World Poverty

The first major problem that faces us is the persistence, and moreover the growth, of world poverty. The world league table of wealth (Table 12.1), drawn up after a quarter-century of postwar capitalist expansion and immediately prior to the oil crisis of 1973, reveals an average global per capita income for the 3½ billion people of the world as about £430. But in the USA 200 million persons had an average £2,000 per head, whilst two-thirds of the world's population, 2·3 billion persons living in the poor countries, had on average a mere £85 per head. Thus average income in the richest country was about twenty-four times greater than that in the poor countries of the world where the great majority of mankind live.

264

Table 12.1   *World League Table of Wealth*
(1972, just before the oil crisis)

Bloc	Population (m.)	Total GNPs (£b.)	GNP per head (£)	Recent % per year growth in real GNP	Recent % per year growth in population
USA	200	400	2,000	4·5*	1·0
Other rich/OECD countries (Western Europe, 'old' dominions, Japan)	500	500	1,000	†	1·0
Newly industrialising countries (Comecon, the Mediterranean, some Pacific Asia, some Latin America)	600	450	750	5·0–10·0	1·0+
Poor countries	2,300	200	85	*c.* 5·0	2·5
TOTAL	3,600	1,550	430	*c.* 5·0	2·0

Notes: *Prior to the mid-1970s
 †From under 2% in the UK to more than 10% in Japan.

How is this vast inequality in the spread of the world's wealth changing? First, population growth is much faster in the poorest countries. Whilst the world's population is growing at about 210,000 every day, or 76 million a year (a doubling of the world's population within thirty-six years), the pace of growth is increasingly diverging between rich and poor countries. It is getting slower in the former, but faster in the latter. The UN four-yearly *World Social Situation* (1975) found that the population growth rate for developed countries fell from an average 1·1% a year in the 1960s to 0·9% in the early 1970s. By contrast, the developing countries, including the 1,400 million in China and India alone, grew at 2·4% a year in the early 1970s compared with

2·3% in the 1960s, and their share of total world population grew from 67·4% in 1960 to 71·6% in 1975.

Secondly, the central resource requirement for this population explosion is an adequate food supply. It is estimated there are some 300–500 million undernourished people in the world, in the sense that they do not get the 1,900 or so calories a day needed merely to maintain the structure of their bodies. It is also estimated that some 100 million children suffer from malnutrition, which in Latin America, for example, is the immediate or associated cause of 60% of infant deaths.[1] The problem of world food shortage is actually growing in the sense that there are twenty-four countries with a combined population of 363 million where improvements in food production are being outpaced by population growth. Then there are seventeen nations (including India) with 957 million people, whose food production has kept pace with population growth, but not with the increase in food demand. Only some thirty countries, containing 380 million inhabitants, are able to feed their own populations.[2]

Thirdly, there are signs that the economic capability of the LDCs to cope with their population explosion is fading. Until the oil crisis of 1974–5 economic growth had advanced relatively well in the developing world. Growth of GDP in the Third World rose from 5% a year in the late 1960s to 6·2% in the early 1970s, which compared in the latter period with 4·8% in the developed market economies and 6·5% in the communist countries. Even when growth in industrial output in the underdeveloped world matched that of the industrialised countries, the latter still achieved a growth in income per head almost half as high again as the former because of differential population increase. Thus whilst the developed capitalist countries, with a 6% annual increase in industrial output in the 1960s, and a 1·3% per year population growth, achieved a rise of 4·5% per head per year in incomes, the underdeveloped countries, with about the same overall annual increase in industrial output but a 2·5% a year population growth, only managed a rise of just over 3% per head per year in incomes.

But as a result of the 1974–5 oil crisis, discussed further below, the gap between the poor majority and the rich minority will widen sharply again in the 1980s. Thus, even on the (certainly wrong) assumption that industrial countries stop growing altogether, Table 12.2 shows that it would take middle-income countries, growing at their 1960–76 average, sixty-five years to match the industrialised countries' GNP per head. For the low-income group, it would take 746 years! Assuming, more reasonably, that all three groups grew at their 1960–76 average rates, it would be AD 2220 before the middle-income countries match the

Table 12.2   *Rich* versus *Poor: Growth and Income, 1976*

Countries (1976 income levels)	Population 1976 (m.)	Area sq. km. (m.)	Average annual growth in GNP 1960–76 (%)	GNP per capita (median values) 1976 (US $)
Low income (<US $250 per head)	1,216	21	3·3	150
Middle income (>US $250 per head, but still recognisably LDC)	895	39	5·8	750
Centrally planned	1,208	35	4·1	2,280
Industrialised	684	32	4·1	6,200
[Surplus oil	12	4	11·4	6,310]

Key: Middle-income countries – includes five southern European countries, Greece, Portugal, Spain, Turkey, Yugoslavia.
Centrally planned countries – Eastern Europe, China, Vietnam, North Korea, Cuba.
Industrialised countries – mostly OECD, covering Western Europe, North America, Japan, Australasia.
Surplus oil countries – Kuwait, Libya, Oman, Qatar, Saudi Arabia and United Arab Empire.
Source: World Development Report, 1978

industrialised ones. Low-income countries would on the other hand fall further and further behind.

Fourthly, as a result of these trends the world has increasingly polarised into distinct blocs. Over the three decades to 1970, North America, maintaining its population at around 7% of the world total, actually pushed up its share of world income slightly to 33%. Other developed capitalist countries, with a slight fall in world population share to about 10·5%, suffered a fall in share of world income of fully a third, though still retaining 22%, more than double their numerical proportion. The Soviet bloc, with a relative drop in population share of a third, achieved the biggest increase in share of world income, by more than a third to 21%. China showed the same tendency, though to a lesser degree, with a smaller fall in population share to 21·5% but a similar or even larger rise in share of world income to 5%. On the other hand, the semi-industrialised countries, with a stable proportion of world population at 12%, took a drop in world income share of about a fifth to 6·5%. The under-developed countries, however, sharply diverged from these patterns by experiencing a huge rise in world population share by no less than a third to almost 40%, though this was matched by a proportionate increase in world income share to some 12·5%. The net effect, however, was that they still retained about a third of world income in relation to their numerical proportion. Thus these shifts have still left the world divided into two quite distinct groupings, rich and poor, except that by the 1970s the rich group, the capitalist states, had been joined by the Soviet bloc, which previously had occupied an intermediate below-average position in per capita wealth.

There has been a similar polarisation too in terms of trade. Broadly, in the 1950s two-fifths of trade generated by capitalist countries took place within the industrialised world, and some three-fifths of their exports were manufactured goods. A decade later these proportions had risen to three-fifths and three-quarters respectively. Moreover, about four-fifths of long-term investment from the capitalist countries consisted of direct company investment, and two-thirds of this lay in cross-investment between the industrialised nations. Such has been the growing penalty of trade exclusion for the Third World.

The consequence of all these trends has been the burgeoning of world poverty on a huge scale. The ILO in its 1976 review *Employment, Growth and Basic Needs* estimated that 33 million persons were unemployed, and a further 250 million (or 36% of the workforce in developing countries) underemployed, in the Third World. Taking a 'poverty line' as equal to the average earnings of unskilled labour in large-scale manufacturing in India, and an even lower 'destitution line' as equivalent to 1 rupee per person per day in Indian terms (when per capita GNP in India was around 2·3 rupees per day), the ILO calculated that two-thirds of the 1,815 million population in developing market economies in 1972 were 'seriously poor', and of these 706 million (or 39% of the total) were 'destitute'. What these figures must mean is that basic needs for the world's poorest can only be realised by the end of the twentieth century through a much more radical redistribution of global income than has ever yet been envisaged.

Rejection of Interdependence: a New International Economic Order

Three postwar decades of adherence by the less developed countries (LDCs) to the Western line – that the shortest route to prosperity was development on the Western model and integration into the capitalist economic system – has signally failed to deliver the LDCs from the bondage of poverty. Bitter experience has shown that subordination to world markets meant in practice for the LDCs the diversion

269

of land, almost always the best arable land, from basic food crops like millet or sorghum to profitable cash crops for export. The result almost inevitably was that an increasing quantity of basic foodstuffs had to be imported from abroad.[3] As a result integration in the world market meant in practice that by the mid-1970s the non-oil LDCs were spending almost as much on imported grain as on imported oil.

Moreover, interdependence within Western capitalism has been seen to lead in practice to redistribution, not from rich to poor countries, but actually the other way round. Thus the French economist Jalée has calculated the overall net effect of money flows between the industrialised and LDC worlds (LDC terms of trade losses, loss of dividends and private repatriated revenue, payment of interest on private loans and interest on export credits, and payment of maritime shipping charges to the industrialised countries, less total aid received from the latter) as a positive surplus in favour of the rich creditor and investor countries.[4] Furthermore, despite pious resolutions calling for an acceleration of capital exports from rich to poor countries, Professor Triffin has calculated that the former received 97% and the latter only 3% of the US $103 billion of international reserves created during 1970–4. At the same time surpluses obtained in Third World countries were regularly transferred to the owners of capital, technology and managerial skills in the rich nations. Also the OECD noted that debt service payments increased by 9% per year in the 1960s, while earnings from exports of goods and services rose by only 7·5% and the GNP of developing countries by only 5%.[5] The differential was largely made up by further loans which could only, in turn, worsen the debt service figure.

For these reasons new Western promises of interdependence, with proposals for a fresh global economic bargain based on complementarity between non-developed and developed countries, have rung hollow in the Fourth World (the non-oil LDCs). While the already industrialised nations continue to appropriate a totally disproportionate share of the world's raw materials and energy output, redistribution is only possible if a 'new economic order' fundamentally reverses this structure. A new development strategy is necessary for the poor countries that does not depend merely on the generosity and goodwill of the industrialised nations, as the first and second UN Development Decades did.

In particular, a new trading structure has been sought. Hitherto, when Western interests have been severely threatened by effective competition, capitalist countries have resorted all too readily to a system of countervailing tariffs, quotas and price-fixing, most notably in the fields of textiles (the Multifibre Arrangement), footwear and consumer electronics. Or they may subsidise domestic industries to counteract cheap imports, in the manner in which the UK set up a highly subsidised sugar beet industry in East Anglia and the ECC has even planned to export its subsidised sugar production under the CAP. Commodity agreements are offered to developing countries to stabilise their export prices, but if a poor country seems likely to make a major breakthrough, rich countries call for the agreement to be renegotiated. Thus after Brazil, for example, set up its own coffee-processing factories and won 14% of the US markets, US soluble coffee manufacturers claimed 'unfair competition' because Brazilian firms could buy coffee beans (in fact used broken beans, unsaleable in the world market) more cheaply than they could; so the USA promptly threatened it would not renew the International Coffee Agreement which maintains stable prices and talked about cutting aid to Brazil.

As a result, the underdeveloped world has come to see, not only that the promised Western strategy has failed, but that it was perhaps mistaken in the first place – that more foreign assistance, more foreign investment and more technology have not solved, and cannot solve, their basic

271

problems without a reordering of international economic priorities. Harsh experience has thus confirmed the theoretical contention of Emmanuel[6] – that the classical economic principle of so-called comparative national advantage – the West specialising in industrial manufacture and the LDCs in raw materials production – is entirely false.

The need for struggle by the poor world is justified by the Prebisch–Singer thesis that the terms of trade between commodities and manufactured goods will deteriorate inexorably given the present balance of world power. This is based on Prebisch's view that benefits from productivity improvement accrue in the developed countries as a result of the exercise of power by labour unions, which is complemented by Singer's view that productivity improvements accrue to the developed world as higher incomes whereas they simply depress prices of developing country exports. Once it is accepted that the power balance is the crucial variable, other instruments, of course, besides commodity agreements require consideration. These must include the threat to expropriate foreign investments, limitations on the repatriation of foreign profits and capital, the threat of the withdrawal of money balances or demand for their conversion into gold, joint action to improve the terms of contracts with multinational companies (for example, removal or reduction of tax concessions, demand for higher royalties, stronger demands for local participation or use of local materials), trade discrimination against exports from industrial countries, demand for higher rents for granting military facilities and other similar demands.

There are perhaps two main ideas for a 'new economic order' being actively canvassed among developing countries. One is to apply raw materials policy – on the OPEC model via price cartels, limitation of production and nationalisation of foreign mining enterprises – as a lever for securing a radical redistribution. A majority of developing countries, however, prefer to campaign for enforcing changes in market rules in their favour by commodity agreements negotiated with the consumer countries. The other view hinges on changes in the balance of power predicated on the projected depletion of Western raw material resources. At present the industrial countries depend on imports from the developing countries for one-third of their mineral raw materials requirements (excluding oil). It is believed that because of the increasing exhaustion of deposits in the West (apart from those in Australia, Canada and to some extent South Africa), and in the light of the geographical distribution of the known reserves, this dependence should increase significantly over time. Indeed, the likelihood of future gaps is signalled by the fact that in 1972–3, for example, whether because of inflation or a more inhospitable investment climate, foreign investments of US mining enterprises fell 20% in money terms compared with the average of a few preceding years.[7] However, this argument can cut both ways in other sectors. In the case of grain, for instance, which accounts for 25% of world exports of agricultural raw materials, the developing countries are net importers.

Nevertheless, there is a range of key materials where developing countries do account for a high proportion of world production – 51% in the case of bauxite, 36% for chromium, 44% for copper, 25% for iron ore, 25% for lead, 30% for nickel, 75% for tin, 24% for zinc, and 30% for phosphate rock.[8] But none of these is quite so high as for oil, where it is 58% (including OPEC alone at 51%), and oil, moreover, uniquely brings together price-inelastic demand, non-substitutability, a politically cohesive cartel and a capacity of the largest producer (Saudi Arabia) to bear whatever cuts in supply are needed on behalf of all the OPEC countries without feeling the pinch.

While restrictive supply action of this kind on the part of the LDCs can be expected to intensify and certainly is needed to redress market forces on a major sustained scale, there can be no doubt that for the rich countries only a socialist approach is compatible with the massive redistributive programme required. For a rich country like Britain a socialist plan for aid to LDCs should include implementing the 0·7% UN target for official aid; encouraging British public sector co-operation with the public sector in developing countries (including subsidies where necessary from the aid budget) to assist the transfer of capital and skills without the disadvantage implicit in direct foreign private investment; accepting the developmental necessity of nationalisation and helping to meet the technical and financial problems thus arising; and waiving interest and repayment of debt or reducing it at least within a maximum ratio of debt service to foreign exchange earnings.[9] But more important than any of these specifics is Britain's will and vision to argue and campaign within the OECD group of Western nations for a massive redistribution of world wealth and power.

Redressing the Powerlessness of the World's Poor

In a fundamental sense the grossly unequal spread of wealth in the world reflects the very unequal balance of power. It therefore has to be asked how far imperialist attitudes and policies are inevitable, irrespective of the type of regime, and whether imperialism is therefore in some sense endemic in the human condition as reflected in international relations. What are the roots of imperialism? Given such a causal explanation, does history or recent experience suggest it is possible that world interrelationships could be constructed on a basis by which the strong nations would not inevitably seek to dominate and exploit weaker nations? To put it another way, is power between nations inevitably and remorselessly expressed in terms of domination, or is it practicable and realistic to conceive of international power being predicated on non-imperialist relationships?

IS IMPERIALISM INEVITABLE?

The different manifestations of imperialism reflect different causal explanations as to whether the political or economic roots of the phenomenon are primary. The classical liberal view regards imperialism as an aberration from capitalism due to the survival of the ambitions of a declining and underemployed feudal class.[10] Keynesians, by contrast, emphasise the dominant motives of personal and national power and prestige in the agents of economic activity, not as an extraneous and irrational factor in economic activity, but as central to its form and direction.[11] They therefore see no exclusive causal connection between imperialism and industrial capitalism. A modification of this view has been to regard imperialism as a continuation of mercantilism by new ruling classes seeking to use the state as a means to extend their own economic power in the special circumstances of nineteenth- and twentieth-century industrialisation. Marxists, on the other hand, have regarded changes in technology rather than changes in ideology or psychology as the key to understanding what determines economic and political structures.[12]

They have therefore regarded capital accumulation as the driving force compelling capitalist societies to strive for trade domination over other nations, just as, for example, territorial aggrandisement was necessarily practised by feudal societies and slave raids were needed by slave societies. For the continuing competitive struggle within capitalism between increasingly large and powerful corporations forces them to seek to incorporate other producers and control their own markets and sources of raw materials, carving up the world in the process. Keynesians, on the other hand, have seen these phenomena as different manifestations of an unchanging human nature.

However, it is relevant to note, against this latter view, that where co-operation is essential to survival among certain existing primitive societies, aggression and struggles for domination are absent from interactions between individuals and groups. If on this basis it is accepted that the structure of economic relations adopted at particular levels of technology corresponds with the legal, political and military institutions in the respective societies, this does at least provide some grounds for believing that if future higher levels of technology required co-operation as a condition of survival, a non-imperialist society need not be purely an idealistic and impractical fancy.

For the immediate future the relevant gauge for the meaning of imperialism will be whether the underdeveloped countries can achieve economic development within the general structure of the capitalist world. Is it inevitable that this structure polarises the world in an artificial division of labour between the wealth of the area where capital is accumulated, where capital goods are manufactured and labour productivity raises real wages, and on the other hand the poverty of the areas where reserves of labour are retained with minimal capital equipment at low levels of productivity? Now that the form of international economic co-operation built on the 1944 Bretton Woods Agreement has faded, will it be replaced by a re-establishment of US hegemony, by the carving out of spheres of influences by an emerging larger group of superpowers, or by some new international institutions that recognise the changed balance of power? Will US capital still dominate because US companies are much bigger, more advanced and faster growing, or will the challenge of EEC and Japanese corporations, with lower wages plus increasing productivity, enable their exports to break the US domination of world capitalism, investing increasingly in subsidiaries in the USA and in areas of the world where currently US companies dominate the market? Will transnational corporations rather than nation-states form the main new sources of capitalist rivalry, dividing up the world according to their current strengths, with US companies extending their domination over the American hemisphere, Japanese companies in South-East Asia, West European companies in Europe and Africa, and a Soviet sphere of influence in Eastern Europe, the Middle East and India?

While direct manufacturing investment ties satellite economic development in the underdeveloped countries more closely into a polarised world division of labour than did the indirect investment in transport and infrastructure in the nineteenth century (for example, by British capital in North America and Argentina), on the other hand large-scale capital plants are real assets vulnerable to nationalisation which local staffs are increasingly capable of operating. Even if the transnational companies in the metropolitan countries retain research and development know-how, spare parts and perhaps some of the main capital equipment production, the Japanese, to quote one precedent, have demonstrated how far technology can be copied, given at least a certain level of know-how.

IMPERIALISM AND WORLD INDUSTRIAL
DEVELOPMENT

As far as the developing world is concerned, the major impact of imperialism was to propel colonies, dependencies and clients into the world capitalist system. That forced them to produce a small surplus, some of which was repatriated to the metropolitan state, another part allowing an elitist form of minor development in the dependent country. In the postwar years the mechanics of the capitalist system have changed. It is now dominated by transnational companies, who have moved from simply utilising cheap labour in the post-independence developing nations and exporting manufactures to them. Now they also deploy capital raised by themselves, the local economy and international sources to initiate manufacturing ventures within the Third World countries. To do this, they rely on sympathetic or bribed independent governments and the members of the tiny elites they have attached to their enterprises. A basic question here for the future is the extent to which governments in both developed and underdeveloped states can control the activities of these companies.

The great problem of the next decade for the industrial workers of the rich world and for the liberation movements of the poor world will be to discover the framework of political and economic co-operation that will allow their long-term common interest to prevail over the short-term interests that divide them. It can be expected that the political consciousness will steadily grow; that it is not any kind of uncontrollable force of nature, but human artefacts, that stand between the unemployed capacity of industrial workers in developed countries to produce goods that the peoples of the LDCs want, and the underemployed capacity of workers and peasants of the Third World to produce goods that the industrialised world wants.[13] There have already been examples of this growing consciousness in Britain, in the struggle of electrical workers on Merseyside, steel workers in Sheffield and shipbuilders on Clydeside to find markets in the Third World for the products of their factories and yards threatened with closure because they were unprofitable in the going markets. Such a view on the internationalisation of contemporary socialist reality effectively bridges the gap between the immediate demands of British workers and the far greater needs of the world's poor. It positively identifies the common interest which unites the objectives of the industrial workers of the rich world with those of the peasants and workers of the poor.

How can this alliance between the workers of both the industrialised and Third World countries be consolidated? At present the giant multinational companies regulate the pace of economic growth worldwide by aiming for a sequencing of markets at different stages of development, so that market domination for new products in the most developed markets can be successively maintained over time down to the least developed. Hence the importance of the communist countries in filling the crucial gap between the least developed markets of the West and the most developed of the incipiently industrial markets of Asia, Latin America and Africa. This gap exists precisely because the underdeveloped countries have failed to develop in the capitalist world economy. Yet at the same time these under-developed markets become increasingly important for the advanced industrialised countries as they increasingly develop conditions of overproduction.

Correspondingly, the giant multinationals also generate an international sequencing of production levels. Those manufacturing processes which can be highly automated with a small and highly skilled labour force are retained in the advanced industrial countries, less capital-intensive processes are exported to intermediate industrial areas of the world and the most labour-intensive processes are reserved for the least developed countries where labour is therefore cheapest.[14] Thus just as mineral and raw material production in these latter countries had long been controlled by expatriate companies, so now manufacturing is initiated in these countries on the same basis. But this pattern of dominance entails severe drawbacks to the process of LDC economic growth. Development is extremely slow, and sales expand slowly precisely because wages are low and profits are repatriated to the metropolitan industrial countries.

Disadvantageous though this is to the LDCs, it is always assumed that this pattern must be beneficial at least to the peoples of the rich, industrialised countries. Yet there are strong reasons for gravely doubting even this. First, low prices received by primary producers for their products or their labour are not necessarily fed through in low prices for consumers in the industrialised countries if large profits are secured by mining or plantation companies or by merchants in the process (for example, the high profits of the oil majors). Secondly, available cheap labour in the LDCs may delay investment in capital equipment which would reduce the price to consumers below what any labour-intensive process, however cheap, could ever achieve. This leads to many natural products from the LDCs being replaced by some of the cheaper synthetic substitutes in the developed world. Thirdly, and most important of all, depressed wage levels in the LDCs feed back in the form of impoverished markets for manufactured exports from the industrialised countries and thus remove new job opportunities, or actually generate unemployment, for workers in the West.[15]

The essence of imperialism is thus, not so much the tribute extracted from subjugated lands, as the wholly artificial world division of labour between manufacturing and primary production imposed by capitalism on the world outside Europe and North America. This assured the capitalist powers, locked in their own competitive struggles, of both sources of raw materials and privileged markets for their manufactured goods. But a division of labour of this kind, once created and preserved by international free trade, served not only to check the economic development of the LDCs, but also to stunt their political development through the propping up of the native feudal and client ruling classes. These distortions were further increased by the various forms of protection used to bolster the agricultural and other labour-intensive industries in the developed economies which undermined the sale on world markets of even those products to which the LDCs were largely restricted.

By contrast, an anti-imperialist, shared, socialist relationship between the peoples of developed and underdeveloped countries would depend on certain conditions. It would require that the LDCs should have the opportunity to increase their earnings for exports, by increasing their agricultural raw materials and foodstuffs output, higher prices for non-recoverable minerals, increased processing and refining of primary products and expanded manufacture of goods for export. It would also require for the LDCs that there should be opportunity to use their export earnings to diversify their economies and develop industries capable of absorbing their underemployed labour and of rapidly raising their living standards without being oppressed by debt to the industrial countries.

For the developed world, on the other hand, it means the opportunity to move to higher levels of technology without unemployment of labour or of existing capital plant. And this means increasing the transfer to the LDCs of technical know-how, and also of capital machinery and transport equipment to pay for imports from them of raw materials, food and some refined products. For the industrialised countries of the West it also means maintaining a level of stable economic development rather below that of the most advanced LDCs, with no population increase and without raising (and preferably with reducing) consumption of raw materials. The last entails using advanced technology to provide more leisure and labour for an expansion of services rather than seeking simply to maximise the production of goods. It means actually reducing spending in certain sectors, for example, supersonic aircraft production, as well as designing goods to last, not for planned and early obsolescence, for example, cars with smaller engine sizes and lower compression ratios. It also means a deliberate, sustained and mass-scale programme for both materials and energy conservation and for recycling.

A SOCIALIST STRATEGY FOR WORLD
INDUSTRIALISATION

How, then, can a balanced development of the world's resources of materials and labour be secured without the distortions created by the sequential planning of the multi-

281

nationals and without dependence on their contingent choice of location for investment to maximise profitability? Equally, at a macroeconomic level, how can a conscious aggregate demand maintenance be achieved for the world markets, so as to reach equilibrium of demand and supply at a high, or the highest, level rather than the current low level of activity?

One main requirement is that LDCs without gold output and with only one or a few commodities to offer on the world market should be able to build up a reserve currency for times when sales and foreign currency earnings are depressed, so that they can then call on this reserve to meet their trade deficits without reducing their imports. If there were also international agreements, for conservation reasons, on the price of scarce minerals, these could, provided they were easily stored, measured and subdivided, very suitably form part of a commodity reserve currency of the kind envisaged here. Thus an UNCTAD paper of 1964[16] was directed along these lines at the lack of gold and currency reserves held by LDCs which forced them to cut back their imports as soon as their balance of payments went into deficit, even temporarily – perhaps from a crop failure. It was aimed to reverse the trend whereby the share of world currency reserves held by the LDCs declined even faster than their share of world trade – a situation which prevailed till the end of the 1960s, and after a temporary reversal became apparent again in the 1970s.

The other, even more important, requirement is that governments, in both the underdeveloped and already industrialised world, should be able to plan in advance for the major structural changes in their economies that are inevitable as the present artificial division of labour between the raw material producing countries and the manufacturing countries is transformed. The need here is for the systematic planning of an expanded level of trade exchanges. It is needed anyway to complement economic planning at home.

The planning of foreign trade might be based on each party to the plan indicating what it required and what it could offer, commodity by commodity, in volume terms, over so many years ahead. Obviously any such trade plans would have to be adjusted by negotiation until a consistent mix was agreed. Governments and their industries would then contract to fulfil their plans, subject, of course, to annual reviews of progress when revised contracts could be negotiated.[17] If aid programmes were also fitted with these plans, the LDC partners would be enabled to expand their output and markets faster, and the commodity reserve currency could be used to finance longer-term credit.

TOO RISKY FOR BRITAIN?

It may, of course, be objected that such a high-risk policy of increasing access to the UK market, albeit on a balanced and reciprocal basis, would be too dangerous, given the secular weakness of the UK economy and the rapid and powerful rise of the more advanced LDCs, the so-called newly industrialising countries (or NICs). These countries may be identified as essentially those with at present only a comparatively narrow range of industries – especially footwear, textiles and electronics – with their main advantage in low wages and living conditions, often allied with modern imported Western machinery and know-how and therefore high productivity. Some of them, though not, for example, Hong Kong or Singapore, are highly protective of their home markets against Western imports. Some, particularly South Korea, may within fifteen years become highly industrialised on the Japanese model, though with their smaller populations they cannot pose problems on quite the same scale.

Perhaps the most significant lesson from recent history is the speed with which competitive threats can emerge. Thus over the fifteen years 1960–75 Japanese exports rose in value by a factor of 14 (from US $4b. to US $56b.), while Korean

283

exports grew at the phenomenal rate, though from a much lower base, of a factor of almost 150 (from US $0·03b. to US $4·5b.). The second issue is the rate at which the NIC economies are expanding, particularly in the manufacturing field. During the period 1963–76 when the British economy grew at only just over 2% on average per year, industrial production in South Korea grew by over 20% a year, in Taiwan by 16·5% and in Hong Kong by 14%. The figures for their rate of growth in manufactures are even more startling. NICs with a growth rate of a staggering 40% or so a year comprise Taiwan, South Korea, Thailand and Turkey. Those expanding at an annual rate of 24–33% a year include Brazil, Mexico, Argentina, Spain, Greece and Romania. Those with a slower but still by Western standards very rapid growth rate of 10–17% a year are Hong Kong, Singapore, Malaysia, Philippines, Pakistan, Portugal, Yugoslavia, Poland and Hungary. Only one NIC has a low annual rate of growth in manufacturing: India, at 3% a year.

Thirdly, given these extraordinarily rapid rates of expansion, what impact has this had on Britain's trade? Surprisingly, recent government surveys have revealed that NICs (comprising the twenty countries listed above plus Iran, Israel and Malta) account for only some 10% of UK imports of manufactures and only 3% of total UK sales.[18] It can be said, of course, that these figures give a false and somewhat complacent impression because they conceal NIC concentration on particular limited sectors where their impact has been very strong. This is a fair qualification. NICs accounted for no less than 58% of UK imports of clothing, 48% in travel goods, 43% in footwear and 25% in textiles. But the overall figures do show how limited this assault has been so far.

The fourth, and central, issue raised by the NIC challenge is what will be the effect on British jobs? In the six years to 1976, whilst NIC exports to the UK rose at about 11% per year, their imports from the UK grew at some 4% a year.

284

This suggests a gross loss of jobs of about 83,000, balanced by a gross gain of 23,000. Thus it can be estimated that the net effect of imports from the NICs, after allowing for the benefits, from increased exports to them, amounted to a loss of some 10,000 jobs per year in the UK in the 1970s.

But it is relevant here that the biggest effect on jobs comes overwhelmingly, not from trade, but from technological change. Thus of the total job loss in the UK of 405,000 jobs in the period 1970–5, government estimates suggest 62% of these were lost as a result of productivity improvements, 18% from changes in consumption patterns and only 20% from the effects of trade (including 6·5% from increased imports from developing countries). Moreover, during the same period 375,000 extra jobs were created, some 88% of which derived from changing patterns of demand, less than 1% from higher productivity and 11% from changes in trade (including 5% from increased exports to developing countries).

However, while the NIC trade effects on British jobs seem comparatively small, what does suggest that this will intensify is that the industries chiefly affected are labour-intensive. Also it can be seen that firms react to NIC competition by switching to more capital-intensive methods. Again, what suggests that a net displacement of labour could develop is that the industries which expand for export to the NICs are likely to be less labour-intensive than those which contract.

One response to this has been the MFA in the field of textiles and clothing, and this and other measures have helped to avoid a net loss of jobs so far in our trade with the NICs. Another, which has been actively pursued by both the British government and the EEC, is a more selective 'safeguard' clause in the GATT to replace the present non-discriminatory Article XIX, so that disruptive imports from one or only a few sources can be checked without impugning wider trade in that sector. But more positively there remains the over-riding need for a country like the UK to move upmarket in favour of more technologically advanced industrial sectors while leaving the basic manufacturing areas increasingly to the LDCs. Such an optional solution not only enhances the export earnings of the latter and hence their capacity for import absorption from the advanced economies, it also offers the prospects of higher wages for workers in the industrialised countries by concentrating on sectors with higher productivity, and preserves access for Western consumers to a cheaper range of manufactured goods. Nor does this policy approach imply, as the Hayes Report has shown, a sharply rising loss of jobs from NIC competition – the pressures of technological change lead to far greater gross (though not necessarily net) job displacement.

In conclusion, it must be said that such socialist proposals for genuine world industrialisation would undoubtedly be resisted by both the international bankers and the multi-national corporations whose power they would challenge. Against this, however, they would offer a rallying focus of common interest for the working people of the rich industrial and poor underdeveloped countries alike. For quite apart from the expanded job opportunities and faster-rising living standards which these proposals hold out for the LDCs, workers in the industrialised West have no less interest when some industries, now largely monopolised by the rich countries, such as the refining and processing of raw materials, oil refining, steel production, and so on, are increasingly transferred to the countries where the materials originate. In other words, in the absence of conscious trade planning, the likely alternative for countries like the UK is the ruthless kind of adjustment to a changed world division of labour which decimated Britain's older export industries in the 1930s – savage and prolonged unemployment.

NOTES: CHAPTER 12

1   P. Harrison, 'An unequal world', *New Society*, 13 March 1975, p. 648.
2   H. Jackson, 'If 1984 is frightening, what about 1985?', *Guardian*, 12 July 1974, p. 14.
3   G. Barraclough, 'The battle for the new economic order', *Sunday Times*, 16 May 1976, p. 63.
4   P. Jalée, *The Third World in the World Economy* (New York: Monthly Review Press, 1969), pp. 114–17.
5   OECD, *Development Assistance Efforts and Policies, 1966 Review* (Paris: OECD, 1967), tables 11, 5, 6, 7.
6   A. Emmanuel, *Unequal Exchange: A Study of the Imperialism of Trade* (London: New Left Books, 1972).
7   O. G. Mayer, 'Towards a new international economic order', *Foreign Trade Review*, vol. 10, no. 4 (January–March 1976), p. 283.
8   World Bureau of Metal Statistics, *World Metal Statistics* (London: World Bureau of Metal Statistics, 1977).
9   J. Hart, 'A socialist plan for aid', *Guardian*, 12 January 1973, p. 12.
10 J. A. Schumpeter, *Imperialism and Social Classes* (New York: Meridian Books, 1955; first published 1919).
11 For example, J. Robinson, *Freedom and Necessity* (London: Allen & Unwin, 1970).
12 M. Barratt Brown, *The Economics of Imperialism* (Harmondsworth: Penguin, 1975), p. 24.
13 ibid., p. 328.
14 M. Barratt Brown, *Spheres of Influence in the Age of Imperialism* (Nottingham: Spokesman, 1972), p. 72.
15 M. Barratt Brown, *Essays in Imperialism* (Nottingham: Spokesman, 1972), p. 98.
16 A. G. Hart, N. Kaldor and J. Tinbergen, 'The case for an international commodity reserve currency', in N. Kaldor (ed.), *Essays on Economic Policy*, Vol. 2 (London: Duckworth, 1964), pp. 131–77.
17 R. Frisch, 'The problem of multicompensatory trade', *Review of Economics and Statistics*, vol. 30 (November 1948), p. 376.
18 Foreign and Commonwealth Office, *Report on the Newly Industrialising Countries* (the Hayes Report) (London: HMSO, February 1979).

Index

Socialism with a Human Face

self-sufficiency
    increasing 16, 184, 185–9
Sik, O. 125
silicon chip *see* microelectronics
social class 6
    and equal opportunities 255–8
    and status hierarchies 252–5
    divisiveness 8
    identity 224, 225
    in 'socialist' countries 143–4
    myths 239–40
    'ruling' 29–32, 196
    see also middle class; working
        class
'social contract' 34
social democracy 94–5
    ideology for 227–43
social goals *see* ecological dilemmas;
    'quality of life'
social inequality 105–6, 234,
    239–40, 247–8
    and wealth 251
    socialist repudiation of 250
socialism 93–4, 183, 223–7
    and accountability of power
        201–22
    critical assessment of 150–61
    definition 95–7
    in China 118–24
    in Czechoslovakia 124–9
    in USSR 113–18
    in Yugoslavia 129–34
    key principles of 98–110, 161–2
    transition problems 162–3
    types of 112–13, 140–7
    see also social democracy
space projects 55
speculation booms 28, 211
Special Drawing Rights 45
stagnation *see* economic decline
standards of living
    and socialism 159–61
    see also 'quality of life'
state controls 18–29
status 252–4
sterling
    exchange rate 8

Stock Exchange 211–12
sugar 9, 135, 271
Surinam 80
Sweden
    insurance companies 213
    post-war growth 6
Switzerland 106

taxation 31
    and resources conservation 187
    and wealth 251
technological advance
    and arms industry 52
    and economic growth 54–5, 275,
        276
    and natural resources 75
    and unemployment 285, 286
    see also microelectronics
Thailand 80
Thatcher, M. 17, 29, 228
tin 9
trade 3
    free 9, 35
    imbalances 49–50
    planning foreign 189–93, 282–3
    polarisation 268–9
    structures 271–2
    surplus 160
trade unions 4, 11, 158–9
    and EEC entry 33
    and industrial democracy 206–7,
        238, 241
    dissent 35
    in Cuba 137
    in Czechoslovakia 127, 128
    in USSR 117
TUC 203
training programmes
    for worker-managers 16, 206–7
Treaty of Rome 181

unemployment 3, 34, 68–71,
    284–5, 286
    and monetarism 63, 67
    cost of 160
    European 17
    in China 121

294